Something for
the acts. Happy
Birthday, Great Heart.
1985.
X M.

DONALD SINDEN

Laughter in the Second Act

Also by Donald Sinden:

A Touch of the Memoirs

DONALD SINDEN

Laughter in the Second Act

HODDER AND STOUGHTON
LONDON SYDNEY AUCKLAND TORONTO

British Library Cataloguing in Publication Data

Sinden, Donald
 Laughter in the second act, or, Another touch
 of the memoirs.
 1. Sinden, Donald   2. Actors – Great Britain
 – Biography
 I. Title
 792'.028'0924   PN2598.S5/

 ISBN 0 340 28540 0

For
Jeremy and Delia,
Marc and Joanne

CONTENTS

ILLUSTRATIONS

Between pages 60 and 61 and 132 and 133

The photographs are drawn mainly from the author's own collection.

For permission to reproduce the following the author and the publishers wish to thank: *Punch* (caricatures on pages 155, 168, 172, 191 and 198); Zoë Dominic (*Henry VIII*, with Peggy Ashcroft); the Tate Gallery (Graham Sutherland's portrait of Somerset Maugham); Douglas H. Jeffery (*The Relapse*); Reg Wilson (*The Wars of the Roses*).

The portraits of Jeremy and Marc Sinden, by Margaret Boden, appear by permission of the painter.

The Brangwyn painting hangs in the banqueting chamber of the Skinners' Hall and is reproduced by permission of the Skinners' Company.

It has not always been possible to trace the copyright holders of certain pictures. The publishers apologise for any inadvertent infringement and will be happy to make appropriate acknowledgment in any future editions.

FOREWORD

My first book, *A Touch of the Memoirs*, related my story only to
1960. If you have a copy of the first impression of the hardback and a
pencil to hand please could you correct a mistake on page 130; the
eleventh line from the bottom of the page should read:
    A. GATE WILL BE AT SIR MARTIN FIELDS AT 11.30
Also, on page 171, the fifth line from the top should read:
        She replied ni huyu, ni huyu, ni huyu.
Thank you.

I am grateful to Messrs Hodder and Stoughton for giving me
the opportunity to continue my Sinden Saga. Many titles were
suggested for this second volume. My own favourites were *Return
to Laughter* and *Cake in the Second Act*, neither of which appealed to
the publishers, but a compromise was reached and so we have
Laughter in the Second Act.

Once again Ion Trewin and my sister Joy have tried to prevent
me from making too many syntactical and grammatical errors, up
with which they will not put, and once again Diana has coped
splendidly with the problems of living with an actor and an author
at the same time. For this I thank them.

D.S.
November, 1984

I

LET COPULATION THRIVE

In the north-west corner of the vast expanse of India (coloured pink in my old school atlas), in what is now Pakistan, lies the area of Sind. In ancient times a type of flax or cotton was grown there from which a material was made called Sinden. In Sanskrit the word is

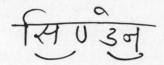

meaning 'cloth from Sind'.
This word was adopted by the Greeks and became

σινδών

meaning 'a type of linen or cambric'.
The main use of this strong material was for shrouds and the word later assumed much greater importance when the Greek Scriptures stated that after the Crucifixion, 'Christ's body was wrapped in Syndon.' Today the Holy Shroud, enshrined in the cathedral at Turin, is called in Italian *Il Santa Sindona*. And in Chinese

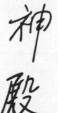

Sinden means 'shrine'.
The first time that we encounter Sinden as a person's name is in

I

1539. When Henry VIII brought about the Dissolution of the Monasteries, the Abbey at Salehurst in Sussex had only six monks in residence; the others must have foreseen which way the ecumenical wind was blowing. One of the monks was William Senden. We will never know what his name was before he entered the Abbey; the theory is that on becoming a monk he acquired the name Senden either as a religious adoptive name (as for example Brother Benedict or Sister Theresa; so William-of-the-Holy-Shroud) or that he was the Abbey's shroudmaker – not exactly a full-time occupation one would imagine. However, William Senden left Salehurst Abbey in 1539, joined the priesthood of the newly formed Church in England as the vicar of the nearby Parish of Bodiam, and set about siring a family. With the customary inconsistencies of spelling during the following two centuries, the name appears also as Sindin, Syndon, Sinden, Syndonne, Syndenne, Sindenne. (The first Queen Elizabeth spelt the word 'soldier' in twenty-six different ways during her lifetime.) All Sindens of today descend from that one man.

I began to unearth all this information in 1970. I was visiting Australia with the Royal Shakespeare Company and met the children of my mother's cousin who had emigrated many years previously. Brian was living in Brisbane and Gordon was an architect in Sydney. They were aware and disturbed that they had never known anything of the background of their (and my mother's) family – the Fullers – and feeling the need for roots, and being so far removed from the sources of information, they pounced upon me as a life-line from England and asked what I knew. Now here was a subject that had never interested me and I had to admit that I too knew nothing of the family history.

The cousins implored me to find out all I could and let them know, so, dutifully, on my return, I telephoned my mother's sister, Aunt Florence, who immediately reeled off scores of names I had never heard of before. Uncles Edward, Henry, George, Arthur, Edwin, William, Sidney and Francis; Aunts Sarah-Ann, Kate, Harriet, Nellie and Edith . . .

It was all too much over the telephone, so at the first opportunity I raced down to see her in Worthing armed with pencil and paper. Slowly we built up a family tree. Many of the people she mentioned should by rights be still alive but Aunt Florence was always a reticent, reserved person, even as a child. At the age of twenty-two she had married a construction engineer, George Edward (Teddy) Rice, and a delightful, carefree and attractive couple they became.

Within months Teddy was offered a splendid job in America and the young couple set sail in the *Mauretania* – the first people we knew of who had been to the New World – it was as incomprehensible to us then as if someone we knew in 1983 were to go to the Moon. (A brother of my Grandmother Sinden had previously emigrated to Canada but as far as we children knew had been eaten by cannibals.)

I never knew what exactly was being constructed, but a deep trench had been dug for the foundations and Uncle Teddy was inspecting the works when suddenly the sides of the trench caved in and he was crushed . . . They raced him to hospital, but he only lived another three days. Aunt Florence, married and widowed within five years, returned to England on the *Majestic* (even the names of the ships are firmly imprinted on my mind) and was met by her father. She never married again, but became the most independent member of the family, joining the Metropolitan Police Force. Attached for some time to Vine Street police station, she threw herself into her work, desperately trying to forget the anguish of watching the only person she really loved die in her arms. Many years later we heard, bit by bit, of the terrifyingly sordid cases in which she was involved – suicides (sometimes a bloated body was recovered after two weeks immersed in the Serpentine); the harrowing details of rapes; the gruesome results of murder – one may read of these cases in newspapers, but just imagine actually having to handle the once-human remains; the sight, the smell, the touch. And then came the war to add to the horrors. She had a breakdown after acting as a decoy in Hyde Park and was retired on a pension. After the war she became a children's officer in Portsmouth, and there she stayed until she reached retiring age. But retirement was not for Aunt Florence: she applied for, and was accepted as, the matron of a boys' school at Tabley House in Cheshire where once again she worked for more hours than there are in a day and became indispensable: a second mother to the boys – many of whom continued to write to her after they left – the confidante of the staff and the right arm of the Principal (and owner of the house) Col Leicester Warren. After his death she really did retire, and eventually came to live near us. Hers was the shoulder to cry on for the entire family. We all knew that nothing we told her would ever be passed on to anyone else. She was totally self-sufficient and never wanted anything that she could not provide herself. As my own children grew up, they too turned to her for advice.

3

Aunt Florence had never concerned herself with other branches of the family – just her immediate small circle: 'Uncle Arthur had a son, Leslie, and a daughter, Gertrude.'

'What happened to them?'

'I have no idea – they lived in Roehampton.'

Returning home, I telephoned all Leslie and L. Fullers in the London telephone directory. 'Are you by any chance the son of Arthur Fuller?' None was. Ah-ha! Was it perhaps possible that he was named after his father Arthur? There was one A. L. Fuller in the book. I tried it. Eureka, it was he.

This Arthur Leslie, astonished and rather bemused at my call, nevertheless put me in touch with other members of the family. Slowly the tree began to grow. All the information I gathered only took me back to the mid-nineteenth century so I began to haunt Sir William Chambers' beautiful Somerset House in the Strand where the Registers of Birth, Marriage and Death were then housed. (They have since been moved to St Catherine's House, around the corner on the other side of the Aldwych.)

From 1838 it became compulsory for all births, marriages and deaths to be registered officially. All the original documents are housed in vaults below ground and only the staff may handle them, but the public may consult the Indexes: vast alphabetical volumes for the four quarters of each year – March, June, September, December. There one may find the Surname followed by Given Names, the area in which they were registered and the number of the volume (in the vaults) in which the details are to be found. Incidentally I must warn you that it is never safe to assume that the first child will be born nine months or more after the marriage of the parents: better start your search immediately after the marriage. In all walks of life it is surprising how many 'premature births' there were among the first-born. When you have found the name for which you are seeking, a form must be filled in and you will receive a copy of the original certificate. When I first started they cost seven shillings and sixpence (37½p) each: now the price is two pounds fifty.

I found myself spending so much time at Somerset House successfully tracing the Fullers, why did I not trace the Sindens too?

With my father and several of his generation still alive I swiftly compiled the nucleus of the Sindens, but again only back to the mid-nineteenth century. Where had they come from before settling in Brighton and Hove in the 1880s? I now needed to consult the censuses at the Public Record Office.

A census of the whole population of the British Isles is taken every ten years. The first one of any real use is that of 1851 in which each householder was asked to state the full names of all residents in his house; their exact ages; their relationship to the head of the house and their exact place of birth. (In 1841 they were only required to state ages to 'within five years' and 'whether or not they were born in the county in which they now resided'.)

Plodding through the returns for Brighton and Hove, street by street, house by house, I came across other Sindens and made notes of them too. I was intrigued to find that they all came from villages within a ten-mile radius of Battle in East Sussex. Checking back I noticed a certain similarity in the Registers at Somerset House and also how remarkably few Sindens there were. It seems to be a rather uncommon name.

I decided to widen my net. Starting with London and gradually moving further afield I telephoned every Sinden in the various telephone directories: 'Do forgive me: my name is Donald Sinden and I am trying to trace the history of the Sindens. Would you please tell me all you can about your own branch?' I made a great nuisance of myself but slowly succeeded in extracting information from them, and many of them became as interested as I. They sent me truncated family trees, letters, birth certificates and photographs – I once received two identical Victorian photographs, one from a family in London, the other from a family in Hartlepool who did not know of each other's existence – almost invariably their information ceased beyond the memory of the oldest member who could remember his or her grandmother or grandfather.

To go further back would have to be my responsibility. I therefore decided to make my own record of all Sindens who were born, married or died during a period of a hundred years – from the start of the Registers in 1838 to 1938. In my limited spare time I spent hours and hours in the echoing, cavernous rooms humping the huge volumes one at a time from the shelves to the desks (there never seemed to be a desk vacant immediately opposite the required volume), making in my own shorthand a rapid copy of the entries and then humping them back to the shelves where quite often someone else had in the meantime mistakenly placed their volume in my vacated space. I needed to copy from four volumes for each year for births, four for marriages, four for deaths. I humped twelve volumes for each year, 1,200 over the hundred years. I then returned home for the entries to be typed and placed in a ring binder.

I met many interesting people during my days there. I got to know the professional genealogists, who were always the noisiest; they walked confidently in and knew exactly where their volumes would be and were then inclined to throw them with a resounding thump on the desk. They could open the enormous volumes to within a page or two of the one they needed. After a few hours I found that I could do this – SINDEN was before SMITH and just after SINCLAIR and a few SINDALLS. Several times I picked the brains of the professionals. They and I soon sided against the crass amateurs – usually women, I'm sorry to say – who arrived in pairs (sisters?) armed with too little information: 'Excuse me – can you help – I'm looking for a Mr Smith who was eighty-three – I think – when he died in – I think – 1952.'

I carried my completed hundred-year file around in my briefcase, and at any spare moment I could check the individual trees that were being sent to me by my ever-growing band of Sinden correspondents. One day, while attending a quite unrelated committee meeting, I left my car, with the briefcase in it, in a multi-storey car park . . . On my return the briefcase had gone! (It was never recovered.) I was shattered. I recalled Kipling's 'Or watch the things you gave your life to, broken, and stoop and build 'em up with worn out tools' and returned once again to Somerset House . . . It was quicker the second time.

To go back before 1838 I had to start on the Parish Registers kept by individual churches. Many, but by no means all, have been deposited with the various County Records Offices, so off I went to the churches around Battle and the Records Office at Lewes. I had soon discovered that my own immediate family came to Brighton from Salehurst after a period of two generations in Hawkhurst (Kent). In the Hawkhurst Parish Registers I made several fascinating discoveries – well, fascinating for me, but probably terribly boring for you; I do apologise: it can only get better in the next chapter.

My great-great-great-grandfather Henry and his wife Philadelphia had obviously moved to Hawkhurst with his brother William who had married a local girl with a most unusual Christian name: Happy. The two families had children at regular intervals: they were sometimes baptised on the same day in a joint ceremony. William and Happy were inclined to give their children unusual names – the first was named Zebulon – but after recording their

6

births the Register was strangely silent. None of their children appeared to marry (Henry's did) and there were no burials recorded for either William, Happy or their children; nor in any other Parish. The family quite simply disappeared. What had happened to them?

In 1974 Diana and I paid our first visit to Canada and once again I made a nuisance of myself by telephoning the few Sindens in the various Canadian directories. (Throughout all my telephone calls I was only once told to mind my own business.) All of them, I learned, had originally come from within the same ten-mile radius of Battle!

In England most of the Sindens I called seemed to *know* of me, but not in Canada. There the Sinden *known* to everyone – indeed with some claim to immortality – is Harry Sinden, the manager of the Boston Bruins ice hockey team, the man who had restored national pride when he led, as a player, the victorious Canadian team to trounce the then unbeaten Russians in 1958, and yet again, as manager, in 1972. Diana and I were subsequently invited by him and his wife Eleanor to join them at matches played by the Boston Bruins. I think I surprised Harry by knowing the rules of the game, having been for years a keen supporter of the Brighton Tigers team, but I was continually unnerved to see people approaching with autograph books – only to pass me by and ask for Harry's signature. Boston's leading player and star of the team was an enormous hunk of masculinity by the name of Phil Esposito. Harry's daughter could never pronounce the name and referred to him as Phyllis Posito.

On one occasion in Toronto my telephone call was answered by a woman – Margaret Sinden by name. She apologised profusely that she and her brother John, an executive with Air Canada, could do little to help in my Sinden researches. They knew nothing of the previous history of their family before they immigrated from England in the 1840s and settled in Prince Edward County; the first ones to arrive were William and Happy and their children, Zebulon . . .

So that is what happened to them! I had, at last, found the branch closest to my own.

Also, outside Toronto, Diana and I enjoyed the hospitality of Donald and Novella Zinkon (her mother had been a Sinden). In London I had already met James Sinden from New York who, now working in Switzerland, is a world-famous mycologist – No, I didn't know what it meant either: he is an authority on mushrooms.

Moving later to the United States I at last met a remarkable lady with whom I had already been in correspondence, Elizabeth Wright (née Sinden). She had caught from me the genealogical bug and had become so infected that she drove her car across America several times in search of hidden Sindens and sent the details of her researches to me to fill in the early background from the Church Registers. Between us we have now nearly completed the Sinden tree. There are still one or two wayward branches, but twigs merely.

Meanwhile, back in England, I continued my researches and made further discoveries. One of my favourites is an entry in the Burial Register at Salehurst: '10.3.1808. William Sinden aged thirty-nine. Blown into five parts: his head; leg and thigh; body and one leg and thigh; arm and arm; from the sudden explosion at Brede Gunpowder Mills, 7 March.'

Another intriguing entry is registered in Brighton: 'George Ralph Sinden died from severe injuries to the neck and left shoulder and other parts of the body caused by a bag containing sand (used as ballast) having accidentally fallen from an aeroplane whilst flying over Richmond Place, Brighton on the 8th day of July 1918.' He was the only civilian casualty in Brighton in the First World War.

While on the subject of graves and worms and epitaphs I must tell you of my Uncle Francis who was a solicitor in Hove. Uncle Francis was enormous, largely the fault of his mother who lived quite near his office and daily took him a basket of fattening goodies because she was convinced that her daughter-in-law was starving her beloved son. Not surprisingly he weighed over twenty stones – we knew this because he could not use the usual bathroom scales with their twenty-stone limit.

When Uncle died in 1956 my father (his older brother) was shattered and with my mother chronically ill at the time he asked me as the only available male in the family to check on the funeral arrangements. The undertaker greeted me gravely: 'I am deeply sorry. When I told my father – who was a friend of your uncle – that Mr Sinden had passed away he was most upset and instructed me, "I want you to make a good job of Francis." I hope I have.'

Uncle was the first dead person I had seen. They had indeed made a good job of Francis: he looked like a Pope in robes with frills at his neck and wrists as he lay in a vast rectangular coffin: it was explained that the usual-shaped coffin would look ludicrous around such a vast bulk. I told the undertaker that my father's one worry was that because of the weight the assistants might drop Uncle as they lowered him into the grave.

'Oh, don't worry about that. I've got six strong men on the job. There's a lot of weight there, and it's all dead weight.'

In Hove Uncle Francis had been involved in public life and when his funeral was held at a Methodist church, the whole of the Hove hierarchy was there; the Mayor and his Corporation; the Police in force (Uncle had been an inspector in the Special Constabulary); the Masons in their aprons; the Rotarians; his office staff and many more. The church was crowded as we sat awaiting the arrival of the procession. The organist played solemn music and we waited, and waited. Black ties were straightened and orders of service were rustled as we continued to wait. The organist, glancing in a mirror to see if the cortège had entered behind us, repeated his repertoire for the third time. And still we waited. Husbands whispered to wives. Official watches were consulted. Seniors whispered to juniors. The relatives of the deceased unnecessarily assumed a responsibility. Still we waited. Suddenly the organist pulled out the stops and the music swelled. The congregation stood and joined in the opening hymn as we stared firmly ahead. Rather self-consciously the vicar rustled past, took up his position on the altar steps and looked apologetically first at the family and then at the Mayor.

Where was the coffin? With no explanation the whole service was conducted in the absence of the principal.

Only later, when we emerged into the bright sunlight, did we discover that the undertaker's six strong men had carried Uncle up the steps of the church, where, after several abortive attempts, they failed, because of its size, to get the coffin through the baize 'baffle' doors. Throughout the entire service Uncle had been left in the porch.

Oddly and sadly enough, I have encountered some of my biggest genealogical problems over two theatrical forbears: Topsy and Bert Sinden. It took me considerable time to discover that 'Topsy' was born Harriet Augusta in 1876. After becoming a Gaiety Girl she achieved some fame as a skirt dancer in the mould of Loie Fuller and preceded Adeline Genée as première danseuse at the Empire Theatre at Leicester Square. Her brother Bert, born in 1878, was a dancer/comedian. I never met either of them but Bert married Gertie Latchford and had a son Albert whom I would like to trace.

Halfway through my self-imposed research the simple fact dawned upon me that, while we have two parents, we have four grandparents, eight great-grandparents, sixteen great-great-grandparents, thirty-two great-great-great grandparents, sixty-four . . . and so on; doubling up with each generation. As a new generation seems to arrive on average every twenty-five years, I calculated that in the year 1500 (about the time that the original William Senden was born) there were 262,144 individuals (with conceivably 262,144 different surnames) who, in couples, engaged in the act of procreation and produced 131,072 children, who, coupled again, twenty-five years later, in

1525 produced 65,536 children
who in 1550 produced 32,768 children

1575	16,384
1600	8,192
1625	4,096
1650	2,048
1675	1,024
1700	512
1725	256
1750	128
1775	64
1800	32
1825	16
1850	8
1875	4
1900	2
1925*	ME

But for a slight imbalance of genes my surname might have been any one of at least 262,143 alternatives. To trace them all would be a hopeless task so I settled for my sixteen great-great-grandparents. I should be grateful for any help with the Fullers, Cadbys, Corneys, Ayres, Aldertons, Browns, Wiltshires, Bennetts, Collins, Grinyers, Harts, Oldhams, Foggs and Frenches.

I told you it was boring, didn't I?

* Actually, in my case, 1923.

2

ONE. TWO. THREE. FOUR.

A telephone call from Terence Rattigan asked, 'Can you sing?'

Now this is one of my claims to fame — not only am I colour-blind, a non-swimmer and a non-dancer, but I can sing out of tune better than anyone else, at least anyone else known to me or my family.

To digress, my colour blindness is inherited from my maternal grandfather: 'egg-shell' blues are identical to 'egg-shell' greens. My wife will say, 'Look how green the sea is today' — to me it looks the same blue that I expect it to look. I have the same trouble with certain reds and browns. In the autumn Diana will say, 'Look at the amazing red leaves of that tree' — to me all the trees look in varying shades of the expected green. Traffic lights present no problem: I see two reds and a blue; I stop when I see one of two reds and go when they change to blue. I once bought some large-scale maps (six inches to the mile) of our particular part of Kent where there are endless man-made waterways. The maps are black and white and every field, wood, house and road is outlined — what fun to colour them! I found the children's paint-box and insisted that I be left alone to carry out my task. Blue for the waterways and grey for the roads was easy enough but what about the fields? I called out to Diana, 'Am I right in saying that blue and yellow make green?' A very tentative and anxious 'Yes' came in reply. I felt that I could not just put one green wash over all the fields — each should be painted separately and preferably in different shades, so I mixed a little blue and yellow and carefully painted six incontiguous, non-adjacent fields. Now was the moment to ask Diana's approval . . .

She could not disguise her horror — 'Which of the paints have you been using?' Confidently I pointed them out. 'But that is purple and that is orange!' she cried and then showed me the correct ones. I managed to wash out most of the old colours on the map and started again using the correct blue and yellow, six fields in one shade, six in another, six in another until I had completed the whole area. Once more I showed it to Diana expecting at least a little praise. Equally she didn't want to hurt my feelings. 'Yes – every one of those fields is green but not one green is the colour of anything that grows in a field.' But I am still very proud of my map.

Terence Rattigan's voice was still ringing in my ears. 'Can you sing?' I could not evade the question. 'No,' I said.

'Good; because Binkie is wanting to put on a musical of *French Without Tears*: Robert Stolz is to compose the music, Paul Dehn the lyrics and Billy Chappell will direct it and we all want you to play the lead. Have you ever appeared in my play?'

'Yes, indeed – at various times in the past I have played Alan, Brian and Kit.'

'Well, you can choose whichever part you like and it will be built into the lead – you know what they can do with musicals.'

I remembered many years before that I had been working with Glynis Johns when she told me that she would shortly be off to New York to see a producer who had some idea – stupid we thought – of setting Bernard Shaw's *Pygmalion* to music and would she consider playing Eliza . . . I realised that musicals could be based on the most unlikely material. I assumed, when Terry had said 'good' in answer to my riposte that I could not sing, that the 'lead' would be a non-singing part; whereas Terry – I later discovered – assumed that I was merely being flippant. I told him that I had most enjoyed playing Brian, the part originally created by Guy Middleton, and before I knew what had hit me I was committed to be the lead in a musical to be called *Joie de Vivre* with the greatly experienced Joan Heal as my leading lady.

Within a week I was trying to get out of it, but no one would take my protestations – that I could not sing – seriously. Of course you can, I was told, anyone can sing – look at Rex Harrison – a few lessons with a singing teacher and you will be fine. I was therefore packed off to start taking lessons from a man who at my first visit told me that my voice was a misplaced tenor.

Really! In 1943 Leslie Charteris Coffin had made me speak as a bass, then in 1953 for films Iris Warren made me a baritone; now I was to sing as a tenor. Way ahead of rehearsals I was sent the words and music of my two solos (solos! It was getting worse and worse. 'A Man Must Be Mad' and 'I'm Sorry, But I'm Happy'), and three times a week the teacher and I trilled through them.

I couldn't yet devote my full time to lessons because I was in the middle of rehearsals for a television play called *Love From Italy*, translated from the French by Kitty Black, with Billie Whitelaw as my leading lady. This was my first meeting with Kitty: many years before she had been the most incredibly efficient secretary to Binkie Beaumont, the czar of H. M. Tennent Ltd: he realised her worth and put her in control of his newly formed Company of Four at the Lyric Theatre, Hammersmith, where, in eight years, she presented successful seasons which included outstanding productions of *Venice Preserved*, *Crime Passionel*, *Richard II*, *The Way of the World*, *Dark of the Moon*, and *The Relapse*.

Love From Italy is forever imprinted on my mind, but it may be difficult for me to explain why: let me try. My character was of a particularly evil young man who manipulated everyone, including his wife, to his own nefarious ends. He treated them like puppets. The play opened with my making a long speech – two whole pages long! – to the viewer describing my plan of campaign and for this the director had a clever idea: my head would fill the right-hand side of the screen and the people I was talking about would be on the left – reduced to the size of puppets. This was done by placing the other characters a good thirty feet behind me and when I turned my head apparently to face them, the focus shifted from me to them. (Do you see what I mean?) Well now: in those days – 1960 – acting on television was a far more nerve-racking business than it is today. An hour-long play had to be recorded in exactly one hour; if anything went wrong there was no chance of a retake, editing was practically unknown, the mistake remained for all time. I have seen actors literally sick with terror: the terror produced panic: in a panic you were more likely to forget your lines: if you forgot your lines the world would know – and you might never work again. For a good hour before the performance, the corridors were filled with actors pacing up and down, no one could relax. So it was in this mood that we approached the hour of *Love From Italy*.

The cameraman who was responsible for the long opening shot was equally agitated: if I were to lean one inch backwards, I would be out of the frame; one inch forward, I would obscure the 'puppets'. He asked me if I would come on to the set a few minutes early so that he could line up his shot. I stood on my marks – they had fixed battens to the floor so that I could not move my feet. 'Could you lean forward a little? – too much – back – ah! – too much – a very little forward – that's it – no – back a smidge – that's it! – can you hold that position? – well, can you see my hand? – good – if I move it to the left, lean in, move it right, lean out – OK?'

It was all very well for him, but I also had to remember an hour's dialogue beginning with a two page speech of some complexity. But at that moment all was ready. 'On your marks, everybody' – I had been on mine for two minutes – the timing mechanism was put in motion. 'We go in one minute from . . . now.'

That was the longest minute I have ever known. Not allowed to move by a half an inch, all my sinews tightened and in some strange suspended way every line I was due to say in the next hour raced through my mind. I hope I never experience a torture like it.

Love From Italy was duly recorded – without incident – but it was never shown: it was deemed, at the time, to be too salacious! But two good things came out of it – I was paid and Kitty Black remains one of our dearest friends.

Two or three days later came the different misery of the first rehearsal of *Joie de Vivre*. Actor/singers of the calibre of Joanna Rigby (of the long legs) and Barrie Ingham, Jill Martin, Terence Alexander, Anna Sharkey and Patricia Michaels were joined by a chorus of sixteen singing dancers who included the young Lindsay Kemp. I have never been more nervous. Joan Heal, with years of musicals and revues behind her, was in her element. The cast sat in a semicircle and, across the diameter, facing us, sat:

Terence Rattigan, the author of *The Winslow Boy*, *Flare Path*, *While the Sun Shines*, *The Browning Version*, *The Deep Blue Sea* as well as *French Without Tears*;

Robert Stolz, the composer of *White Horse Inn* and *Wild Violets*, had also conducted the original performances of *The Merry Widow* and *The Chocolate Soldier*;

Paul Dehn, one-time film critic of the *News Chronicle*, had also written the lyrics for *The Lyric Revue* and *Penny Plain*;

William Chappell, director of innumerable plays, had first joined the Sadler's Wells Ballet in 1934 as a dancer, and later designed the scenery and costumes for *Les Patineurs*, *Giselle* and *The Merry Widow*;

Peter Rice, the designer of *Time Remembered*, *The Winter's Tale* and *Much Ado About Nothing*;

the musical director Michael Steyn;

the choreographer Ross Taylor (he was later to become an impresario); and ten members of the production staff; from the illustrious Bernard Gordon, general manager of H. M. Tennent Ltd, down to the dogsbody, Alexander Schouvaloff (who was one day to become the director of Britain's first theatre museum).

Nervously – well I certainly was – we began to read the script, when, to my horror, as we came to a solo the singer strode across to the piano and joined the pianist – who had been playing the overture and chorus numbers – where they immediately broke into song. I began to tremble: we were coming to my first solo: and argh! There it was. I funked it. I made some lame excuse and we moved on. A week later, when none of the hierarchy were present, I did my solos for the first time. Nobody said anything. *Nobody* said *anything*. It was ominous.

For my two dance numbers with the chorus Ross Taylor prepared some miraculous steps which he illustrated.

'All right, boys and girls.'

Immediately every one of the chorus appeared to do them perfectly while I was still trying to work out which was my left leg. I had to pirouette. If I began facing front, I always ended up facing the back of the stage. To overcome this difficulty Ross arranged for me to begin facing the back. But it made no difference. Ingeniously I still finished facing the back. Although I was quite unable to master the simplest steps, I was reasonably athletic, so Ross gave me a lot of jumping up and down, running about and leaping on tables – all this disguised by the real dancers around me.

Then came the first dress-rehearsal and sheer panic. Up to this moment I had been accompanied by a charming and most helpful gentleman playing the piano; now there was a conductor with a full orchestra. The pianist had played the same notes that I was singing (singing?). Now the orchestra were playing something I had never heard before – to my ears it was an entirely different tune! No one had explained to me that it was I who sang the tune – the top line – and the orchestra played an accompaniment: Robert Stolz had written it and arranged it – at great expense of time, spirit and genius. I explained that I would do my best to sing whatever they played – but not something different. Fortunately the conductor had already perceived that I was no ordinary singer and he changed it all to suit me so that once again I could hear the tune.

We opened in Oxford. With boundless enthusiasm I threw myself into the part and managed to get through by sheer ebullience. But during the second week . . . near disaster.

One of my solo numbers, accompanied by a dance routine for myself and chorus, was preceded by a dialogue scene with Joanna Rigby and Barrie Ingham played to background music. At the end of the dialogue the other two exited and I immediately had to launch into my solo number, 'A Man Must Be Mad', joined by the dancers who were already assembled. This had caused me great trouble the previous week – I could never be sure when I was supposed to start because the 'intro' dissolved into my number. Thankfully the conductor had helped me out again by arranging for the drummer to give four loud bangs on his big drum, ONE. TWO. THREE. FOUR. and on the imaginary FIVE I would begin. But during a performance in the second week, one of the actors entered late which meant that the dialogue was late in starting. The blasted orchestra kept grinding inexorably on. The dialogue overran my music 'intro'. While we were still talking I heard my ONE. TWO. THREE. FOUR. go past! The actors made their exit and I was left alone with sixteen dancers behind me. The orchestra was playing – music that I didn't recognise. I was looking at the conductor who, while still waving his baton, was nodding at me. What was he nodding for? He then took to raising his eyebrows as he nodded. I was rooted to the spot. The seconds which seemed like minutes ticked by. He then started to grimace fiercely as he nodded. The orchestra continued to play a very repetitive tune. Perspiration was running down my face. At last, at long last, one of the dancers, bless her heart, tripped across to me, held my arm firmly and suddenly said, 'Now!'

Like an automaton I began, 'A Man Must Be Mad . . .'

During the interval the conductor arrived in my dressing-room torn between apoplexy and genuine concern for my sanity.

'Why didn't you watch me?'

'I did!' I screamed, 'but you just nodded at me.'

'I was giving you your cue – watch my baton.'

'But what was the music you were playing?'

'It is called "vamping till ready", we play the same bars over and over again until you are ready.'

Two performances later the same thing happened again. Someone was late; the dialogue overran; I heard my ONE. TWO. THREE. FOUR.; the others exited and I looked at the baton. It was going up, down, to one side, then the other. Up, down, side, side. Up, down, side, side. But which of those movements was my cue?! I looked at the conductor: he was nodding again. The blessed dancer was already at my side holding my arm – 'Now!'

Only later did I discover that I could take any of his nods as my cue.

We rehearsed the show every day and it got better and better. In each city the theatres were full for every performance. In Liverpool we had our first free days and Joan Heal asked me to join her in a round of golf. I explained that I had never played, but Joan was undeterred and I drove her in my car through the Mersey Tunnel to Hoylake where we spent a very happy four hours playing three holes. Joan had lent me a number 7 iron and I managed all my strokes with that; she was most complimentary and told me that I had probably created a record for those three holes and suggested that I should be given a handicap of 180.

At four o'clock we thought we had better leave to be in good time for our seven thirty performance. Driving into Birkenhead we encountered a traffic jam – not serious to begin with, but it slowly became worse and worse. Rounding a corner, a long straight stretch of road lay ahead and as far as I could see was a solid line of cars. Perhaps there had been an accident. A policeman was trying to control a crossing and as we slowly moved along, yards at a time, I asked him what the problem was.

'It's like this every night – three lanes of traffic coming out of Liverpool at the rush hour – only one going in.'

Still nose to tail at six o'clock we began to get worried: both of us were strangely silent. Contractually we had to be in the theatre at six fifty-five, but we both knew that we needed to be there by at least six thirty to prepare for the performance. We tried to reassure each other. We listened, apparently calmly, to the six o'clock news. Would it be simpler to park the car in a side-street and walk? No, this hold-up couldn't last long. But it did. I turned off the engine and got out to look: over the tops of the stationary cars I could just see the entrance to the tunnel. It was six thirty. We talked nonchalantly of our children, interspersed with remarks like, 'This is absurd!' 'Shall we telephone the stage door?' – 'No, we're moving again.'

We then started to laugh and by the time we actually entered the tunnel at six fifty-five we were hysterical. Cold sweat broke out under the middle of the Mersey at seven ten. At seven twenty we emerged to find the roads that formed the roundabout ahead quite deserted – no sign of a hold-up. With tyres squealing, I raced the car around St George's Hall, skidding to a halt outside the stage door at seven twenty-seven where we found a furious reception committee of the entire management: what could we say? – and

17

there was no time to say it – but before we could try, the tension was broken by a tight-lipped sibilant voice, trying to be authoritative, screaming, 'That's the lasssst time you two play with each other!'

The performance began at seven thirty, but the two leading players wore no make-up and clothes which appeared more suited to a golf course than an idyllic island off the South of France.

On Thursday 14th July, 1960, *Joie de Vivre* opened at the Queen's Theatre in London's Shaftesbury Avenue to a glittering first-night audience – Binkie Beaumont and Terry Rattigan had 'dressed' the stalls and circle beautifully. Adrenalin was running high and we threw ourselves into our task. Our first premonition of impending disaster came as the curtain fell on Act One. The applause of our friends seemed desultory. Act Two confirmed our suspicions as the audience failed to laugh – even the fact that I came in perfectly after ONE. TWO. THREE. FOUR. didn't cheer them up.

We fought on and arrived at the last line . . . In retrospect I wondered how Terry had been brave enough to use that same line as the final curtain of the original *French Without Tears* in 1936 – he must have been very confident of success.

The character of Alan has spent the play trying to avoid the seductress Diana; he has arranged secretly to return to London, sure that Diana will turn her attentions to a new arrival, Lord Heybrook. Heybrook enters. He is a schoolboy of fifteen. Diana triumphantly announces that she will join Alan on the London train.

'Stop laughing, you idiots,' Alan screams to the assembled company. 'It isn't funny. It's a bloody tragedy!'

Actually this was not quite the ending that Rattigan first intended. Talking to George Astley who was to have played Lord Heybrook, he surprised me greatly by saying that his part had been cut from the original production. In spite of my interest in theatrical history, I had heard nothing of any variation in the original text and could hardly believe it until George sent me his own copy of the script.

> Lord Heybrook enters with a Borzoi on a lead and says to the dog – sibilantly:
> 'Come along, Alcibiades. Follow your master.'

Apparently Bronson Albery, who presented the play, objected to this; George Astley was out, the character of Lord Heybrook became a schoolboy and the play a great success.

But on our first night when Alan screamed, 'Stop laughing! It isn't funny. It's a bloody tragedy,' that was all the audience needed. The gallery went mad – 'Too bloody right,' roared a solo voice above the collective boos. The curtain fell and rose again for the calls. Joan gripped my hand and with tears running down her face hissed, 'Smile!' And we did.

Amid the flowers and first-night telegrams Binkie, Terry, Robert, Billy, Paul, Peter, Ross appeared in my dressing-room, where Diana had joined me, to commiserate. And then off to a twinkling party given by Terry in his penthouse in Eaton Square. On all sides people were searching for excuses: 'the booing only came from a very small section of the audience'; 'the play is old-fashioned by today's standards'; 'whoever thought of Robert Stolz? – he was passé twenty years ago'; 'they don't want Rattigan today'; 'I spoke to one of the Sunday critics and he liked it'. Nobody said (to me), 'You can't sing and you can't dance.' Rex Harrison told me not to worry – the public will like it. Rex had only recently spent several years in *My Fair Lady* and we discussed some of the hazards of musicals: I told him of the great difficulty I had had of watching and following the conductor.

'Oh, you mustn't take any notice of him,' said Rex. 'You don't have to follow him – he has to follow you. In New York our conductor always wore a dinner-jacket but one night he turned up in tails with white tie and waistcoat. I sent a message down, "Tell him to take that damn thing off; I can see him!"'

For some years before this time I had ceased to read my newspaper reviews – I found them too disturbing. My natural resilience enabled me to rise above the bad ones – they could affect the box office of course, but I would not change a performance on which I had worked for weeks because one, or even more, of the critics might not like it. What always worries me are the good reviews. Invariably critics will single out a line or scene or a piece of 'business' as being worthy of praise and from that moment I become self-conscious and can never do it as well again. Diana orders copies of all the newspapers on the day following a first night; she then sits up in bed, reads all the reviews and while I stick my nose in a book she gives me a thumbs up or thumbs down for each critic's personal comment on me. All the reviews are then cut out, put in an envelope, and stored away until the play comes off when I then settle down and read them avidly, but quite uninfluenced.

As Diana read the reviews of *Joie de Vivre* her thumbs stayed down but at 11.30 a.m. there came a telephone call from Emlyn Williams, whose son Brook was playing Kit in our production. I had spent some time talking to Emlyn at the party the night before but now he was asking Diana and me to join him and his son for supper at the Caprice restaurant that evening. The Caprice had taken over the position, previously held by the Ivy, of being the smartest restaurant in London – you needed to be successful to go there. I shall never forget that heart-warming gesture: he knew that we had a flop on our hands and at the moment when everyone was deserting a sinking ship he threw a lifeline of friendship and with his charm and wit that evening he succeeded in raising us out of our unhappiness. However it was still a shock the next day when I made my fairly buoyant way to the stage door of the Queen's Theatre ready for the Saturday matinee to be greeted by three young girls asking for autographs. One of them said as I signed, 'Sorry to hear about the play.'

'What do you mean?'

'Well . . . coming off tonight.'

Fifteen weeks' slog. Eighty times ONE. TWO. THREE. FOUR. My voice a well-trained tenor – all collapsed in three nights. Six months later I asked Binkie how he could have been so certain that it was not worth trying to keep it going.

'By four o'clock on Friday afternoon,' he answered, 'not one seat had been sold for the following week.'

Diana wisely summed it all up when she told me later, very kindly, 'When you opened in Oxford it was quite awful, none of your real friends wanted to hurt you so we ended by saying nothing. Someone should have been brave enough to cancel the whole thing before coming in to London.'

Peter Willes always says that the best moment to ask an actor to do a play is when he has just returned from holiday or immediately after a flop.

Peter Willes was then Manager of Light Entertainment for Associated Rediffusion and had had a splendidly exotic career – why hasn't he written his memoirs? In his youth he was a matinee idol in Hollywood. Tall and unbelievably handsome with a shock of wavy blond hair, he was persona grata at all the smart parties which he enlivened with his caustic wit. He had an excellent war record until his armoured car was blown up in the desert. His legs were shattered and he was taken prisoner by the Germans. After being repatriated he spent some time with the Rank Organisation, learned shorthand and typing, became manager to Vic Oliver and then in 1955 joined the newly formed commercial television company Associated Rediffusion. I had first met him with my mentor Charles F. Smith in Brighton when he was on leave during the war and now, in my moment of misery, he extended a helping hand. Within two days of *Joie de Vivre* closing he asked if I would play the lead in an eight-part serialisation of Charles Dickens' last novel, *The Mystery of Edwin Drood*.

Dickens died in 1870 leaving this novel unfinished. What was left was published after his death and a very exciting story it proved. Dickens, however, carried to his grave the identity of the murderer thus leaving the reader with the mystery unsolved. Many writers have completed *Edwin Drood*; Associated Rediffusion commissioned John Keir Cross to dramatise their version with a new ending based on an idea from John Dickson Carr. It was recorded and shown in eight half-hour episodes plus the clever idea of having a discussion, just before the new ending was shown, between a panel which included Ngaio Marsh and Raymond Francis (who was then the most famous detective in Britain thanks to the TV series *No Hiding Place*) on who they might think was the guilty party. For the first time in many years I had a part I could get my teeth into: Jasper, a cleric addicted to laudanum.

The BBC was simultaneously screening a serial of Dickens' *Great Expectations*, but we were attracting the larger viewing figures. One day at rehearsal Peter asked me if I was happy with our production. I replied that surely it was not so necessary to hammer home each point and to underline so many details. 'Ah, but you have to remember,' said Peter, 'that the BBC can assume that their viewers have read the book; we assume that our viewers have never heard of Dickens.'

All too soon I was likely to be unemployed again – a London cab driver, referring I supposed to the last episode of *Edwin Drood*, said, 'Cor, it's you. I thought you hanged yourself last night!' – but my time spent in 1948 understudying nine parts in *Off the Record* paid unexpected dividends: the same manager, Daniel Mayer, produced *Peter Pan* at the Scala Theatre every Christmas and I was invited to play Mr Darling/Captain Hook to Julia Lockwood's Peter and Juliet Mills' Wendy. Wonderful play though it is, the same old production with the same old scenery had been resurrected every Christmas since 1904, so it was not exactly the most exciting offer. But there was nothing – absolutely nothing – else.

A young man by the name of Peter Hall had become the administrator of the Shakespeare Memorial Theatre at Stratford-upon-Avon – how splendid it would be, I thought, if I could get back into the classics, and prove myself. My agent contacted Mr Hall and shortly I had a telephone call from him, but not quite the call I expected. Had I expected to be asked to play Mark Antony, or Hamlet? I don't remember, but I didn't expect, 'Will you come to audition next Thursday?' Audition!! I hadn't auditioned for fifteen years. After eight years of having my name in lights over cinemas in London's West End I fondly hoped that I would never have to audition again. Audition? Had the theatre I had known before changed so completely – or had the ill-fated *Joie de Vivre* so reduced my marketable value? Audition! Of course, Peter Hall was a very young man who had made his name as the director of Samuel Beckett's *Waiting for Godot* in 1955 and I had spent eight years making films; he could not have seen any of my work in the theatre (he would have had to have been very quick to catch *Joie de Vivre*).

I remembered that the delightful Athene Seyler, shortly before this, had gone to see a young director who asked her, 'What have you done?' The astonished Athene, who had by then been an actress for fifty years, replied, 'Do you mean this morning?' And I remembered Frank Pettingell who when asked the same question, 'What have you done?' would not allow the young director to interrupt while he enumerated every play he had done since 1910.

Audition! I realised that I was in some danger of being labelled as reactionary. I had to admit that I had failed to understand the new movement in the theatre: when my friend of Bristol Old Vic days, Donald Pleasence, appeared in Harold Pinter's *The Caretaker*, I had gone to see him and sat through the first act mystified. During the interval I thought I saw the light and at the end of the play I raced round to his dressing-room, flung open the door, and said, 'Donald – you clever bastard! You've taken this play and shown what a real actor can do with a load of rubbish – you've exposed the lot of them!' Donald blanched and his mouth moved as he tried to find his words – 'Ah – Ah – Hello – er – erm – do you know the author – Harold Pinter?' – whom I had just squashed behind the door.

I swallowed my pride and went to meet the young Peter Hall.

At a flat in New Cavendish Street, four floors up in a birdcage lift, I was met by two young men: one introduced himself as Peter Hall, the other as John Barton. Both had eager, beaming faces. The Peter Hall one, although not quite asking me what I had done, plied me with so many questions that his enquiries elicited the same answer. The John Barton one tripped over a briefcase as he lumbered into the kitchen and after a lot of banging and crashing emerged a few minutes later with three mugs of coffee.

I discovered later that P.H. was thirty years old and J.B. thirty-two: I was thirty-seven but they made me feel as if I were ninety-seven.

'Have you prepared something?' asked the Peter Hall one, as he stretched himself full-length in an armchair.

I had mugged up the Crispin speech from *Henry V* which I had half-remembered from the time I had understudied the part in 1946.

The John Barton one hunched his shoulders eagerly, sank his chin into his chest and, peering through his eyebrows, said with a self-conscious chuckle, 'Then give us a taste of yer quality!' He then stood on a kitchen chair, lit a cigarette, and squatted on his haunches.

> . . . What's he that wishes so?
> My cousin Westmorland? No, my fair cousin:
> If we are mark'd to die . . .

I was doing it rather well I thought. The Peter Hall one nodded sagely and flashed an encouraging smile whenever I happened to look in his direction. The John Barton one beamed continuously as the ash fell on the carpet and the chair creaked ominously as he tipped it precariously on two legs.

> . . . And gentlemen in England now a-bed
> Shall think themselves accurs'd they were not here,
> And hold their manhoods cheap whiles any speaks
> That fought with us upon Saint Crispin's day.

I finished heroically. The Peter Hall one leaped up and cried, 'Yes. Yes . . . Yes . . . Thank you.' The John Barton one said, 'I'm jolly pleased with the way you coped with the parentheses . . . and the imagery . . . have you noticed . . .?' and he was away on a textual nicety.

'I'd like to talk this over with John first – can I telephone you on Saturday?' butted in Peter Hall.

On Saturday I was told that there was nothing they could offer me for the next season.

Oh golly – I've done it again! I've digressed. A real whopper this time. What was I saying? Just a minute – I'll have to check back . . .

23

Oh yes – I had been asked to play *Peter Pan* . . . I accepted and rehearsals began. Another 'young' man, Toby Robertson, then aged thirty-two, was the director, a fact that he omits in his *Who's Who in the Theatre* entry, which is strange considering the success he made of it.

One must never forget that the original production of *Peter Pan* in 1904 took place in a relatively small West End theatre – the Duke of York's in St Martin's Lane – so giving us the clue that J. M. Barrie intended an intimate setting. An Edwardian couple, Mr and Mrs Darling, are going out for the evening, leaving the maid in charge of their three children. The family also have a large sheepdog named Nana, who is really a sort of Nanny to them all. The children have fertile imaginations and no sooner are they asleep than their collective subconscious takes over: a 'boy' – the child they and we all wish we could remain – appears . . . He *flies* in through the open window and for the next two and a half hours we are in the world of make-believe. The boy is Peter Pan and, having taught them to fly, he takes the children off to Never-Never Land where they soon encounter the Pirate Chief, Captain Hook (who is really their father in disguise).

On several occasions in the past, certain leading actors have chosen only to play Captain Hook leaving a lesser actor to play Mr Darling – this of course makes nonsense of the whole story. How often in real life a father has to pretend: at different times I have been for my own children a lion, a tiger, a bear, an ogre, a gorilla, something from outer space – even a motor-car or a train: what fun to be a wicked Pirate Chief! This set me thinking about my appearance as Hook. I have seen Hooks dressed in superb Restoration costumes with immaculate Charles II wigs. Where would Mr Darling have found all that? I decided not to wear anything that could not be found in an Edwardian dressing-up trunk. My wig had long straight black hair. (Where would Hook have found a hairdresser in Never-Never Land?) We are told that Captain Hook lost an arm in a duel and in its place he wore a large hook. Now if he was (as I am) right-handed, I worked it out that it would be more logical if his left hand had been cut off by a cutlass; I therefore wore the hook on my left arm (it was made up from a butcher's hook), becoming, it transpired, probably the first Captain Hook in the fifty-six year history of the play not to wear his hook on his right arm. But an infuriating thing happened: I was photographed facing to my right so that the hook could be clearly seen, but when the management needed to use this photograph in the souvenir programme, they wanted me on the left-hand side of the page facing to my *left*. So they reversed the negative! Future theatrical historians will therefore assume that I wore the hook on my right arm like all my predecessors. For my facial make-up I used burnt cork – which any father could find.

Julia Lockwood (Toots as she is known to her friends) as Peter and Juliet Mills as Wendy were neither of them at the time far removed from childhood and they eagerly joined the 'young' in the play's battle against us, the 'adults'. Among my pirate band I was fortunate to have a number of actors of the older school, for some of whom it was the only work they did in a year. Nearly all of retirement age, they sat at home for eight months of the year and each Christmas they came out of hibernation for the annual production of *Peter Pan*. Their duties were not exactly onerous: they entered collectively and rarely had more than one line apiece before they made their collective exit. Having worked together for years, they always arrived early at the theatre to chat to their old friends, but as their first entrance came at least an hour after the play had begun, and as they all shared a dressing-room, the steady drinking there created many problems on stage . . . During the scene on board the ship, when the drama is mounting high, the dialogue should run:

> HOOK: *Something* blew out the light!
> FIRST PIRATE: Some *thing*?
> SECOND PIRATE: Where is Cecco?
> HOOK: He's dead!

One evening they were all very-nicely-thank-you when the Second Pirate, just – only just – standing, with a glazed look in his eyes, failed to say his line. There was a long pause. Everyone looked towards him. His eyes stared out into space. The pause continued until another pirate who was sitting down at the back (he couldn't stand) thought he could save his old chum's embarrassment and shouted, 'Where is Cecco?' whereupon the Second Pirate crashed into consciousness, wheeled upon his rescuer, and roared, 'That's *my* line!'

The most conscientious of the pirates – the one all the others relied on to listen to the cues and herd them in on time, was Lionel Gadsden. Gaddy, as he was known to us all, was by then in his eighties, a delightful, courteous old gentleman who sat so quietly at rehearsals that I didn't know for three weeks that he had himself played Captain Hook for nearly 2,000 performances – from 1913 to 1934 – a record unlikely to be broken. He it was who while appearing in another play in Canada was called upon to direct *Peter Pan* in Vancouver: the management had failed to obtain copies of John Crook's splendid music so Gaddy hummed all the tunes to the local conductor who wrote them down. Luckily Gaddy approved of my interpretation of the part and, when asked, gave me all the help I needed. For instance, in the Lagoon scene Hook, Smee and Starkey are hot on the track of their arch-enemy Peter, who mimics the voice of Hook.

> HOOK: Have you another voice?
> PETER: I have.
> HOOK: And another name?
> PETER: Ay. Ay.
> HOOK: Vegetable?
> PETER: No.
> HOOK: Mineral?
> PETER: No.
> HOOK: Animal?
> PETER: Yes.
> HOOK: Man?
> PETER: No.
> HOOK: Boy?
> PETER: Yes.
> HOOK: Ordinary boy?
> PETER: No.
> HOOK: Wonderful boy?
> PETER: Yes.
> HOOK: Are you in England?
> PETER: No.
> HOOK: Are you here?
> PETER: Yes.
> HOOK: Uvulas and Tonsils – where?
> PETER: Can't guess – Can't guess! Do you give up?
> HOOK: Yes, I give up.
> PETER: Well then, I'm Peter Pan!
> HOOK: PAN!

Surely, I said, that dialogue goes on too long – there is only one person to whom that voice could be ascribed, and once he gets the admission that 'it' is a boy – not an ordinary boy but a wonderful boy – he must know who it is – why go on?

'My dear Donald,' said Gaddy. 'You are a father yourself. Have you never played hide and seek with the children? You know perfectly well that the child is under the table but you still search everywhere else, even in the bread-bin. The one place you never look is under the table, but you still express the greatest surprise when the child reveals itself.'

He was perfectly right and the proof was that the hundreds of children in the audience all entered into the game.

One of the joys of this production was working with Russell Thorndike who played my right-hand pirate, Smee. The part had been created in 1904 by George Shelton who continued to play it until 1929. He was followed by a series of different actors until 1941 when Russell took over and he appeared in the part, off and on, for the rest of his life. He was born in 1885, the younger brother of Dame Sybil Thorndike, and they both made their professional debuts in 1904 in Ben Greet's production of *The Merry Wives of Windsor*. As a boy Russell had sung in the choir at the Chapel Royal, Windsor Castle, was boy soloist to Queen Victoria, and sang at her funeral. The choirboys were allowed the run of most of the castle with the one proviso that if the Queen should appear, they were to disappear – on pain of death. Russell told me of a most strange encounter.

At that time amateur performances were frequently staged in the castle with members of the royal family and others in the cast, and arrangements had been made for the celebrated wig-maker Willie Clarkson to make and dress the wigs. Now Willie Clarkson was a homosexual with a predilection towards choirboys – and Russell and his fellow choristers were eminently aware of this: each new boy joining the choir was warned, watch out for Willie. One day Russell and another boy were nearing the end of a long gallery (half a mile long, Russell used to say) when they heard Willie's mincing voice calling from the other end, 'Choirboy – choirboy!' Russell's friend was off like a shot but Russell was trapped as the panting Willie caught up with him and pleaded, 'Choirboy – help me – you must do something for me. My inside has been in a terrible state and only this morning I took some tablets, then on the way down I could feel them beginning to work – there was no lavatory on the train; the one at the station is out of order and I need one desperately – now!'

Russell, who knew the castle well, said, 'The nearest one is the other side of the courtyard . . .'

'I can't get there,' simpered Willie.

'Well, there is one here but it is for the private use of the Queen.'
'I don't care – I'll have to go – where is it?'
'Just up that little flight of stairs, on the right – but you'll be shot.'

'Then keep guard for me,' groaned Willie as he shuffled up the steps.

Russell stood there apprehensively when suddenly from the distance he heard a voice, a voice crying, 'Make way for the Queen!' Terrified, Russell looked around. It was now too late to run, but a large tapestry hung on the wall: he slid in behind it and flattened himself to the wall ('I hid behind the arras,' said Russell in later years). Through the crack he saw the royal party come round the corner and advance down the gallery – the procession was headed by the Lord Chamberlain with his Ward of Office followed by some Gentlemen-at-Arms; then came a wheelchair of basketwork in which was seated the aged Queen Victoria, Empress of India, Defender of the Faith. At the four corners of the chair walked four enormous Sikhs resplendent in their turbans and uniforms, sabres at their sides . . .

'Make way for the Queen!'
Russell trembled as they moved slowly along. But then, horror upon horror, as they drew level the procession stopped and he heard the creaking of someone getting out of a basketwork wheelchair and then the tap-tap of an ivory mounted ebony cane helping someone up stone steps, followed by the sound of a brass handle being turned . . . A Germanic 'Aarghh!' rent the air . . . Willie Clarkson's plaintive voice could be heard saying, 'It's only me, Your Majesty – Willie Clarkson – Your Majesty's Perruquier – sitting on his own initials.'

In 1911 Russell Thorndike joined Matheson Lang's company for a tour of South Africa where he understudied Lang as Hamlet. In Johannesburg this play was to be given at a gala performance attended by a glittering array of everyone in full evening-dress. That morning Lang sent for Russell and croakingly explained that it was quite impossible for him to play that night, his voice would not last out – Russell would have to go on in his place! It was a terrifying injunction. The audience had paid a great deal of money to see Lang himself. Before the performance commenced he peeped through the curtain: tiaras, necklaces, earrings, medals and decorations sparkled among the white ties and tails; in the stage box sat, alone, a magnificent-looking Boer with a mane of white hair, bushy eyebrows, moustache and goatee beard and wearing a voluminous black cape. Russell, young and undaunted, rose to the occasion and gave the performance of his life – it would serve Lang right. At the final curtain he returned, happy, to his dressing-room where a few minutes later someone knocked at the door and in came the magnificent-looking Boer and closed the door behind him . . . 'Very good, my boy – very good – I'm proud of you,' said Matheson Lang as he peeled off his mane of white hair, bushy eyebrows, moustache and goatee beard.

On being invalided out of the army after Gallipoli in 1916, Russell joined the Old Vic Company and in two seasons played an astonishing number and range of parts: Joseph Surface; Aegeon (*Comedy of Errors*); Campeius (*Henry VIII*); Cassius; Iago; Caliban; Hamlet; Richard II; Richard III; King John; Macbeth; Wolsey; Mark Antony; King Lear; Brutus; Touchstone; Launce; Launcelot Gobbo; Mercutio; Lysander. How about that for two years' work?★

A second career opened for him in the 1920s when he invented the character of the smuggler Dr Syn on whom he based a series of highly successful novels – some of which were filmed.

So this was the man who was now playing, at the age of seventy-five, the lovable Smee to my Captain Hook. We both shared a passion for Shakespeare and we both collected relics of past actors (theatricalia, as I call the junk I collect). Russell had at one time acquired a costume at the auction sale of Henry Irving's wardrobe which his knowledge and intuition told him was indeed the costume that Edmund Kean had worn as Richard III.

I think I must be eccentric; I always try to wear or carry something used by an illustrious predecessor, and on the first night of *Peter Pan*, Russell's wicked little hunched figure sidled up to me in the wings just before our entrance and he pulled out his dagger. 'My old Shakespearean [as he always called me], you'll never guess what this is . . .'

'No – what is it?'

'Irving's Macbeth dagger.'

I pulled out my dagger. 'Snap!' I said, 'Irving's Hamlet dagger!'

During a performance nothing could 'throw' Russell – if the theatre had burst into flames or if all the scenery had fallen down he would have continued as if nothing had happened. One day

★ Russell it was – as I mentioned elsewhere (*A Touch of the Memoirs*, Hodder and Stoughton, 1982) – who some years later, on a tour of American universities with the Ben Greet Company, created another sort of record playing Hamlet three times each day: the 'bad' Quarto version in the morning, the 'good' Quarto in the afternoon and the full Folio version in the evening.

during the run Lionel Gadsden asked me, 'Did I ever tell you the gag that du Maurier put in to the Frozen River scene?'

'No, you didn't,' I replied, eagerly hoping for a new laugh.

'Well; when Hook sends Smee to "call back the men" at the end of the duologue, du Maurier shouted after him, "Et tu Brute."'

I must admit I thought this rather disappointing – I would have expected something more amusing from du Maurier – but I thought the gag might provoke a reaction from Russell who would know the context of the original quotation.

'Have you ever mentioned this to Russell?' I asked.

'No, I haven't.'

That evening I told Smee to 'call back the men' and as Russell started to plod off upstage I called, 'Et tu Brute.' The reaction was electric . . . Russell stopped dead in his tracks and just stood with his back to me – for ten seconds; twenty; thirty. What had I done? Forty; fifty; I was genuinely worried. Slowly – oh, so slowly – the aged Russell turned and looked at me: a look of 'You whippersnapper – fancy trying something like that on me!' Then slowly he advanced (meanwhile the play had come to a standstill) . . . right up to me until, by standing on tiptoe, his nose practically touched mine. His face broke into a grin, he spluttered a raspberry into my face, turned and slowly made his way off. I never tried another on Russell.

Towards the end of the play when Hook has 'walked the plank', Smee discovers that his beloved Captain has been eaten by a crocodile, and says '. . . it has got him. The gentle Captain is inside! Thus crime is punished and all villains die! O tempora O mores, O cui bono cui! Och ay!' Our director, Toby Robertson, thought that the final 'Och ay' was too cheap a gag – as indeed it is, just to finish the scene on a laugh – and in the most wonderfully diplomatic way said to Russell, 'In your youth did you ever see any of the great "melodramatic" actors?' (He could have said 'ham' but didn't.)

'Oh yes – of course I did – Henry Irving, Wilson Barrett, many of them.'

'Then could you do that last line – the Latin line – as they would have done it – leaving out the och ay?'

With the idea of copying his heroes, Russell was in his element. At the end of the scene, as the lights faded leaving only a spotlight on his face, he looked up to the back of the gallery as he reverently removed his hat and with the utmost gravity intoned the requiem, 'O tempora O mores, O cui bono cui.'

ONE. TWO. THREE. FOUR.

It was one of the finest pieces of acting I have ever seen.

Certainly *Peter Pan* is one of the most rewarding of plays – the sheer magic of the piece pervades the theatre. Children – now adults – who came to see it have never forgotten it. I received a most magnanimous letter (remembering *The Caretaker*) from Harold Pinter: '. . . just a word to say that my wife, self and our son thought you were a marvellous Captain Hook. It was a splendid performance and we all enjoyed the show tremendously. Daniel, who is not yet three, sat entranced for two hours twenty minutes, which is a hell of a compliment to you . . .!'

My memories of this production would all be rose-coloured, but for the fact that just before the end of the run, in the middle of a performance, I opened my mouth to begin my soliloquy and no sound came out! I tried again but still nothing. The curtain had to be lowered and an explanation made by the manager: the understudy was rushed into my costume and within minutes the curtain rose again and he continued the performance. I retired to my dressing-room to await the arrival of a throat specialist who had been telephoned. Within half an hour the door opened and a bird-like man in black jacket and pinstriped trousers darted in and began to unpack his black case. 'Well – what have you been up to?' asked Norman Punt FRCS(Ed): MRCS: LRCP: DLO . . .

'   ,' I tried to say.

'Have you had any throat trouble before?'

'   ,' I answered.

'Good! – well let me have a look.'

Wearing a headband to which a large disc was attached in the centre of his forehead making him look like an Inca priest, he selected some instruments from a drawer in his case and lowered the disc on a hinge to a position in front of his eyes. I could then see that the disc was a convex mirror and, while peering through a hole in the centre, he directed a reflected light beam into my throat. 'Put out your tongue.' Before it could slip back he caught it by wrapping a piece of gauze around and held it firmly with his fingers. He then eased another tiny mirror on the end of a long handle past my uvula and down my throat: 'Say "ah".'

It was a damn silly thing to request under those conditions, but I tried.

'Mmm – yes: it's a Vocal Abuse Nodule – benign. In other words it is a corn on your vocal cords – usually caused by misusing your voice.'

ME – with vocal cords like old boots! When had I misused it?

'You will either have to rest your voice completely for about three months, or the nodule can be cut off.'

I could not afford to sit around for three months. There was no alternative. Within days I found myself in hospital – the nodule was cut off – not without some misgivings, and for the next three weeks I was not allowed to utter a sound. But would I ever be able to speak again?

On the strength of my salary from *Peter Pan*, Diana and I had bought a washing-machine which was installed towards the end of my convalescence, while I was still having to write everything I wanted to say. (Why did everyone in turn take to whispering to me?) My brother Leon had joined us and the three of us sat in the kitchen reading the instructions and experimenting with the new machine. Suddenly I noticed Leon about to do something contrary to the instructions. 'Don't do that!' I shouted . . . My voice was back!

Only then did Diana, Leon – and everyone else – reveal how worried they had all been. 'Don't do that!' had rung out loud and clear. I could return to work. Thank God!

Returning to work meant a six-week provincial tour of *Peter Pan* with Captain Hook rasping his voice nightly to the delight of the audience, but the anxiety and apprehensiveness of the actor. Norman Punt had, however, done his job well and my voice lasted out. Subsequent discussions with him brought to light my singing (sic) as a tenor in *Joie de Vivre* 'That was it,' declared Mr Punt, 'you were rubbing together two parts of your vocal cords that had never been rubbed together before.'

Still there was no further employment on the horizon until we heard that a new manager, David Hall, was to mount a production of *J.B.* – a play in verse by the American poet Archibald MacLeish. The play is set in a deserted circus ring into which two unemployed actors enter, Mr Zuss and Mr Nickles, who are now selling popcorn and balloons. They begin a theological discussion, with Mr Zuss assuming the role of God and Mr Nickles the role of Satan. Their world of the circus becomes the world of Job who is seen as J.B., a successful business man, and his trials are all given modern connotations. By the end of the play Zuss and Nickles have almost changed places – 'God' is quite disillusioned and 'Satan' is filled with compassion for the predicament of J.B.

John Clements was to play Zuss/God, Paul Rogers Nickles/Satan, and I was asked to play J.B. with Constance Cummings as my wife Sarah. Here, I thought, was the opportunity I had been waiting for: a play of consequence, directed by Laurier Lister, with a smashing cast. Yes, please!

There was a large cast – twenty-three speaking parts – including J.B.'s five children. The small parts of two messengers were played by young actors who were later to make names for themselves: Patrick Garland who was to become the director of the Chichester Festival Theatre and Peter Bowles who frequently occupies the centre of our television screens. The Voice of God had to be heard castigating J.B. It was to be prerecorded and played through loudspeakers dotted about at various points of the auditorium, but where could we find the Voice of God? The words were taken straight from the Book of Job – and how magnificent they are: 'Where wert thou when I laid the foundations of the earth . . . when the morning stars sang together and all the sons of God shouting for joy . . .?' and so on. I suggested that we might try my old friend Baliol Holloway, who could easily produce the grandeur, the command and sense of awe that was required.

(Some actors certainly can't: I remember that when John Wayne appeared with a host of other leading players in 'cameo' parts, in the film *The Greatest Story Ever Told*, he was only required to look at the crucified Christ and say, 'Surely this was the son of God.' His flat Western accent robbed the line of all sense of sublime wonder. The director George Stevens tried to advise him, but to no avail; for take after take he gave the same, 'Surely-this-was-the-son-of-God.'

Stevens, in desperation, said, 'We must have a feeling of . . . awe – yes, awe – can you give us awe?'

As the cameras turned Wayne advanced to the foot of the Cross and said, 'Aw-surely-this-was-the-son-of-God.')

I took a tape-recorder along to Ba Holloway's flat, where he gave a splendid reading of the lines. Laurier Lister had meanwhile already asked Sir Ralph Richardson to record them and I must admit that he was superb – his wonderful, idiosyncratic voice had such 'authority' in lines like 'He saith among the trumpets, Ha ha; He smelleth the battle afar off, the thunder of the captains and the shouting. Doth the eagle mount up at thy command . . .?'

Left alone on the stage I had to play this scene to the echoing voice of 'God' and I knew that my lines, by Archibald MacLeish, were no match for Ralph's from the Bible.

We took the play on a short provincial tour. We all had great faith in it, but something – none of us knew precisely what – was wrong. We rehearsed every day while we performed at night. We could not understand where the problem lay. Here was a play that had been an enormous success in the United States – indeed, one of the four most successful dramas in the history of American theatre – but the British public was not to be convinced.

The tour had its lighter moments, of course. In the first act, when J.B., his wife and five children always made their entrances and exits as a team, our waits off-stage were never long enough to return to our dressing-rooms so we used to gather in a remote corner and gossip in two groups: Connie Cummings and I in one, 'our children' in another. One evening Connie and I were so totally absorbed in what we were saying that I feared we had missed our entrance. I clutched her arm, 'Is that our cue?'

One of our daughters assured us that it wasn't. What a clever, responsible little girl she is, I thought, but to make sure, I said, 'Do you know what the cue is?'

'Oh yes,' she replied. 'When the actors on the stage stop talking.'

The play opened optimistically at the Phoenix Theatre in March 1961, but the next morning the reviews in the newspapers were not exactly geared to drumming up business at the box office.

'It is a bold concept,' wrote W. A. Darlington in the *Daily Telegraph*, 'for a modern poet to seek to write a parallel to the Book of Job in terms of the present day . . . does it come off? Not entirely, I think. Its best moments are very fine but there are passages which are hard to follow at first sitting, and one feels that this might be better to read than to hear.'

'What Mr MacLeish has given us is not so much a play as a dramatic poem . . . the result is a jerky, strident, narrative style that fails to engage the audience as it should' (Robert Muller, *Daily Mail*).

'Let me first of all declare my disinterest. If there is anything that bores me more on the stage than religious parables, it is religious parables in verse' (Milton Shulman, *Evening Standard*).

'. . . we may still be impressed with the ambitiousness of the attempt and impressed indeed we remain to the end. But not quite held and not, alas, satisfied. I would like to praise this play more wholeheartedly than I can. For it aims high and, as a piece of stage-craft, it is an achievement of which the company can be proud. Even as it is, and in spite of its shortcomings, many people will, I think, find it a rewarding experience' (T. C. Worsley, *Financial Times*).

The actors on the whole were praised for their work. Robert

Muller made the comment I was rather expecting: 'Donald Sinden offered workmanlike acting as J.B., a far better performance than one had reason to expect from an actor condemned for most of his career to peer into a Pinewood periscope.'

As I arrived at the theatre for the second performance I called upon my colleagues in their various dressing-rooms: none was exactly optimistic about our future, but John Clements was the most philosophical. 'Look Donald, this isn't going to run – I give it a couple of weeks – but you have a golden opportunity: don't waste it. You haven't played a dramatic part like this for years so use this time to experiment, to stretch yourself, to take risks – I'll help you if you want me to . . .'

So every night for the next two weeks (he was right, the play ran for two weeks and two days) we met in his dressing-room and conducted a post-mortem on the previous performance and with his encouragement I tried to make myself theatrically brave – to 'dare'. For instance at the end of my scene with Job's 'comforters' I had to weep. I had not been required to weep on stage for twelve years so I did the old trick of turning my head away from the audience and burying my face in my hands while my shoulders heaved in simulated sobs.

'It won't do,' said John. 'Don't be a coward – the audience want to see your face – give it to them – tears and all.'

All the advice that John gave me in those two weeks has proved invaluable. I will always be grateful to him for his kindness, his interest, his generosity.

With the exception of *Peter Pan*, which had a guaranteed six-week run over the Christmas period, my record in the West End theatre was not very impressive: four performances in *Joie de Vivre* and twenty in *J.B.* I was very depressed, out of work, with a family to keep. It is true that I had acquired a little cottage in Kent and it was there that I went to vent my frustration on the garden where I exhausted myself digging. Then came a telephone call from my friend and agent, John Cadell, to say that he and his wife were driving to Birmingham to see a new play called *Guilty Party* performed by Derek Salberg's repertory company: would Diana and I like to join them – just for the trip? Reluctantly I agreed, but by the time we left in the car I was in a bad temper. We drew up outside the Alexandra Theatre and made our way into the foyer. A tall, dark-haired ebullient stranger bounded over to us: 'Donald – my name is Peter Bridge and I am presenting this play in London. You are going to play the lead.'

35

3

THE FAULT OF ION TREWIN

Do you get the impression that you have read the final lines of that last chapter somewhere before? Well you probably have: they appear at the end of the first volume of these memoirs. In fact, everything you have been reading about *Joie de Vivre*, *Edwin Drood*, *Peter Pan* and *J.B.* should also have been in volume one but I cheated. I have to admit it: I cheated. I apologise, yes, but I cheated. It was all the fault of a Hodder and Stoughton director, one Ion Trewin by name.

Well, it wasn't really. I had promised to let him have the manuscript of my memoirs by a given date and I was hopelessly behind. I worked on, writing in my longhand 250 words to a sheet of foolscap: sometimes 249, sometimes 251, but on average 250. I must admit that I was enjoying it enormously, but I was behind-hand. One day I telephoned Ion: 'I know it is a silly question, but how many words make a book?'

'We are expecting about 85,000,' replied Ion.

'Hold everything,' I said. 'I have written 110,000 and I am only up to 1960.'

'Good God – let me see it!'

Ion seemed reasonably pleased with what he read and felt that Hodder and Stoughton could publish that amount – after some judicious pruning and editing – but was 1960 a convenient date to round off that part of my story? Indeed it was – I had completed the section dealing with my time at the Rank Organisation – but it was at a low ebb in my career. Two important things had happened in the 1950s. Television had come into its own – it seemed that no house was complete without one with the family huddled around it – and this resulted in cinemas being closed all over the country; practically no films were being made and the studios dispensed with the services of contract artists. Also, in 1956, John Osborne had changed the face of the British drama with his play *Look Back in Anger*. Whites for tennis by day and black ties for dinner by evening were theatrically 'out'; jeans, T-shirts and long hair were 'in'. Nobody thought of asking me to grow my hair and put on jeans. I was labelled as a light comedian. In 1960 I was a has-been.

Ion felt that this was too depressing an ending for my book – could I not give it a final upturn: a gleam of hope on the horizon? In fact the gleam of hope in the shape of Peter Bridge did not manifest itself until some time later and publication date was imminent so I cheated and moved Peter forward by twelve months. Now I have had to extricate myself from that tangle.

May I tell you a fascinating tale about the printing of that first book? You can't very well stop me . . .!

Over the years – quite accidentally – it has been my privilege to have encountered a number of extremely famous typographers (the men who actually design the lettering used by printers): Edward Johnston who in 1916, at the time when Frank Pick was changing the image of The Underground Electric Railway Company of London Ltd (later London Transport), designed their lettering; Eric Gill who, when unoccupied as a sculptor, had designed several typefaces and the lettering (now replaced) for the stationers W. H. Smith & Son; and Stanley Morison, who, when not helping to expose the Wise forgeries, designed the type used by *The Times*. Even before setting pen to paper I had suggested to Ion that it would be a delightful conceit if my book could be printed in a type designed by one of these men: indeed, to be specific, could I have the title and chapter headings in Johnston's London Transport lettering, and the body of the text in Gill's 'Perpetua' type?

The final manuscript, by now typewritten, was sent to Hodder and Stoughton's Production Department. Suddenly there came a panic phone call from Ion: there were problems; perhaps it would be easier for me to call Rob Dixon directly at his office in Sevenoaks (why Sevenoaks?). Yes indeed there was a problem: Johnston's lettering is copyright to London Transport. Would I be prepared to accept instead Gill's 'Sans Serif' (which Gill had originally based on the incised letters on Trajan's column in Rome), and which is very similar? Of course I would. Ah, but there is another problem, Rob continued: Gill's 'Perpetua' type is only available in Monotype – hot metal printing type – and has never been transferred to the modern photosetting process.

I was lost but did not want to admit it. 'What do you suggest?' I asked.

'I think the best thing for me to do is to send you some specimen typefaces and let you choose.'

Two days later through the post came ten sheets of paper each printed with a sample type.

Now I was really lost. To my inexperienced eye they looked practically identical. Rob thought I knew what I was talking about, but now I was about to be found out . . . In desperation I telephoned Nicolas Barker who, when not otherwise engaged at the British Library, wrote the biography of Stanley Morison. I told him my problem: 'What have they sent you?' he asked. I read out the heading at the top of the first sheet . . .

'No good,' said Nicolas.

I read out the second heading . . .

'Too black and white.'

The third . . .

'Absolutely dreadful!' his voice thundered.

The fourth . . .

'Bad Ws,' was the short answer.

The fifth was headed BEMBO ROMAN.

'Perfect! – just what you want. A splendid typeface and it has the added interest that it was designed by our mutual friend Stanley Morison.'

I made a note of 'Bembo Roman' and quite as an afterthought said, 'By the way, do these hieroglyphics at the top of the page mean anything?'

'What hieroglyphics?'

'In the top left-hand corner is printed 11 stroke 12.'

'Well, that's no good,' said Nicolas with authority. 'You want 12 on 13½.'

'Do I? – Very well,' and I made a note of 12 on 13½.

'What else does it say?'

'In the top right-hand corner is printed 28 ems . . .'

'Disgraceful!' screamed Nicolas. 'Oh no! You want 25 ems.'

'Do I?'

'Oh yes; insist on 25 ems. Of course your publisher will hate it – he'll fight tooth and nail – but insist on 25 ems – if he is intractable, settle for 26 but first insist on 25. I must go.'

And I was left holding the phone. I then telephoned Sevenoaks (why Sevenoaks?) and tried to summon up a little of Nicolas' authority. 'Hello Rob, Donald Sinden here. Look, I'll be happy

with the Bembo Roman ('Bembo Roman,' noted Rob) but I want
12 on 13½ (there was an ominous silence from the other end) and
I want 25 ems.' The continuing silence deeply worried me: had he
rung off? Or had a heart attack?

At long last a barely audible voice croaked, '25 ems?'

'Yes – 25 ems.'

Still more silence and then the croaking voice said, 'Well now
– look – I think I can get you 12 on 13½ – but 25 ems! Hodders
won't stand for it – they'll kick up a terrible fuss – 25 ems!! – I
might be able to get 26 . . .'

'All right – I'll settle for 26,' I hastily accepted, still without
having the remotest idea of what he was talking about.

It is now of little importance to say that I later discovered that
'ems' refer in printers' parlance to how many letters M would fill
up a line of print (how long is a piece of string?). This paragraph
is printed in lines 26 ems long. Printed in lines 28 ems long it looks
like this:

It is now of little importance to say that I later discovered that 'ems'
refer in printers' parlance to how many letters M would fill up a line of
print (how long is a piece of string?).

So there!

12 on 13½ is slightly more ludicrous. Each letter has to be cut
out of a block: 12 is the height of the letter; 13½ is the height of
the block. But 12 on 13½ what? Aha-ha! – 0.013837 (or 1/72) of
an inch is deemed to be a 'point': 12 of these would be the height
of the letter. (In fact, 1/6 of an inch high.) The block must always
be slightly bigger than the letter or the print would look thus:

Tyger! Tyger! burning bright
In the forests of the night

Now isn't that fascinating! We live and learn: I wonder if that
information will ever be of any use to me? At least it has helped
me to explain how I deviated chronologically at the end of volume
one. I am now back on the tracks.

There were still four months before *Guilty Party* could be re-cast
and re-produced for London – just time to fit in a delightful play
called *The Glove* for BBC Television with Herbert Wise directing.
In this production I worked for the first time with the legendary
Marie Löhr, who was then seventy-one years old. She had made

her first appearance on stage as a child in 1894 and later toured with the Kendals – Madge and William. (Madge was a very domineering woman totally preoccupied with the running of their company, with the result that poor, henpecked William was rather starved of affection. The story was told that in bed one night William plaintively tried to insist on his conjugal rights. After his repeated attempts Madge uncooperatively agreed saying, 'All right, but pass me my script.')

In 1908 Marie Löhr was engaged by Sir Herbert Beerbohm Tree at His Majesty's Theatre and there, among other parts, she appeared as Lady Teazle in a production of *The School for Scandal* which has gone down in theatrical history as one of the greatest productions of all time. From old photographs we can see that, as a young girl, she must have been entrancing: when I knew her she was a Grande Dame of the British Theatre.

The Glove was intended to be sixty minutes in length but when, on the day before the live performance (it was not prerecorded) we ran the play for the first time, it lasted seventy-five minutes! Fifteen minutes too long: and fifteen minutes represent a lot of lines: lines we had swotted away to learn.

Herbert Wise called his cast together, 'Get out your pencils, my dears – there must be a lot of cuts.'

'But we do it *tomorrow*!' cried Marie.

'That's right.'

'But Herbert, my dear, I can't do it – I'm an old lady – it is all I can do to learn the lines in the first place – I can't be expected to remember cuts at this late stage. I can't do it . . .'

Herbert realised that he had a very serious problem and cogitated for some time. His solution was that all the other actors had their lines cut drastically and Marie's were left intact.

At the camera rehearsal the next day Marie showed signs of being agitated and in the afternoon Herbert took me aside privately and said, 'Look, I'm very worried about Marie – she might crack up during the performance. I have arranged to have an extra camera which I will keep focused on you the whole time so if Marie goes wrong I will cut to you. Can you keep talking?'

I was nervous enough on my own account without the worry of this extra burden but what could I do but agree? That evening, in the studio, the seconds ticked up to starting time. An anxious cast launched themselves into the play and I could see the spare camera tracking after me wherever I went. Everyone was tense. The only person who displayed no trace of nerves and who sailed through the play like a battleship was Marie – the complete professional.

But *love* is what we all felt for Marie.

4

'ALF A BOOBULL OOP

Just after our second son, Marc, was born in 1954 I was invited by our friends, Jean and Gerry Campion, to visit them in Kent. It seemed a good excuse to escape from a house which at that time was inundated by females – mother and grandmother, nanny and daily lady – all looking after the new baby.

The Campions had bought two dilapidated semi-detached cottages in a remote area. Although an elderly retired farm-worker and his wife still lived in one half, Gerry set about restoring the other half based on plans which took into account that one day the whole building could be incorporated into one dwelling merely by the removal of a couple of walls, and judging by the age of the elderly couple next-door, that day would not be far off. Gerry's first step was to put two rooms in the communal roof space. Within a year or two the old lady died so Jean and Gerry took over the care of the aged widower. Gerry's abiding passion is food – it was no accident that he was cast to play Billy Bunter on television – so he built himself the most sophisticated and elaborate kitchen. Rather than attempt to tell you what gadgets he had, it would be easier to challenge you to say what gadgets he hadn't; and here Gerry prepared meals of astounding splendour. Old people being what they are, the elderly man next-door became something of a recluse and frequently rebuffed the care and attention that the Campions were prepared to extend to him. It was, therefore, rather macabre that when he eventually died his official 'cause of death' was given as malnutrition.

In that part of Kent a number of old and increasingly dilapidated farm cottages in the more remote areas were becoming redundant as the farm-workers naturally preferred to move to the new council houses in the villages. The Campions were idyllically happy in their rural retreat – why didn't the Sindens also buy a cottage? So Gerry and I explored the area and saw at least a dozen empty properties – all without bathrooms, indoor lavatories, electricity and drainage, and all falling into disrepair. Many were similar to the Campions': pairs of semi-detached cottages only one of which was vacant – and the other half? – Gerry's experience was not to be wished for. We drove for miles along the narrow lanes that interlace that part of Kent: originally mere cart-tracks, they lead from nowhere to nowhere. On one of our intrepid journeys, heading nowhere, my eye was caught by a glimpse of a chimney above a tall hedge . . . We pulled up and fought our way through brambles to find a long low building, little bigger than an old cowshed, huddled at the foot of what on the Romney Marsh constitutes a hill. It lay on a triangular plot of ground: on one side the tiny lane, on another was what I first took to be a stream until I learned that it was man-made at the time when the marshes were drained (these waterways are known locally as sewers), on the third side was the rising ground where sheep grazed amid a group of ancient oak trees.

Perfect! But who owned it? At the nearest house three-quarters of a mile away we were told the name of the farmer, Mr Ashby of High House Farm. The perfect stereotype of a working farmer – a round sunburned face topped by pure white hair – he had been born on this farm and here he lived with his wife and teenage son Derek, who was precariously poised on an enormous tractor as we approached. Yes indeed, Mr Ashby did own the deserted cottage.

If I had returned home to tell Diana that I had bought a country cottage only months after embarking on a mortgage for a house in London she might think I had gone raving mad, so to be on the safe side I asked Mr Ashby if he would rent it to me. He forestalled Diana by saying that I would be mad to take on such a property – it had no water, drainage, electricity or gas – but he would be prepared to let me have it for what the previous tenant, an old retired woodman, paid – six shillings and sixpence (32½ new pence) a week. I paid him a year's rent in advance, took some photographs of the cottage, thanked Gerry and Jean for their hospitality and returned to tell Diana of my escapade. I had underestimated Diana: she said I had gone raving mad even to *rent* a country cottage – until she saw the photographs and then nothing could stop her racing down with me to see the real thing.

I had been correct in saying it was a long low building: the entrance was at one end opening directly into a small room, which led into the largest room where the ingle-nook fireplace took up one entire wall. Beyond this room lay two more rooms each opening from the other. In fact there were four rooms in a straight line with no passageway. We could only afford to do the minimum amount of work on it. The ceilings had to be replaced or repaired and we installed a calor gas system of lighting and cooking, paraffin oil stoves provided the heat and in a corrugated tin shed at the back we put an Elsan lavatory – it was found necessary to beat the corrugated iron with a stick to ensure that no rats popped out while the loo was in use. There remained the problem of water until the splendid Mr Ashby provided us with a vast galvanised tank which stood in the yard and was filled every week by Derek who brought a fresh supply which was syphoned into ours from another tank on a tractor-drawn trailer. All drinking water, there-fore, had to be boiled first. We took down some junk furniture and carpets and moved in.

Jeremy, by now aged five, and Marc, aged one, had a nanny in London but this formidable woman refused to join us in Kent: 'I will not sleep in the middle of a field!' Just the four of us drove down through the apple blossom and hop vines and I don't think that before or since have we been happier.

The Ashbys allowed us the run of the farm where the children gambolled with the newborn lambs, Jeremy rode behind Derek on the trailers, Marc, quite unafraid, chased enormous bullocks from the patch of field he considered to be his, and at the end of a muddy day they were bathed in a tin tub in front of a blazing log fire with water heated in kettles and saucepans on the gas stove.

Diana was only mildly perturbed by the isolation – for two and a half miles the tiny lane only led from A to B, and there was no good reason for anyone to travel from A to B or even from B to A. The only cars to use the lane were the few residents, most of whom were abed by ten o'clock. At night we could stand outside our door and not see a single light except for the moon and stars.

At one time when I was working in London I drove down late at night to join the family. I arrived after midnight and thoughtfully turned my headlights off as I rounded the corner so that they would not wake the sleepers by shining through the windows. I then turned off the engine and coasted the last hundred yards to the cottage rather than wake anyone. Silently I unlocked the front door and closed it behind me. If I turned on a light Diana would be sure to wake so I undressed in front of the glowing embers in the ingle-nook, put on my pyjamas, crept through the room where the boys lay curled up, and stealthily opened the door into our bedroom. Not a sound did I make as I raised and lowered the latch and not a move came from Diana. Softly I moved back the bedclothes on my side of the bed and carefully sat on the edge and eased my legs between the sheets. I had performed the whole operation immaculately: I could now relax: I sank back on the pillow and – CRACK – the back of my head painfully struck something – Ouch! Lying on the pillow was a poker from the fire, placed there by Diana to be in easy reach should a marauder enter the house. But I was already in bed beside her and Diana had slumbered on.

We began to explore the neighbourhood. The nearest village was three-quarters of a mile away – and one could hardly call it a village. No shops – just six houses and a pub kept by a man known by all as the Sergeant – and it could hardly be called a pub; just a small room with a counter dividing it with a cellar below. The landlord, who had been a sergeant in the First World War, was a short round man with a bald head set on a bull-like neck and he had small piggy eyes. He lived all alone – which was not surprising as he was a man of most changeable temper, one minute wickedly acid and amusing, the next he could be so insufferably rude that one would vow never again to set foot inside his pub. Either because of this or because there was no passing trade, he had very few customers – in fact he discouraged them and took little notice of licensing hours, never erring in favour of the customer. He was addicted to horse-racing and when he could persuade a crony to drive him to a Meeting the bar remained closed until he returned – or later.

The Sergeant would let the children have bottles of Coca-Cola on a Sunday afternoon if they knocked at his back door, but if a bona fide customer arrived during opening time when he happened to be watching racing on television in his back room, he would roar out, 'Who is it?' If the customer was a stranger he received the unequivocal answer, 'I'm not open!' If the customer was someone known to him he shouted back, 'Help yourself!' Many times I have taken friends in especially to meet the eccentric Sergeant and left an hour later after serving ourselves and leaving the money in the till and only having heard his irate voice muttering away when his horse failed to win.

All the water in the Sergeant's pub came from a well in the garden. After a visit from a Public Health Authority Inspector the well was pronounced to be contaminated and the water undrinkable: any water served to the public must first be boiled. This so infuriated the Sergeant that for many years when, for example, someone ordered a whisky-and-water they were subjected to a lengthy tirade against the hapless Inspector; only then would the Sergeant retire to his kitchen to fill and boil a kettle and the customer – like it or not – got boiling water with his whisky.

Sadly the pub and the Sergeant are no more.

Of the six houses in the village one of them is known as The Manor, and here live a retired Indian Army Colonel and his wife, Charles and May Armstrong, who are at the centre of all village activities. Charles first called on us by water like a Venetian Doge, having paddled a canoe along the interconnecting waterways from his house to ours – a journey of three-quarters of a mile by road but about two miles by sewer. Charles is a 'pillar' of the village church, which was moved to its present position in 1854. Previously it stood as the last vestige of a monastic building on top of a hill a mile away, surrounded by fields, where the old graveyard still is and anyone with ancestors interred there is entitled to be buried with them, the coffin being placed on a farm wagon and drawn through the corn by a tractor. Once a year a service is held there and the villagers process from the church to the hilltop where some kind person has scythed a clear patch amid the overgrown tombs; a harmonium wheezes out the tunes as the congregation lustily sings the hymns, their voices carried by the wind across the surrounding marshes.

The oldest house in the village was once the home of the actor Harcourt Williams, who had been director of the Old Vic pre-war Company. Sadly, he died before we moved there, but how I wish I had known him – what a beautiful actor he was. Some of his performances have been captured on film; the French King in Laurence Olivier's *Henry V* for instance. Once, when in his house, I made a most awful remark. Have you ever done it? To say something unknowingly, although you should have known. Something so hurtful that you could have bitten off your tongue. A remark that for the rest of your life you will never forgive yourself for having made.

The contents of Harcourt Williams' house were to be sold and I was privileged to be shown round by his son. On the stairs hung a framed playbill for a performance during the First World War at Tenterden Town Hall. The cast list contained some legendary names, Harcourt Williams, Edith Craig, Gordon Craig and was headed:

ELLEN TERRY
and
JEAN STERLING MACKINLAY
in
A SHAKESPEAREAN RECITAL

I said, 'How amazing! That the little Town Hall at Tenterden should be the scene for all those famous people to appear in a single performance! The great Ellen Terry, the Craigs, Harcourt Williams . . . but who the hell was Jean Sterling Mackinlay?'

'My mother,' said her son quietly.

Ironically someone bought that playbill and quite unknowingly presented it to me. It now hangs on my wall as a permanent reminder of my faux pas.

Another of the six houses is occupied by Sheila and John Clark: he is a veterinary surgeon and Sheila is the hub of a social whirl. Between them they have made the house and garden quite delightful – I find it difficult to remember that in 1954 I could have bought the dilapidated property for five hundred pounds.

As the years passed we became more and more attached to our cottage – surely it would be sensible to incorporate a few mod. cons., like a bathroom and running water. But would it be worthwhile as I had no lease – I just paid my rent of six shillings and sixpence a week. The Ashbys by now were almost part of our family and one day I asked Mr Ashby if we could come to some contractual arrangement: could I take a long lease? Say for ten years. Slightly suspiciously he asked, 'Why? What do you want to do?'

'Build a bathroom and lavatory: lay on water and drainage – even electricity if possible . . .'

Mr Ashby pondered the question for some time – he never hurried over anything – this was a matter of serious import. Something was worrying him. Several times he seemed about to say something but changed his mind. At last it came.

'Just a minute. You mean you want me to let you have the cottage for ten years and in the meantime you will build a bathroom and lay on water and electricity – at your own expense?'

'Yes.'

'And at the end of ten years it will all be mine?'

'Well, yes.'

'But that is stupid! – why don't you buy it?'

Absurdly enough, that had never occurred to me. 'Ah. Yes. I'd love to – but how much do you want for it?'

47

'What do you say to two hundred pounds?'

I wrote out a cheque for two hundred pounds and the cottage was mine.

First I asked a London builder to come down and give me the benefit of his advice. He was clearly unimpressed: he looked all over our beloved, but rather pathetic little structure and joined me in the garden. 'You want to know what to do with this place, Donald? You see that field over there; if I were you I'd dig a big hole and push it in it.'

A local builder proved to be far more helpful and prepared to start work, but we had to obtain permission from the local authority who decided that the wall running the full length of the four rooms was structurally unsound and would have to be rebuilt. When it was removed we realised what a beautiful view we had been missing for four years and decided there and then to replace the wall with enormous windows. Water was laid on from the Ashby farm but electricity proved to be rather expensive: it had to be brought across a field, necessitating the erection of two poles, at the cost of two hundred and fifty pounds. A telephone proved to be an agreeable surprise. At that time the GPO guaranteed to provide a service for anyone, anywhere, for a standard connection charge of thirty shillings (£1.50) – we quickly took advantage of this and fifteen telegraph poles were erected to join us to the nearest supply.

We needed a fence to prevent the children falling into the sewer and we were lucky to find Mr Wilkinson. Old Wilkie was over eighty and lived with his equally aged wife – who wore thick pebble spectacles – in the same small cottage in which he had been born. All his life had been spent among saplings which he cut and made into fences and gates. I have spent many happy peaceful hours in his company watching his expert hands cut and fashion the green timber, but only once were Diana and I invited into his cottage. In his broad Kentish accent he told us that he and his wife had never been to London: they had once moved from the village for a couple of years just after they were married, but they didn't like it so they moved back.

'Where did you move to?' I asked.

'That were up Rolvenden way,' he said in a voice that could not have been more scornful if he had said Alaska. Rolvenden was only three miles away.

'Would ye take a glass of cider? I make it meself.'

Three minute glasses, the size of thimbles, were produced and gripping the neck with his thumb he slung the flagon over the crook of his elbow and carefully filled them: 'Bless ye,' he said as he clinked glasses.

I took a sip politely but it felt as if I had thrust a red-hot poker into my mouth: it was too late to stop the process of swallowing and the 'poker' seared its way down my throat: I caught my breath and couldn't speak. I looked at Diana but it was too late for her also. She was spluttering and tears started from her eyes. Wilkie's eyes were twinkling. His wife then joined us, picked up a tumbler, crooked the flagon on her elbow and glug-glug-glug filled her glass. 'Cheerio!' she said as she downed it in one long gulp. I think we had discovered the cause of the thick pebble spectacles.

Young Derek Ashby now had an 'intended' – a delightful girl named Judy who was teaching in a local school – but Derek was slow in popping the vital question. To bring him to the boil Judy and Diana devised a scheme. Judy packed in her job and came to stay with us in London. That did the trick: the telephone line between the farm and London positively smouldered. Oh, the deviousness of women!

But suddenly tragedy struck. Derek's father died and within a year his mother was killed in a car crash. Not only was Derek – an only child – left to run the farm, but because of the iniquitous tax laws of the time, he had to find double death duties on their estate. It is greatly to his credit that he succeeded in doing so with the help of the redoubtable Judy whom he subsequently married. Their children, Louise, Rebecca, Mark and Jocelyn, are now around the age that Derek was when we first met him.

The rejuvenated Ashby farm is still our first port of call each time we arrive in Kent.

Each side of our triangular plot is owned by a different farmer. Across the sewer is Forty Acre field owned by the Withers-Greens: we have now known three generations of the family. On her father's death, Brenda took over until her son Paul was of an age to run the farm and he is a great friend of our son Marc. Behind us, the rising ground is owned by Charles Bates, who married Joyce, built himself a house on the top of the hill and lives there with their daughter Elizabeth. The steeply sloping field on which, at different times of the year, the sheep graze and bullocks crop the grass around the oak trees, is for us the most peaceful spot in England. We sit on the bank and gaze across the valley and a walk around the perimeter is always the first thing we do on arriving at the cottage and the last thing we do before returning to London.

From Charles Bates' father we bought a small part of the field on which to build a garage. To facilitate this we had to erect a new five-barred gate – surely these are the most beautiful man-made objects to be found in the countryside – and I asked a local firm to do this for me. A lorry arrived early one morning and deposited the gate, ten feet long and four feet high; a great baulk of oak nine feet long on which to hang it; and a seventy-six-year-old man with a severely humped back, to do the job. The top five feet of the hanging post had been neatly cut into a nine inch by nine inch square section but the lower part was still as it had grown on the tree and this had to be securely embedded in the ground. The little bent old man took a spade and slowly began to dig down into the hard earth, moving around the hole in a circle as he cut down inch by inch. He then took a shovel and removed the loosened soil before resuming his slow encircling.

Chop, chop, round. Chop, chop, round – shovel, shovel. Chop, chop, round . . . Inch by inch he dug into the ground. I had been watching him, agonising for the poor old man. I could bear it no longer. 'Would you like me to do a bit for you?' I asked, flexing my muscles.

The old man raised his head as far as his humped back would allow and narrowed his eyes as he summed me up: 'Aye . . . Aye . . .' and he passed me the spade.

Less than half his age, I threw myself into the task. My arm juddered each time the spade struck the ground, chop-chop-chop-round-chop-chop-chop-round-shovel-shovel-chop-chop-chop-round at considerable speed. Within ten minutes my right arm had seized up from the wrist to the shoulder. The old man just stood still watching me. 'I think I heard the telephone,' was the only excuse I could think of.

'Aye . . . Aye . . .' he said and carried on slowly. Chop, chop, round . . .

The next time I looked out, four feet of solid oak was embedded in the ground and he was stomping the earth around it. I watched him as he bored two holes for the L-shaped hinges which he bolted in. He then picked up the ten-foot-long gate as if it were a child's bicycle, lowered it on to the hinges, and placed a spirit-level along the top. Peering at it, he uttered a phrase that I will never forget, 'Oo – ah – half a bubble up.' (Except that it sounded like, 'Ooer 'alf a boobull oop.') A calamity, I thought; the poor chap will have to dig out the post and reset it ''alf a boobull doon'. I had not calculated on the ingenuity of the old craftsman. He removed the gate, took a sledgehammer, struck the bottom hinge a resounding blow, replaced the gate, applied the spirit-level, peered at it and muttered a satisfied, 'Aye . . . Aye . . .'

During our holidays in Kent we found time to explore the area around: visited Canterbury, Bodiam Castle, Knole and Hever; rode on the Romney, Hythe & Dymchurch miniature railway; bathed from the safe shallow sands at Littlestone and Camber; experienced the tranquillity of the Romney Marshes; discovered the churches of Barfreston, Brenzett, Brookland, Ivychurch and New Romney; climbed the cobbled streets of Rye; puzzled the origins of the grid-like pattern of streets in Winchelsea.

Several of our friends had moved to the area. In 1953 the opening of Butlins' hotel at Saltdean near Brighton was celebrated with a weekend of festivities to which Diana and I were invited. There we met a young couple who, we discovered, lived only a hundred yards from the flat in Chelsea which was then our home. Donald Derrick was – is – a dentist with a practice in Park Lane and his wife Patricia Lambourn was a journalist with – is now a director of – the International Publishing Corporation. They were kindred spirits and a firm friendship developed between us; Don became the family dentist and agreed to be godfather to our son Marc. We discovered that they too rented a cottage in Kent and in the course of time they too bought one of their own.

There are problems in having a dentist for a friend. I was seated in his chair of torture one day, my mouth open, with rolls of cotton-wool jammed around my gums and a suction tube hooked over my lower teeth, a nurse had another vacuum cleaner operating near the back of my throat as Don leaned over me with a screaming, water-cooled, high-speed drill which began to grind nearer and nearer the nerve. Above the racket I heard Don's voice say, 'Will you make an after-dinner speech for me?'!! Did he seriously expect me to say 'No' at a moment like that?

In 1956 I waited one afternoon with other parents for our children to come out of school. Occasions such as these produce a sort of camaraderie and I found myself talking to a pretty woman in a blue dress with big blue eyes. Her name was Wendy Batsford she told me, and her husband, Brian, was a publisher – but of course, Batsford Books, I had a shelf full of them – and who would in time become Member of Parliament for Ealing. We exchanged addresses and shortly afterwards Diana and I were invited to dinner, and thus began another family friendship. Brian and I shared an abiding interest in the history of architecture – he once organised a dinner-party to which he invited a number of well-known contemporary architects. Brian and I should have been in our element but we were saddened to find that the professionals knew remarkably little of their historical background; they knew all about stresses and strains, quantities and bending moments and cubic footage but none of them could name the architect of the Victoria and Albert Museum* for instance or define Palladio's modular system of proportion.†

Many years later when the Theatre Museum project was about to falter, Brian was instrumental in preventing its demise by asking the right questions in the House of Commons and lobbying his influential colleagues. We have much to thank him for.

One day in the early 1930s Victoria Sackville-West was out driving with her diplomat husband Harold Nicolson when they detected the ruins of an old castle. They bought it at once. Only later did they find that it had originally been built by one Thomas Baker who was an ancestor of Vita on the distaff side. They set about making Sissinghurst Castle one of the most unusual residences in England. She was a superb gardener and, to the designs made by Nicolson, she turned the overgrown deserted area into the splendid showplace that it remains today. On one of our first visits, Diana and I had the pleasure of meeting the Nicolsons and from then on we spent many hours in their company. Vita rather liked our children and took them up the seemingly secret staircase, past her study, to the roof of the tower, while Diana and I talked to Harold sitting on one of the garden seats, specially designed for Sissinghurst by Edwin Lutyens. Since their deaths one can hardly move in the endless crush of tourists up and down the tower and I am told that it was most unusual for Vita in her lifetime to allow anyone to go up.

* Sir Aston Webb, 1849–1930. Also designed the Admiralty Arch and the façade of Buckingham Palace.

† Ackerman in his biography of Palladio defines it thus: 'A proportion, in the system of Belli, of Palladio, and also of Barbaro's commentary on Vitruvius, is the relation of two quantities (eg 6:4) such as the height and width of a wall or the length and breadth of a room. To extend a proportional relation into three dimensions so that the wall and the floor plan could be integrated, they used what they called a "proportionality", or "the relationship of proportions" in which three or more terms could be linked (eg 9 : 6 : 4).'

I'm not surprised they didn't know!

At the turn of the century, on a similar journey of discovery from her house in Winchelsea, the actress Ellen Terry saw a beautiful timbered farmhouse in the village of Small Hythe and immediately – impulsive creature that she was – fell in love with it and asked the occupants, an elderly shepherd and his wife, if they would sell it to her. No, they wouldn't. But, insisted Miss Terry, if ever they thought of selling would they please let her know. Some years later she received a postcard addressed to ELLEN TERRY, LONDON saying simply, 'Willing to sell'. She had quite forgotten about the whole thing and had to rack her brains to recall the significance of the postmark. Luckily she did, and the house became her home for the rest of her life – she died in the room to the right of the front door in 1928. Her coffin was drawn through the Kentish lanes on a farm wagon to Tenterden Station and thence to London: after the cremation her ashes were enshrined in the Actors' Church, St Paul's in Covent Garden. Her daughter Edith (Edy) Craig continued to live at Small Hythe with the two ladies who were her lifelong friends: Christabel Marshall, who, having assumed the pen name of Christopher St John, was known as Kit, and Clare Attwood, who was known as Tony. There they entertained their friends: Radclyffe Hall and Una Troubridge; Virginia Woolf and Vita Sackville-West.

Over the years Ellen Terry had bought several adjacent cottages and when Edy died in 1944 she bequeathed the entire property – nearly the whole village of Small Hythe – and the contents of the farmhouse, to the National Trust as an Ellen Terry Museum, with the proviso that Kit and Tony should be entitled to live in one of the cottages known as the Priest's House for their lifetime.

Ellen Terry's niece, Olive (Terry) Chaplin, was installed as curator of the museum. She was no longer young when I first met her in 1954 and as she guided me round the house so full of Terry memories I mused on the fact that this woman was the daughter of one of the famous Terry sisters, Florence, who for years had been the mistress of the actor/manager Sir Charles Hawtrey and had borne him a son Anthony, who in turn had become an actor/manager. The fact that I too was an actor nurtured our friendship and we spent many hours together gossiping about people she had known in the theatre of the past. She let me loose in the library among books signed lovingly and presented to Ellen. She would suddenly come flying in carrying a bundle of old clothes, 'Have you seen this, Donald?' as she shook the dust from an exotic costume – 'Nell wore this as Lady Macbeth at the Lyceum,' and there was the actual beetle-wing costume that I had so often seen in Sargent's painting at the Tate Gallery. Today this and other costumes she shook out for me are mounted on dummies behind glass. Much safer for the costumes of course, but lacking the element of discovery and the thrill I had in actually handling them.

Several times I tried to meet Kit and Tony, but was always warned off by Olive: 'They see no one – the door is permanently on the chain.' Kit St John had edited the famous correspondence between Ellen Terry and Bernard Shaw; she had 'ghosted' Ellen's autobiography *The Story of My Life* and had also written a biography of Ellen. She had known Henry Irving and presumably knew a great deal of the suspected relationship between the famous pair so when Laurence Irving was writing the definitive biography of his illustrious grandfather he called on the eccentric Kit and Tony at the Priest's House. He knocked on the door and after a lengthy pause he heard shuffling, bolts were drawn and the door creaked open a few inches. 'Good morning – my name is Laurence Irving . . .' The door was slammed in his face. So what chance had I of meeting the pair who represented a vanished era?

Some years later I heard that Tony Attwood, by then in her nineties, had gone into a nursing home and feeling that my chances of meeting the equally aged Kit were slipping away, I girded my loins and nervously hammered on the door of the Priest's House . . . No answer. I hammered again. But still not a sound. I would have been quite thrilled if I had even heard a shuffling. At that moment someone walked down the lane and enquired my business. I explained, and was told that Miss St John had been taken the week before to Tenterden Hospital. Off I raced. I felt like someone in a Brontë novel as I approached the grim Victorian building which I later learned had been the Workhouse before being converted to a hospital. On hearing my enquiry for Miss Christopher St John, the porter, instead of giving me simple directions, referred me to a nurse who, after some indecision, asked me to wait. On her return several minutes later she requested me to follow her to the matron. This tall, authoritative woman said, 'Thank you, nurse – close the door. Now, Mr Sinden. Do you know Miss St John? Are you a relative?'

I began to wonder what all this was about – was every visitor cross-examined in this way? – but I gave her a brief run-down of my various attempts to visit Miss St John over the previous six years.

'Yes. Well. I don't know what to suggest, but I can only tell you that she has been insufferably rude to the other patients. She is quite impossible to my staff – she refuses to do anything she is told. She has twice thrown her tray – containing her lunch! – at one nurse. She has only been here a week and I am beside myself. She's a terrible woman. But if you insist I will take you to the door of the ward and point out her bed, but then you are on your own. I refuse to speak to her!'

I think she expected me to retire hastily, but I was determined. Through the glass panel of the door we looked into a ward containing twelve elderly ladies in twelve beds. 'Hers is the third from the end on the right,' said Matron, disappearing in a cloud of ether. Several rheumy pairs of eyes turned as I opened the door and followed me as I moved forward to the third from the end. Propped up on four or five pillows was a bony head like the head of an unwrapped Egyptian mummy, sparse white hair very closely cropped betrayed that it had fairly recently been washed; red blotches showed through the parchment skin. A nose, the like of which I saw only many years later on a Mayan woman in Southern Mexico, stood out from her prominent cheek-bones like a sickle, her lower lip protruded and drooped flabbily. It was purple in colour. How many young girls – many with famous names – had been first seduced by this woman and kissed by those lips? Her bloodshot eyes stabbed at me as I stood beside her, her claw-like hands twitched on the sheet . . .

'Good afternoon,' I said quietly, 'my name is Donald Sinden and I have come to visit you.' She continued to look at me coldly. I sneaked a look around – there was nothing for her to throw. Gingerly I sat on the chair. 'I would like to talk to you about Ellen Terry . . .'

At the mention of the magical name her face softened and tears welled in her sagging eyelids. A claw reached out and clutched my hand: 'Did you know Nell?'

She didn't hear my reply – her mind had locked into a period when they all danced attendance on the divine Ellen: 'Oh. She was so beautiful. She said to me . . .' Prompted every now and again by me, she talked about 'Nell' for nearly two hours and I heard first-hand many anecdotes of the Lyceum days. She told me about two of Nell's disastrous marriages, first to Charles Wardell and then to James Carew.

'You know that Edy and Teddy were illegitimate? Well, Nell had always loved and remembered Ailsa Craig in Scotland so she invented the surname Craig for her children, but when she married the man Wardell, it was the first time the children had a legal father and Edy even called herself Edith Wardell for a time. I never liked him . . .

'Long after Nell's death the man Carew died and we received a visit from his executors or relatives or something saying that he had requested that his ashes should be scattered on the farm at Small Hythe – and there they were in the nasty little box: well, we didn't want to have anything more to do with the horrible little man so I told them to be off and I shut the door on the lot of them. The next morning I went out to the garden and do you know what they had done? – they had thrown the box over the hedge and there it was in the middle of the lawn. I buried it in the rubbish dump over by the hedge.'

A bell announced that visitors must leave: as I rose she gripped my hand and her nails cut into my flesh, 'Oh, please come again – they are so awful here,' she pleaded.

The matron had been waiting for two hours expecting me to be ejected at any moment. 'What on earth did you do to calm her down?'

'We talked about a very beautiful mutual friend,' I replied enigmatically.

Kit St John died before I could visit her again; followed shortly by Tony Attwood and they were buried side by side in the little graveyard at Small Hythe.

Olive Chaplin and her husband Charles had the awful job of clearing out the Priest's House. When I next saw Olive she reported that it was 'in a terrible state – filthy – and you remember the shed in the garden? – well, when we succeeded in opening the door we found that it was full – full – of old copies of *The Times*, jammed floor to ceiling! We had a lovely bonfire. But right at the bottom of the pile we found a rusty old tin box. Charles wanted to open it but I said throw it away – it wouldn't be down there if there was anything in it. But Charles wouldn't do as he was told; the lock was rusted solid so he got a hammer and chisel and broke it open. What do you think was in it . . .? Well, guess . . . You can't? All of Nell's letters to her last two husbands!'

Some weeks elapsed before I saw Olive again. 'Have you been through those letters yet? Will you deposit them in the museum?' I asked.

'Oh no, my dear! I burned them – Nell would have wanted me to.'

I bought many things at the sale of the contents of the Priest's

House including a large quantity of blue and white Worcester cups and saucers and Diana arranged them around the pelmet boards at the cottage but unfortunately, during our absence, a bird got down the chimney and, terrified, flew around the room and every cup and saucer crashed to the ground. Olive assured me that she was expert in repairing broken china but sadly she joined the wrong pieces together and we were left with oval saucers and more cups than had been broken.

At Olive's house one day, having tea from her own repaired china, she embarked, 'I was going through one of my boxes of treasures the other morning – I have several boxes of treasures I must show you – I came across a tin box: I wondered what on earth it could be, so I opened it and there was a lot of dust inside. Then I remembered – it was Edy Craig's ashes. When she died she had asked for her ashes to be buried with Kit and Tony. I have hung on to them all this while but when the time came I forgot all about it. Too late now. I'll nip across one day and scatter them on the grave.'

A large country house in Kent had been sold and all the contents were to be auctioned – Diana and I adore auctions so off we went. Unfortunately we had been unable to attend the viewing on the day before, so had to depend on the sight of something being held up a few seconds before it was sold. We were all assembled in the Great Hall as the porter held up a representative drawer: 'Lot three – carved oak sideboard, seven feet long, as viewed in the basement.'

'Five shillings,' I said optimistically, receiving the laugh I had expected.

'Ten shillings,' said a man on the other side of the room.

'Fifteen shillings,' I retaliated.

'Sold, to the gentleman down here,' rapped the auctioneer. The last thing I wanted was a carved oak sideboard, seven feet long – but at fifteen shillings it had to be a bargain. Meanwhile we had reached, 'Lot nine, quantity of carved oak as viewed in the stables.'

'Five shillings,' I said again, receiving the same laugh.

'Ten shillings,' upped the man on the other side of the room.

'Fifteen shillings,' I countered.

'Sold, to the gentleman down here.'

It must have been my lucky day for carved oak.

As the auction progressed several pieces of furniture were shown which Diana coveted, but a dealer seated behind us always topped our limit. Diana glowered at him, but he still won.

'Two plaster statues of goddesses, six feet high, over there by the fireplace. What am I bid?'

We certainly didn't want them, but the dealer did.

'Five pounds,' in a voice of quiet expertise.

Aha, thought Diana. I'll teach him. 'Seven pounds ten shillings,' she called out maliciously while flashing a look at the dealer.

Ignoring the look he merely replied, 'Ten pounds.'

'Twelve pounds ten shillings.' Diana's voice was gleeful.

'We don't want them!' I hissed at her.

'Fifteen pounds,' from the dealer.

'Of course we don't, but that beastly man does,' she hissed back. And then out loud: 'Seventeen pounds ten shillings!'

Silence. Where was the dealer's next bid? His face was buried in the catalogue. Horror! He had opted out.

'Sold to the lady down here – are you two together?'

I wished we weren't.

That afternoon the sale continued in the garden. We bought several Lots of odds and ends before a large 'Ali-Baba' urn was indicated.

'Five shillings,' from me.

'Ten shillings,' from the original man.

'Fifteen shillings.'

'Sold. To the gentleman who didn't like the statues.'

Next day when we came to collect our purchases we were shattered. The carved oak filled an entire truck; the 'sideboard' was all in pieces and there was nothing of any interest in the 'quantity of carved oak from the stables'. To our horror we found that the 'Ali-Baba' Lot included a massive amount of polished granite which looked like assorted tombstones. Not only that, but among another Lot were included two millstones each weighing seven hundredweight.

'They'll cost you a fortune to move them,' said a man who turned out to be the former owner of the house. 'I had to pay to have them brought here and, by the way, that polished granite is the original front entrance of Harrods – I bought it when they redesigned it and took away the steps.'

After several abortive attempts, the removal man agreed that it was better to leave the millstones behind, but the Harrods front steps made very good garden seats. The six-feet-high statues of

goddesses have remained white elephants gently to reproach Diana
as she passes beneath them.

At two o'clock the following Sunday afternoon I answered the
telephone to hear a slurred voice saying, 'I'm the removal man –
you remember them millstones? – well, I'm down at the pub and
my mates reckon they know a way of lifting 'em. Would they be
worth a fiver? – delivered.'

The idea of two beautiful millstones – delivered – for a fiver
was very attractive. 'Done,' I said.

Three hours later a large cattle truck swayed up our lane, veering
from side to side. Inside were five farm-labourers singing at the
tops of their voices. 'We're pissed,' smiled the driver in an attempt
to apologise. The tail of the truck crashed down and formed a
ramp normally used to get cattle on board. The two weighty
millstones, each ten inches thick and four feet in diameter, were
standing on edge inside. Through the hole in the centre of one of
them a stout pole was inserted to form a long axle and with three
staggering men on each side, the giant wheelbarrow started to roll
down the slope. But they had overlooked that it would gather
speed and before they could stop it they were two hundred yards
further down the lane. They wheeled it back into the garden
leaving a deep trench behind them, and let it fall. The operation was
repeated, five pounds were handed out, black coffee consumed, and
the waving team zigzagged their way back up the lane leaving us
to design a garden around two immovable objects and two long
trenches.

Also at this time, Diana's parents sold their house and the new
owners did not want the enormous amount of beautiful York stone
paving which formed the paths so, as I was severely out of work,
we decided that, to utilise my time, we would transfer this paving
to Kent. As the contractors would only pick up from point 'A'
and deliver to point 'B' we called upon all our friends who manfully
– and womanfully – helped us to lift the massive slabs of stone
from the garden and moved them down to the roadside at point
'A' where they were carefully loaded on to a thirty-ton lorry.

The next day Diana and I awaited their delivery in Kent when
up the lane came an entirely different lorry containing an apparently
entirely different load of York paving. Puzzled, we tackled the
driver. 'Ah well, you see, the thirty-tonners only operate between
depots. This load was tipped out at the Kent depot last night and
loaded on this lorry this morning for local delivery.'

Tipped out! Every one of the large rectangular pieces that we had loaded in Hertfordshire was now broken in two or three pieces. We could have cried. But before we could remonstrate the driver had pulled a lever, the back of the lorry rose up, and the entire load was tipped, for the second time, on to the roadway. Hardly a piece was left larger than twelve inches across – and I was left to hump the entire lot into the garden. We now have crazy-paved paths.

Diana's parents had also given her some lovely things – china and copperware – which embellished the cottage, but sadly we were burgled and the whole lot was stolen. If these people only knew the heartbreak they cause. Whether or not one is insured is beside the point. Things which had been lovingly collected and which had been in her parents' house before she was born, and over which she had guardianship, had been stolen – for what? Not, I am sure, by someone who is short of the next meal but by someone whose instinct is merely to destroy – to destroy enviously the pleasure and pride of others.

But we learned our lesson. Now there is nothing in our cottage of any value – intrinsic or sentimental. It doesn't look so attractive but we are spared another possible heartbreak.

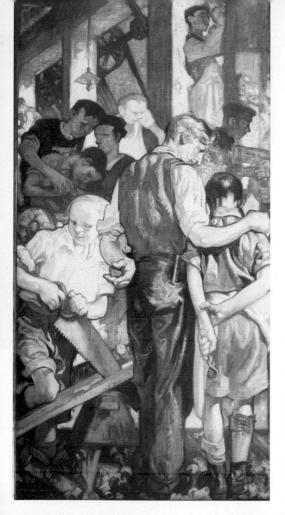

Since the publication of *A Touch of the Memoirs,* I have discovered the whereabouts of the painting (Left) by Frank Brangwyn for which as a boy I posed in 1933. Some ten feet tall, it is one of several murals in the banqueting chamber of Skinners' Hall in the City of London.

Below are two photographs of me used by Brangwyn to build up his composition. The man with his arm around my shoulders is his assistant, Kenneth Center.

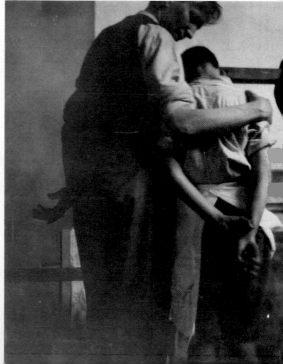

Me, Diana, Peter and Rosalyn Bridge about to be presented to Her Majesty Queen Elizabeth, the Queen Mother by Lord Willoughby de Broke (back to camera) at the St Martin's Theatre, 1961, during the run of *Guilty Party*.

The cast of *Guilty Party*. Standing: Ralph Michael, Hugh Cross, Duncan Lewis, Me, Michael Bates, Peter Stephens. Seated: Hugh Sinclair, Frances Rowe, Melissa Stribling, Ann Firbank, Anthony Woodruff.

Richard Plantagenet, Duke of York, in *The Wars of the Roses*, 1963.

Bernard Cribbins, Jill Melford and me in *Not Now Darling*, 1968.

John Barton, Stratford, 1963
(Chapter 7).

Charles F. Smith, Majorca, 1966 (Chapter
16).

Patrick (Tiger) Halsey, Lancing, 1968
(Chapter 9).

Russell Thorndike, Chelsea, 1965
(page 27).

'...And I tell you it wasn't Donald Sinden.'

Fame at last. The Rev Stephen Young in *Our Man at St Mark's*, my first television series, became the subject of a cartoon in the *Daily Sketch* (Chapter 10).

Captain Hook in *Peter Pan*, 1960. This is the first published photograph showing the hook on my left arm (page 24).

How to break an egg in mid-air with one hand. *There's a Girl in My Soup*, 1966 (Chapter 15).

The intrepid travellers set off for the palazzo in Naples. The Sindens: Diana, Marc, Jeremy; and the Cadells: Selina, Jill, Patrick (my godson), and Simon (Chapter 14).

The family in the garden, 1966.

Including Robbie the dog, we climbed to the top — but we came down by train (Chapter 9).

The Mayor and us at Shakespeare's Birthday Celebrations, Stratford-upon-Avon (Chapter 11).

Two portraits
by
Margaret Boden

Jeremy

Marc

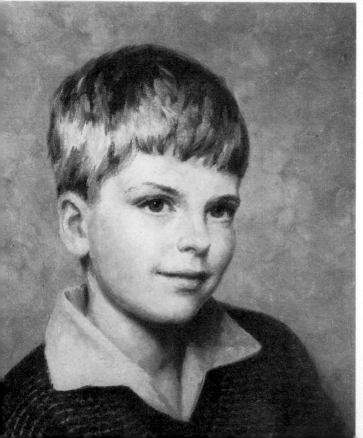

5

'WE COULDN'T GET SEATS FOR "THE MOUSETRAP"'

I do apologise – I have digressed appallingly, my worst digression so far. I'm blowed if I can remember what I was telling you about – will you excuse me while I flip back to remind myself.

So sorry. I won't be long.

Good Lord! I had to go back to Page 35. I was telling you about Peter Bridge and the play was *Guilty Party*. Yes. Well. Peter had assembled a splendid cast. Hugh Sinclair, whom I had first met in 1946 when he was married to Valerie Taylor, our leading lady at Stratford (he was later married to the painter Rosalie Williams), Ralph Michael, Frances Rowe, Ann Firbank, Melissa Stribling, Michael Bates (who had married a schoolfriend of Diana's, Margaret Chisholm), Hugh Cross, Peter Stephens, Anthony Woodruff and Duncan Lewis.

The play, written by accountant George Ross and actor Campbell Singer, and directed by another old friend Anthony Sharp, was a whodunnit of a different type: gathered at a party in one room are the directors of an important firm from which a very large sum of money has been embezzled. Someone in that room is the guilty party; the question is – who? No one is allowed to leave the room during the course of the play and gradually we learn of the private lives and motives of all the characters. The suspense becomes electric and the culprit is not discovered until the last moment.

We didn't do the usual pre-London preliminary tour but opened 'cold' at the St Martin's – one of the West End's most beautiful theatres: the auditorium is panelled in mahogany and the acoustics are perfect. All the men in the play were required to wear dinner-jackets and as the custom was, each actor was expected to provide his own. I took mine (a very expensive and beautiful one made by Hawes and Curtis) to the first dress-rehearsal, two days before we were due to open, but to my horror, all the heavy garden work I had been doing in Kent had developed my muscles alarmingly – my shoulders and biceps positively bulged out of the sleeves; and I was supposed to be an elegant, immaculately dressed man. (Hugh Sinclair meanwhile looked as if he had been poured into his suit.) It was far too late to have another tailored so off I went the next day to hire one from Moss Bros. In my pre-first-night state I failed to mention this to Diana or she could have prevented the calamity. After the second dress-rehearsal in my Moss Bros outfit I decided that the new jacket was a great improvement but I would wear my own trousers because they were better cut and hung better than the hired ones. So it was that I faced the sophisticated first-night audience and the nation's critics in a black jacket and midnight-blue trousers! One member of the press asked Diana if I was starting a new fashion, but nothing could stop *Guilty Party* being a success and we settled in for a year's run, thanks almost entirely to Peter Bridge. It was his first success and it pulled me out of the doldrums.

Peter had had a chequered career: in the RAF during the war, he later became a theatre manager, of the Arts and the old Winter Garden theatres, before selling the best seats to those who wanted them in a famous ticket agency. He then took a chance with the new Independent Television Company, Associated Rediffusion, as their Manager of Sport. In 1957 he returned to the theatre and in the following twelve years put on no less than sixty productions; an astonishing record. He it was who first presented an Alan Ayckbourn play in the West End; who brought over Hugh Leonard's *Stephen D* from Ireland, which launched T. P. McKenna and Norman Rodway on their careers; who first put on (unsuccessfully) Barry Humphries as Edna Everage; who produced successes such as *Relatively Speaking, Say Who You Are, Wait Until Dark*, and *How The Other Half Loves*.

The Bridge children, Michael, Andrew and Chris, were of an age with our two and the whole family soon became regular visitors to the cottage in Kent, but unlike his wife Rosalyn, Peter could never adjust himself to life in the country; tramps over the fields were not for him – he was an urban man and was never happy until he had driven off to the nearest town each morning and returned with every available newspaper.

There was no doubt that he was egocentrically bossy – the whole household, his or anybody else's, had to revolve around him. He lived and breathed theatre and knew everything that was going on – not only in the West End but all over the entire country. Managing on too little sleep, he regularly set off in his car to visit provincial companies which he made more difficult for himself by paying no attention to their geographical location. London – Edinburgh – Scarborough – Liverpool – Chichester – Bristol. He also saw all the end-of-term plays at the drama schools and helped many young students to find their first jobs. He was addicted to the telephone; his day always began at 7.30 a.m. with an hour-long conversation with his old friend and backer Edward Sutro. Frequently he would wake us (and other friends) late at night or too early in the morning with a call that never announced the name of the caller; a bright voice launched into mid-sentence, '. . . actor who worked with you at Stratford in 1963 – you know very well who I mean – wants to know . . .'

He was also the most generous of men, always returning from his regular trips to America armed with presents for the entire family. But as an impresario he was often too generous with the result that a play might run for a year or more but make no profit because he was paying the actors more than the box office would take. At other times a play had to run for months to pay for the parties he gave at the launching. Unfortunately, by the time of his premature death in 1983 he had spent all his own private money – but Peter could have given you a cast-iron reason for the necessary expenditure of every penny.

The theatre was his life. He was fascinated to know what made the public tick and during the run of *Guilty Party* he had a questionnaire inserted in every programme asking patrons: How often do you go to the theatre? Which newspaper do you read? Which critic do you follow? Do you go to a play because of the author or the names in the cast? Are you a visitor to London? and so on. One evening Peter and I left the stage door together and some young girls asked for my autograph but Peter grasped the opportunity and grilled them. 'Did you like the play?'

'Yes.'

'Why did you come to see this particular play?'

'Because we couldn't get seats for *The Mousetrap*.'

I have often been told that it was a delight to watch the old actor Richard Goolden (probably best known as Mole in A. A. Milne's *Toad of Toad Hall*) working on a new director. During the weeks of the rehearsal period the director would be asked a series of seemingly innocent questions: 'On my first entrance, could I be wearing a battered old hat – I could place it on that chair as I come on.' 'Don't you think this character would wear rather old baggy trousers?' 'Do you think an old shapeless jacket would be right?' 'I think this man's shoes are none too clean – do you agree?' 'Wouldn't it be jolly if he had pieces of string and a penknife in his pocket?' 'If you agree – I would like to wear a woollen shirt and a cardigan under the jacket.' 'When I go off, shall I take the old hat with me?'

The director, who had other things to worry about anyway, always deferred to the old actor's suggestions with the result that Richard Goolden, who in private life wore a battered old hat, shapeless jacket over a woollen shirt and cardigan, baggy trousers and none-too-clean shoes, and who rarely wore make-up, wandered into the theatre two minutes before the play began, went directly down to the stage, made his entrance, took off his hat, played his part, put on his hat again and went straight home.

In *Guilty Party* the script called for my character to have a small, neat beard and moustache, so, in emulation of Goolden, I grew my own and as I needed no further make-up all I had to do was put on my dinner-jacket. On matinee days this meant that at the end of the play I could walk directly from the stage across to the Garrick Club nearby for an early dinner and get back to the theatre just in time for the next performance to begin. As I entered the club one Wednesday, Michael Redgrave happened to be standing in the hall.

'Disgraceful!' he cried, 'coming in here with your make-up on!' and he attempted to pull off my beard.

'Ouch!'

'I'm so sorry – I thought it was false.'

It so happened that the following week I was due to begin work on a film – I could work at the studio at Pinewood each day and still do the play each evening – and for that I was required to be clean-shaven, so my own beard had to come off and I had to stick a false one on for the play. The next Wednesday I again went into the Garrick and by coincidence Michael Redgrave was again standing in the hall, this time with a group of other members. As I joined them Michael remarked, 'I did a terrible thing last week, I accused Donald of coming in here with his make-up on and I pulled his beard like this – Oh my God!' My false beard had – you guessed it! – come away in his hand.

★

It was another 'whodunnit' that gave rise to one of my favourite anecdotes.

The play concerned the theft of £500,000 from a safe to which there were two keys. These keys have at different times been held by all the characters in the play and if the detective can establish who had them at the precise time of the theft he can reduce his list of suspects. During the second week of rehearsals one of the actors suddenly stopped and asked another actor, 'Sorry to stop, but do you have one of the keys at this moment?'

'Yes.'

'And do you have one?' he asked another.

'Yes.'

'Well, I have one too.'

In great consternation they began the Act again and sure enough at that point of the play there were *three* keys. The rehearsal was broken off while a very worried director telephoned the author. 'One of the actors has just discovered that in Act Two – on page forty-seven – there are three keys.' A long silence was broken by the author hissing, 'Bloody actors!'

A play written by Patrick Cargill had had an extremely successful run in London under the title *Ring for Catty*. The story was used as the basis for *Carry On Nurse* (the second in the 'Carry On' series) and now I was to return to the fold at Pinewood to make another film with the same story, *Twice Round the Daffodils*, produced by Peter Rogers.

Here was nepotism at its best. Betty Box had become a producer under the aegis of her famous brother Sydney. She went on to make the highly successful 'Doctor' films with Ralph Thomas as director and his brother Gerry Thomas as cameraman. Now Betty's husband Peter Rogers – already a successful writer and producer in his own right – was my producer and Gerry had been translated to the role of director. As a team Peter and Gerry also made all the 'Carry On' films. And as I write Betty and Peter remain the most delightfully genuine couple we met during my time with the 'Rankery', as we affectionately termed the Rank Organisation stable.

I proved to be tougher than I suspected and coped with my double life pretty well, but – not for the only time – it was Diana who bore the brunt as she hardly saw me for four weeks. I left the house at seven thirty each morning for my drive to the studio; one hour's break for lunch, finished filming at six p.m., drove immediately to the theatre for the play to begin at seven thirty, home at about eleven p.m. and straight to bed. However, *Twice Round the Daffodils* was a great success at the box office, even if it failed to be nominated for a Venice Film Festival award.

I have to admit that since my eight years with the Rankery I have never enjoyed going to the cinema: for conjurors and magicians, I am the perfect audience, the complete sucker. I sit transfixed as doves are produced from pockets and rabbits from hats. I once spent hours watching a man doing the three card trick outside the stage door of a Shaftesbury Avenue theatre – he was there every Saturday and I came to know him and his colleagues, two of whom formed the nucleus of a 'crowd' and placed bets of five or ten pounds to encourage the unsuspecting who joined the group like moths, and two who watched for the police. It was to one of the latter I was talking as his eyes darted about looking for a tell-tale helmet. 'They can't win, Donald – George's hand is so quick.'

'Yes – but is it a trick?' I asked ingenuously.

He looked into my eyes briefly as he turned his head to peer up the road – a look of incredulous disbelief – 'Course it is, you twat!'

Nevertheless I decided to pit my wits against George and went over to the intent little group. 'I'll put 10p on that one.'

'10p?!!' hissed George through clenched teeth, 'do us a favour, Donald – bugger off.'

Their best trick of all was to disappear totally, cards, upturned orange box, and five men, at the first sign of a policeman. After he passed by there they were again: the box upturned, the three cards dealt and the betting under way.

As a boy I had gone many times to the Hippodrome in Brighton to watch the man who called himself The Great Dante performing spectacular tricks using the whole stage and more recently I have sat wide-eyed watching the late Tommy Cooper and Paul Daniels doing mystifying things in close-up for the television cameras. Of course it is all trickery and I don't know how it is done – and I don't want to know. I am a child in their dexterous hands and I want to stay that way: I still want to believe in the magic. But sadly I no longer believe in the illusion of the cinema – I know how it is done.

During my time in the Rankery I spent many hours in the cutting room and special effects department. I know when doubles and stuntmen have been used and I can pick out a 'model' shot a mile away. I met the man who painted by hand on the negative the flight of hundreds of British arrows that defeated the French cavalry charge in Olivier's *Henry V* because the eye of the camera could not pick out real ones fired from the bows. I have seen Clark Gable having to act in reverse as spears were pulled out from a wall behind him instead of being thrown at him and missing him as they appeared when the film was projected backwards. I have seen stuntmen fall out of windows and leading men then lifting themselves 'painfully' from the ground; have seen leading men say, 'Come on, let's go,' and a double riding away into the sunset. The editor of *The Cruel Sea* showed me a clip of film in which the *Compass Rose* was sailing from left to right across the screen. 'Now, that is exactly the shot I need to show the ship returning to Liverpool – but the ship is going the wrong way.'

'What do you mean?'

'You ought to know by now – the eye of the viewer accepts anything travelling from left to right as going *away from home*; anything going from right to left is *returning home*. What I shall do is reverse this piece of film and the ship will be going in the required direction.'

I have seen actors of note give performances of such ineptitude on the studio floor, only to be rescued at last by judicious editing in the cutting room. I have seen actors need twelve takes to say 'good morning'. I learned fairly early on that, just as in family snapshots, there are those who are photogenic and those who are not, so those who are photogenic make the successful film actors. The camera either loves you or it does not; it is as simple as that. Acting has nothing to do with it – in fact it shouldn't even be called *acting* – *behaving* would be a better word. The world's greatest actor and a truck driver from Ohio are all one through the lens. A film was exhibited recently called *Dead Men Don't Wear Plaid* in which the makers had used old off-cuts of performers such as Humphrey Bogart and stuck them together with new shots of contemporary *behavers*. It is therefore conceivable that a dead actor could win an Oscar for a film he never made. Farcical.

It was Eisenstein, I think, who made a short demonstration film showing various emotive subjects: a beautiful girl; a sumptuous meal; a yacht on a placid sea; a young child; a car crash; a body in a coffin etc; and between each shot he showed a young man in close-up reacting to each of the subjects. He later admitted that he had used precisely the same shot of the young man each time – it was the viewer who read into his face the expected emotion.

Roger Livesey told me that he was at one time engaged to play a small but good part in a film with Charles Laughton. He arrived on the set at eight thirty and Laughton took him aside saying, 'Roger, what are we going to do with this scene?'

'Well, Charles, I thought I would just learn my lines and do nothing.'

'Oh no – no – I'm the one who's doing nothing!'

That story contains the seeds of all the best film acting and all the best leading film actors have learned the art of doing nothing – it is the small-part character actors who must graft away as best they may.

I also learned that a film is photographed (and projected) at a speed of twenty-five frames per second: a frame is exposed and then a shutter/gate comes down behind the lens while the film is moved up to the next frame; the shutter goes up and the new frame is exposed, and so on. The shutter remains down for the same length of time as the film needs to be exposed; frame-shutter-frame-shutter, twenty-five frames and shutters a second.

The speed deceives the eye, but if you could blink twenty-five times a second you could sit in a cinema and see nothing!

Again, if you think about it, as the shutter is down for the same length of time as a frame is projected, a ninety-minute film is actually only forty-five minutes long. Perhaps you should ask for half your money back.

Diana now refuses to go to the cinema with me: while she sits with tears of laughter or sadness running down her cheeks, totally absorbed in the story, I sit chuntering away about the editing, speculating on how many takes were required to achieve a certain effect and counting the number of misplaced inflections.

On 26th January, 1962, during the run of *Guilty Party*, Diana arranged a splendid party at the Garrick Club to celebrate the twenty-first anniversary of my first appearance on the professional stage at the Theatre Royal, Brighton on 26th January, 1941. All our friends and colleagues turned up and Peter Bridge arranged for an illuminated scroll to be inscribed, recording all the plays in which I had appeared. This was presented to me with a glowing speech. It was not until twenty years later when I mentioned in my book *A Touch of the Memoirs* that my first appearance had been in 1941 that I received a letter from Geoffrey Spence, who had known me in my amateur days, pointing out that the date was in fact 1942. Happily, his letter enabled Diana and me to celebrate my fortieth anniversary for a second time.

While *Guilty Party* was at the St Martin's the lease of the theatre expired and after many years reverted to the owner of the freehold, Lord Willoughby de Broke, whose father had built it in 1916 for the impresario Bertie Meyer. The entire theatre was redecorated and Bertie Meyer, by now considerably advanced in age, returned as general manager. A magnificent party was given by John Willoughby de Broke. After a performance, the curtain fell, the audience left, the actors retired to their dressing-rooms, and forty-five minutes later the guests arrived to find all the seats in the stalls area removed, the curtain up again, our scenery gone, staircases led up to the stage – the whole building had become one vast ballroom. Long tables had been placed around the perimeter on which caterers had arranged a gorgeous array of goodies and champagne was popping all over the place. In the centre of the stage was a large round table for the use of the chosen few who were to join the guest of honour, Her Majesty the Queen Mother. A small reception committee, of which I was part, formed in the foyer to await the arrival of Her Majesty, and having been presented, the group moved down the stairs to the stalls. At this moment John Willoughby de Broke came up beside me and quietly said, 'You are to sit on the Queen's left . . .' Until then I had no idea that I was even to be at the main table. I need not have worried – the Queen Mother was enchanting and we nattered away like old friends – but I found myself at the receiving end of an occupational hazard: throughout the time, people were continually being brought up to be presented on the Queen Mother's right-hand side. Invariably they arrived as the Queen Mother or I was in the middle of what seemed a riveting anecdote, but dutifully Her Majesty turned to the new arrival. After a few minutes' talk she turned back to me and had to ask what we had been talking about. Many good tag lines were ruined that evening.

The only regrettable thing was that Diana was unable to join the select group, because of the presence of two inveterate social climbers who literally elbowed their way to seats at the table and who were firmly snubbed by the Queen. Except for that, it was a memorable evening.

It was not only the parts of the theatre used by the public that were decorated; the whole backstage area was done up as well and I was asked by the company manager if I would mind moving to another dressing-room for a week while mine was painted. My own dressing-room (comprising two small rooms with a connecting door) had walls and ceilings covered with cream and brown paint which made them look like an old-fashioned hospital corridor, so I asked the painter which colours he intended using this time.

'Oh, same as before.'

'Could it not be done more tastefully – perhaps one room in pink, the other in an egg-shell blue?' I suggested tentatively.

'I'll have to ask the gov'nor.'

The following day I was told that I could have any colour I wanted – if I paid for the paint. I couldn't understand the reasoning behind this but I thought that for the benefit of future generations I should agree.

The next day the painter informed me, 'The gov'nor says you can have your pink and blue but when you leave it will have to be put back to cream and brown – at your expense.'

The rooms remained cream and brown. I would just like future generations to know that I did try.

The pattern of an actor's working life is like a see-saw – one minute up, the next down. In 1960 no one wanted me. In 1962 I was wanted by everyone. The biggest problem was to equate my income for tax purposes; except that it was not just a problem – in those days it was impossible. In 1960 my earnings were well below the national average and I was required to pay practically no tax at all but in 1962 I was in the supertax bracket with no way of spreading the load.

That year I was asked by the producer Victor Saville to make another film, *Mix me a Person*, while still doing *Guilty Party* in the evenings. The story concerned a married couple; she is a psychiatrist, he a barrister. She becomes professionally involved in the case of a young psychopath (played by Adam Faith – this leading pop singer's first essay into straight acting) and so obsessed is she with the case that her own marriage begins to founder. I was to play the barrister and once again it was back to the treadmill: rise at six thirty, drive to the studio, on the set at eight thirty, one hour's break for lunch, finish work at six, drive to the theatre, curtain up at seven thirty, home soon after eleven. My only enduring memory of the film is the pleasure of working with the American actress Anne Baxter who played my wife. She told me a story which I still consider one of the three best I have ever heard – and that is a dangerous beginning – it really needs acting but I will attempt to tell it to you.

The American inventor, Thomas Edison, is in his cellar laboratory. His fertile brain is teeming and he has several experiments going at the same time. His long-suffering wife calls down the cellar steps, 'Thomas, you really must come up and eat.'

'No, no. I can't stop. Go away.'

'But Thomas, you have been down there for three days and nights.'

'Go away!'

'But you must get some sleep.'

'Go away! – I'm nearly there . . .!'

On the bench in front of him is a glass sphere; inside it is a filament to which two wires are connected. With trembling hands and sweating brow, he takes the other ends of the two wires and tentatively holds them to a small electrical generator . . . And the filament glows – it GLOWS! Beside himself with excitement, Edison picks up the glass sphere, holds it to his ear and cries, 'Hello? Hello?'

Yes. Well. As I said, it works better when it is acted. Sorry.

Here is a paradox. I was now working harder than at any time in my life, but I was dissatisfied. When I first went into the theatre, there were two categories of actors, modern and classical, and very few actors bridged the gulf between the two. I always imagined that an actor should be able to do all things, but I had started in the modern mould and had had great difficulty in breaking into the classical. Once there, I stayed for five years and became labelled as a Classical Actor. I had then broken into films and eight years later I realised that there was a third category – I was a Film Actor. I wanted to extend my horizons, but memories are short in the entertainment world; people had forgotten my five years in the classics. I determined at that moment to do all I could to keep my feet in as many different acting areas as possible.

My friend and agent John Cadell and I had many long talks on how to achieve this objective and we resolved once again to confront Peter Hall, enthroned at Stratford-upon-Avon. Peter showed a limited interest: would I be prepared to do an audition? (Had he forgotten my last one?) But what had I to lose? Pride is one of the stupidest deadly sins, so why not do it? And I did.

Off again to the flat in New Cavendish Street, where John Barton succeeded in opening the door while spilling coffee from the mug he was carrying, and there was Peter Hall smiling benignly from the depths of a very easy chair.

'This *is* good of you, Donald – what are you going to do for us?'

I still had only the same old speech from *Henry V* – it was a part that I had always wanted to play – so why not sow the seeds? They might mount the play specially. John Barton lumbered out, a tin was heard crashing from a shelf, a chair fell over and he emerged with another mug of coffee. He delved into a cardigan pocket and produced a cigarette only to find that he already had one in his mouth. An inch of ash hung from another smouldering in an ashtray. The seat of his trousers only just allowed him to put one foot in a shiny suede ankle-boot on top of a desk while remaining standing on the other; his shoulders hunched and he beamed.

After a few pleasantries I launched into '. . . What's he that wishes so? My cousin Westmorland? . . .'

Due, I am sure, to John Clements' schooling, I did it very much better than on the previous occasion.

P.H. looked at J.B. who beamed back at him as he tried to drink his coffee through his cigarette. An unspoken agreement was reached. 'Thank you,' said P.H. 'At Stratford you know we ask all our actors to play small parts as well as large – we are an "ensemble" company, so what about Sebastian in *The Tempest* – Mmm?'

My heart sank. Sebastian is one of the followers of King Alonso and those 'lords' scenes', as they are known, are quite unbelievably boring. I had spent two years, 1946 and 1947, playing one of the other lords, Adrian, and I know, better than most, just how tedious they are. And I said so.

'Ah,' smiled P.H., knowingly, 'but not in this production. Peter Brook is directing and he sees the lords as the focal point of the whole play: he has some wonderfully exciting ideas for those scenes. Also we are repeating last year's *Comedy of Errors* – I'd like you to be in that, but all the leading parts are cast . . .'

Unfortunately I didn't then know the play, but asked if there was a good 'character' part. P.H. looked at J.B. and asked/suggested, 'What about the Duke?' J.B. raised his eyebrows and beamed a sort of 'Yes.' 'Then halfway through the season I am going to direct the three parts of *Henry VI* which John is editing – do you know them? No? Well read them through and let me know which part you would like to play. You can't have Henry – that's cast. Can you let me know by Friday?'

I raced home, not altogether exultant, and in my free hours began to plough my way through the interminable pages of the three long plays that make up Shakespeare's *Henry VI*. When

Friday came I was not halfway through the trilogy but I had made up my mind and telephoned P.H.

'I would like to play Richard Plantagenet, Duke of York.'

'What a wise fellow you are − I bet it was the death scene that convinced you.'

I was clever enough not to admit that I had not reached that scene in the plays. Had I done so, I might have been so overawed to have opted out of the whole venture. But more of that monumental scene anon.

John Cadell was left to negotiate my salary and his not overjoyed voice announced, 'I don't know how this will affect your tax situation but they won't pay a penny more than sixty pounds a week.'

6

SIX LORDS A LEAPING

My brother Leon had been a member of the Royal Shakespeare Company at Stratford-upon-Avon the year before, in 1962. Soon after he arrived he telephoned me to say that it was almost impossible for actors to find reasonably priced accommodation. The season now lasted most of the year and people were not so prepared to rent cottages and flats to actors as they had been when the season was a bare six months long. Also a new law gave sitting tenants the right of tenure: a householder couldn't get his own house back if the tenant chose to sit tight. Leon had seen a house that was for sale quite cheaply in the village of Tiddington, a mile and a half outside Stratford, and suggested that we might buy it between us. I was in the funds and it seemed a good idea.

It was to this house that Diana and I moved at the beginning of March 1963: not an attractive house but it backed on to fields and the village shops were charming.

I don't know why an actor gets married – his family life is continually disrupted. Nothing is ever secure. Most other professions have a recognised structure: a businessman, a solicitor or an accountant can expect to move, however slowly, up the ladder of success and can expect to earn more this year than last. When he goes on holiday he still receives a salary and someone else will take over until he returns. When he retires he is cushioned by a company pension. Not so the actor. Whatever success he has achieved can be nullified by a set of bad reviews and the next week he is quite simply out of work. He may be lucky to be paid quite handsomely for a year's work and then be on the dole for the next year. He will be taxed on his working year on the basis that he earns that sum every year. He can contribute to a pension scheme one year and not be able to afford the premium the next. The only holiday he gets is when he is out of work and the next job may be one day or one year ahead: not knowing, he hesitates to spend money or time on a holiday. Certainly this element of 'not know-

74

ing' is a great incentive – if we don't deliver the goods we may not work again. When the solicitor or businessman/accountant takes a client or prospective customer to lunch, it is paid for by his firm. An actor has to pay for it himself – and it is not deduct-able. When the businessman (or the others) is required for pro-fessional reasons to be away from his office, abroad or within the United Kingdom, his fares and hotel accommodation are also paid for by his firm. If an actor goes on a ten-week tour or if his play is transferred to Broadway he has to find and pay for all his own food and lodgings.

For me to go to Stratford I could not afford to keep two establishments going, so reluctantly we let the house in London (with fairly disastrous results – the bath was allowed to overflow, which brought down the sitting-room ceiling). I hated having to subject my family to making stringent economies, but I knew I had to take this step. I just prayed that it was the right decision.

I was thirty-nine, but I felt like a boy going to a new school for the first time as I made my way to the first rehearsal of *The Tempest*. I had heard so much of this company of young actors whom Peter Hall had fashioned into something called an 'ensemble'. This was different, I gathered, from the 'star'-orientated theatre where a production was mounted and revolved around two, or perhaps more, leading players and the company was in the shape of a pyramid – the base supporting the apex. What I found was a group of actors identical to those with whom I had worked in 1946. They were mostly very young and dedicated to their job – and so were we in 1946. But this time they made my life miserable. From all sides I could feel antagonism and I was treated with utmost suspicion. I was a 'film actor' – the lowest of the low. I was a has-been – so why bother with me. I had worked in the commercial theatre – a dirty word. I had my own car – I was a capitalist. I wore a suit – I was an Establishment square. I was happily married with two children – there was something wrong somewhere.

The only person who bothered to greet me as I entered the room was Ken Wynne whom I had first met when he was a call-boy at Stratford in 1946. He had always dreamed of being an actor and over the years he has become not only one of our finest character actors, but is one of the best farceurs I have ever seen. I will always be grateful to him for extending that first hand of friendship. All the others stood around in animated groups and I felt sure they were sniggering at me.

There was no sign of Peter Brook, the man who was going to make the lords the 'focal' part of the play, as we sat round in a semicircle to be shown the model of the set in which we were to work; instead a strange, frenetic young man by the name of Clifford Williams expounded at length on the intricacies of the scenery, designed by Abd'elkader Farrah, and which was to be made of perspex. Apparently, at certain moments, Ariel would 'explode' through the scenery. Ah . . .

We broke for lunch and I learned that Peter Brook was held up elsewhere and his assistant – the frenetic young man – would direct the play in his absence. I hoped that he had the same ideas about the lords. In the afternoon we read through the play: Tom Fleming was splendidly sonorous as Prospero, but all the time I was judging his performance against Robert Harris who had played it in 1946 and John Gielgud whom I had seen in 1957.

It had been to this last performance that we took Jeremy, then aged seven, for his first taste of Shakespeare. We went round to John's dressing-room afterwards and, knowing that we were coming, he kept on his magnificent costume. Jeremy gazed at him awestruck: this was not an actor – this was indeed Prospero, the weaver of spells: 'Have a chocolate, Jeremy.'

Jeremy took one apprehensively and continued to gaze as the three adults talked. Suddenly he blurted out a question that undermined the whole premise of the play. If Shakespeare had asked himself the same question he could not have written the play. It was a question that John had never asked himself. But Jeremy asked the question of Prospero himself, not the actor: 'If you were so clever, why didn't you just magic yourself back to Italy?'

But back to our rehearsal. Roy Dotrice sounded as if he was going to be good as Caliban. Derek Smith as Stephano spoke as if his cues were coming to him from a tape-recorder. A very private young man named Ian Holm was most interesting as Ariel. A tall spotty youth, who looked as if he had not yet woken up, gave a dull reading of Trinculo.

(Lilian Baylis once said to a young understudy who in an emergency went on as Juliet, 'Well dear, you've had your chance; and you've missed it.' The spotty youth named David Warner might miss his chance, I thought.) Next to the lords, the dullest parts are the three goddesses, and three young actresses, Janet Suzman, Susan Engel and Cherry Morris, did their best. I had nearly forgotten the lords – but John Welsh, Ken Wynne, Nicholas

Selby, Roy Marsden, John Corvin and I read our scenes as if we had all been told that they were the 'focal' points of the play.

That evening I went home to Diana nearly in tears. What had I done? I had stepped back seventeen years; but then I was young and the world was my oyster. Now I felt as if I had an allergy to shellfish.

If there is one irrefutable fact of the lords' scenes, it is that the two villains, Antonio and Sebastian, are a 'double act'. They are always conspiring together. They attempt the murder as a two-some and they share their come-uppance. When the lords gathered for the first staging of the play's 'focal' scenes, the frenetic Clifford addressed us saying, 'In every production of *The Tempest* I have seen, Antonio and Sebastian always seem to be played as a double act. We must get away from that – it is a cliché – so old-fashioned, so I want Antonio on one side of the stage and Sebastian on the other.'

Nicholas Selby and I found ourselves trying to insinuate our conspiratorial lines to each other over the heads of four other characters. Surely somebody would notice that it doesn't work? But I kept my mouth shut. I was frightened to appear old-fashioned.

In the final 'focal' scene the lords are required to enter 'with frantic gestures' and 'stand charm'd' as if in a trance. The frenetic Clifford told us that the designer had arranged for a section along the front of the stage to be constructed as a conveyor-belt (like a flattened escalator); we were to stand on this in the wings doing our 'frantic gestures' and at the press of a switch we would be conveyed 'standing charm'd' on to the stage; the belt would stop when we arrived in position. Of course for rehearsals we didn't have the conveyor and we all felt pretty stupid standing in a line making 'frantic gestures' and then having to walk to our positions. Remember, this was a 'focal' scene.

In the final week the mercurial Peter Brook suddenly appeared: still with the same cramped movements that I remembered from 1946, but now with considerably more authority gained from successful experience. We were asked to run through the entire play, for him to see what we were doing. Endless notes were given afterwards and when he came to the lords' scenes he said, 'What are Antonio and Sebastian doing so far apart?! – they can't be conspiratorial at that distance – they are a double act!' I promise you, I only *thought*, 'I told you so'. But Peter Brook said nothing

77

at all about our scenes being the 'focal' point of the whole play. I knew they weren't.

Next came the dress-rehearsal and we saw the scenery for the first time. The part of the perspex through which Ariel was to 'explode' had been carefully cut through in a jagged outline, which left a frosted edge all around it, perfectly visible to the audience, and when poor Ian Holm tried to 'explode' the section merely clattered to the ground and he tore his costume on the serrations. Then came the conveyor-belt. It was there all right, but instead of extending into the wings it began only a couple of feet off-stage, so that only one lord could mount it and had practically no time to make a frantic gesture before being propelled, 'standing charm'd', in front of the audience, allowing the next lord to jump on. However, six lords one by one succeeded and were moved, like targets at a funfair shooting-booth, across the front of the stage – and straight off the other side! Somebody had failed to turn off the switch. The embarrassment – and this a 'focal' scene. We had to begin our entrance all over again. Six lords were for the second time conveyed 'standing charm'd' across the stage. Somebody turned off the switch: the belt stopped dead and six lords fell over.

That was to herald the end of the conveyor-belt.

The Tempest, in the 1963 season, was only a mild drizzle – as it had been in 1946.

John Cadell had come up for the first night and afterwards, rather mournfully, he, Diana and I repaired to the Dirty Duck for supper. Sitting at the other end of the room were Clifford Williams and his young French wife, Josie-Anne. He no longer looked frenetic: he was now grey and sunk in gloom. For the first time it dawned upon me that others concerned with the production had been just as worried as I. Clifford had been expected to take over someone else's ideas at the last minute and the production had fallen between the Brook and Williams stools. I suddenly felt terribly sorry for him. A little later there was a sound of breaking glass, a chair was knocked over and Clifford rushed from the room leaving his poor wife in tears. Diana was quickly to the rescue, gathered up Josie-Anne, who was heavily pregnant, and did her best to comfort her. A foreigner, totally alone in Stratford and inexperienced in the neurotic world of the theatre, she was obviously frightened. None of us knew where Clifford had gone, so rather than leave her alone, we took her back to our house to stay the night. We left messages everywhere for Clifford, who after

driving a hundred miles up the M1 and back again, failed to receive
any of them, and was not aware of her whereabouts until the next
morning when he found her having breakfast with us. Clifford
was deeply grateful to Diana for her solicitude and sent her flowers
with a message, 'Thank you for calming my Tempest.'

It was an emergency that had brought Clifford Williams to the
fore. The previous year a production was cancelled (or postponed)
at the very last moment and he was called upon, as Resident
Associate Director, to mount an alternative play – any play –
with no time for preparation. He chose *The Comedy of Errors*
because the parts would suit the actors who were suddenly available. Time, again, prevented the designing and making of the
many costumes required, so the entire company were kitted out
at a shop in Stratford High Street with black polo-necked sweaters
and black trousers for the men and long black skirts for the ladies.
To these basics were added small colourful bits and pieces, hats,
cloaks, epaulettes, ribbons, ruffs, etc, to differentiate the characters. A bare stage with one or two box-like benches was all the
scenery. The company threw themselves into the task of opening
a play with minimal rehearsals and the day was saved. The production was an enormous success.

I had asked Peter Hall for a 'character' part – and I got it. I was
to take over the role of Solinus, Duke of Ephesus, from Tony
Steedman who, with several other members of last year's cast, was
no longer in the company. The Duke is the grandfather figure in
the play, removed by his rank from the day-to-day activities of
his state, he only appears at operative moments to pass sentence
or be justifiably mystified at the events which round off the play.
I was determined to enjoy myself. With Clifford's connivance (I
now had a new friend) I contrived to look like a tall thin black
candle that had softened and drooped in the sun: a lank white wig
and beard were topped by a conical hat-cum-crown and a long
black cloak without shoulders hung in swags to my feet and
overflowed on the floor. I used a thin, high-pitched voice. The
actor who plays the Duke is faced with two alternatives in the
opening scene: either to appreciate the underlying humour of what
he says, or to say his lines straightforwardly and allow everyone
else on stage to react in a comedic vein. I chose the former. Only
two people actually speak in front of the assembly, the Duke
and Aegeon of Syracuse. Although the italics are mine, the Duke
says:

79

> Well, Syracusian; say, in *brief* the cause
> Why thou departed'st from thy native home,
> And for what cause thou cam'st to Ephesus.

Aegeon then speaks for sixty-five lines! Whereupon the Duke says:

> Nay, forward, old man; *do not break off so* . . .

Aegeon then goes on for another twenty-three lines about his sons, to which the Duke answers:

> And, for the sake of them thou sorrowest for,
> Do me the favour to dilate *at full*
> What hath befall'n of them and thee till now.

Aegeon then follows with another sixteen lines . . .

For this production we were joined by several new members of the company, Diana Rigg, Madoline Thomas, Ian Richardson, Alec McCowen and Clifford Rose among them (I had first worked with Alec in *The Cruel Sea* ten years before), but I still felt from all of them that I was an outsider. I was a fallen 'star' reduced to playing small parts. All the others had private jokes from which I was excluded.

But then the battle for laughs was on and I seemed to be getting my fair share: this is the moment when we acknowledge each other's expertise and at last I was 'accepted'. In the final scene, as I listened to a long speech from Diana Rigg, I was able, due to the fact that my voluminous cloak hid my body completely, gradually to 'lose' height by bending my unseen legs, until I was eighteen inches shorter than when she started. It was then my turn to make a speech and Diana, who was standing behind me, 'goosed' me . . . The ice was broken.

During rehearsal Madoline Thomas, who was in her seventies, had some difficulties with her characterisation of the Abbess. Young Clifford gave her a lot of intellectual advice which she failed to understand. I broke in by saying, 'Maddy, darling – it's a Sybil Thorndike part,' whereupon Clifford cried, 'Oh Donald – no externals – please!'

But Maddy came to me later and thanked me, 'That was just the sort of advice I wanted!' But then you see we both came from a different era.

The whole production had such youthful gaiety and we all remember it fondly, but for me, the abiding memory is of Ken Wynne's pronunciation of the word 'chain'. He had to say it several times during the play and evolved a way of saying 'cheaaain' until it was five minutes long.

No sooner had *The Comedy of Errors* opened than I received a letter from a Countess Fortescue asking me to open the village fête at Ebrington. In each of the seasons I have spent at Stratford Diana and I have tried to involve ourselves with the various activities in the town. One cannot spend eleven months of the year in a place and remain insular. Ebrington is a village only a few miles away from Stratford; I was free on that Saturday afternoon, so I agreed to do it. It held no terrors for me – I had opened hundreds of fêtes, bazaars, shows, shops and sporting events during my time with the Rankery. The only part that worried me was the impersonal aspect: the Rankery would send us off in a car to an unknown destination; on arrival we would be introduced to some twenty local people involved in the organisation of the event, most of whom we would probably never meet again; our presence would then be announced over a microphone, we would step forward and in a few well-chosen (we hoped) words, declare the said fête, bazaar, shop, show, sporting event open. This was followed by a conducted tour around the stalls at which one must always buy something (this is where Diana came into her own – I always bought the most useless things). Then followed a session of auto-graph signing for a fee, all proceeds going to the fund, then back into the car and we would be swept off to London.

My biggest problem is that I am frightfully bad on names. I can forget a name three seconds after having heard it, and it was always during the first ten minutes after arrival that one met those first twenty local people. On one occasion I remember hearing the word 'Brigadier———' during the introductions and while talking to some other local dignitaries I discovered that not only was 'Brigadier———' the President of the organisation for which the funds were being raised, but he also owned the enormous house and grounds in which the fête was being held. It would be politic, to say the least, to mention his name in my speech: but what was it?! I went over to two ladies sitting at the side and said, 'Excuse me, but can you tell me the name of the Brigadier?'

'Oh yes – Brigadier Brkstdl' (well, that is what it sounded like).

'I'm so sorry, I didn't quite . . .'

'Brigadier Brkstdl.'

'Would you mind spelling that?'

'B-R-E-A-K-S-T-E-D-D-L-E.'

'. . . and how do you pronounce it?'

'Brkstdl.'

'You must be joking!'

'No. He's my husband.'

On another occasion, at a charity ball, I was taken in hand by a charming lady who was completely in control of the situation – she was the Lady Bountiful – she knew everyone by name, where they lived, what they did, to whom they were married, how many children. I clung to her like a limpet – 'Who is he?' – 'Who is she?' – she always knew the answer. The one moment I left her side I found myself talking to two men, when one of them faced me with that unforgivable phrase, 'You don't remember where we last met, do you? – Well, you stayed the weekend with us in Suffolk . . .'

'But of course!' I cried. 'Yes, yes. I remember . . .'

I raced back to my Lady Bountiful. 'Quick – quick – who the hell is that man standing in the corner?'

She looked at me in disbelief. 'My husband, of course.'

Two stories, both true, with the same tag line.

Back to the Fortescues. Before opening the fête, we were invited by the Earl and Countess to lunch at Ebrington Manor. Did Osbert Lancaster know them? They were the archecartoonal Earl and Countess: Sybil was tall, elegant, wan, and slightly absent-minded; Denzil (Denny), 7th Earl (motto: 'A strong shield is the salvation of leaders'), was Eton, Army (MC, TD), bluff and, when we met him, rather deaf – a disability he preferred or pretended not to concede, with frequent hilarious results. For instance, a relative of his, Peter Lord, is married to an important theatrical agent, Patricia MacNaughton. Denny asked him what Patricia was doing at Stratford, to which Peter replied, 'She looks after some of the cast at the theatre.' Denny failed to hear the final 't' of 'cast' and from then on always referred to her as 'the person who looks after the cars at the theatre – damn silly job for a woman.'

Denny showed me round the Cotswold stone house, built originally in the fourteenth century, which has a galleried great hall and views across the Gloucestershire countryside. I asked him how long he had lived there but never expected the show-stopping answer – 'Well, my ancestor bought this place in 1456 – Sir John Fortescue: he was Chancellor to Henry VI.'

The village of Ebrington – which is pronounced by the locals as 'Yebbrrtun' – is built on the slopes of a series of small but steep hills and is absolutely beautiful. What a lovely place to live! Sybil said that there was a derelict cottage for sale, she explained exactly where it was, so I arranged to return the following week. I found the rough stony track she had described and started to walk along it; a man was leaning over a gate of one small cottage and as I passed I asked if there was an empty cottage in that direction. He looked at me quizzically, 'Aye. Aye. Yonder.' I continued up the lane for some distance and around a corner the track petered out beside a ramshackle building. The thatch was missing from several parts of the roof, exposing the rafters, some of the stonework was crumbling, windows were broken and weeds and brambles grew high all around. It was eerie to say the least – almost spooky. I climbed over the gate, which hung only on its bottom hinge, and fought my way through the undergrowth and peered in at a cobwebbed window. The last occupant had left an old wooden table and some boxes in the room and there were bottles and mugs around as if some tramps had used the place. The ceiling had collapsed at three points and there was a pile of straw and twigs in the fireplace as if a bird's-nest had fallen down the chimney. I trod down the brambles to get to the back of the house and tried to look in at the kitchen window, first pulling away a clump of creeper. I then pressed my face to the glass to find myself looking straight into the eyes of a terrifying apparition: an old crone, like one of Fuseli's witches from *Macbeth*; thin straggly hair started out of a skull, with a hooked nose and sunken cheeks around toothless gums; her bloodshot eyes glowered back at me . . .

I gulped and stumbled away as fast as I could. When I reached the other cottage the man was still leaning on his gate. 'There's-someone-living-in-that place,' I stammered.

'Aye. Aye.' He looked at me keenly. He seemed to think that I should be warned, but was it his job to tell me? He decided it was. 'She's a witch, you know.'

'A witch?'

'A witch!' he said categorically.

I have heard many people talk of witches in Gloucestershire and many people believe in them. I have seen one.

The Fortescues refused to believe a word of it and invited Diana and me to spend as much time as we liked at their house during the season and it was always a pleasure to get away from the grind at the theatre to spend a few hours in the elegance of Ebrington Manor.

Meanwhile we were eking out our existence in our Tiddington

semi-detached. The other side of the adjoining wall was occupied by a young couple with two small children and over the garden fence we got to know each other. They rarely smiled. The wife was painfully thin and harassed by the children: the husband was almost as thin and had a receding hairline – in fact it had already receded. He looked like an emaciated curate attached to some lesser-known Abbey in the outskirts of an industrial city. He was actually the drama critic on the *Stratford-upon-Avon Herald*.

Diana has an uncanny knack of putting her finger on people's psychological problems – much more so than can be attributed to feminine intuition – and she was certain that next door there was some deep-seated malaise. I, of course, failed to notice anything: the husband and I would spend hours discussing the theatre but it was to Diana he came one day and handed her a typescript which he asked her to read.

So absorbed was she that she stayed up most of the night to finish it. The typescript was his autobiography. Our neighbour was an alcoholic.

It was the first time we had encountered the disease. He never appeared drunk or even tipsy, but secretly he was consuming vast amounts of alcohol. Due to this he had already lost several jobs and he had nearly succeeded in reducing his family to penury. He had at last acknowledged his problem and had consulted several doctors in an effort to conquer it. A psychiatrist had suggested that, as he was a writer, one way to help himself would be to write down his own version of the events that had led to his collapse – to make, as it were, a written confession.

Why had he wanted Diana to read it? He told her that the psychiatrist had been so impressed by it that he suggested it should be published – under an assumed name – so that others with a similar problem might be helped; now a Sunday newspaper was prepared to pay a very large sum of money to serialise it, but only if he used his real name. What should he do?

No one in the town knew of his problem. Should he keep his guilty secret to himself or run the risk of losing his present job and having his wife and children pointed at in the street and possibly ostracised? In confidence, he was asking Diana's opinion.

Diana thought deeply on the situation but was really in no doubt: he should publish. The money could pay all their debts and even allow them to move away from the area if necessary. Diana was certain their real friends, and these by now included us, would stick by them.

The husband and wife were deeply grateful to Diana. The book, published under the title *Spin the Bottle* and duly serialised in the Sunday paper, was a great success and a heavy load was lifted from the author's shoulders. Within months an extension was built on to their house for the children, all the rooms were decorated, and in place of lean and haggard looks, smiling faces appeared over our fence. It was a fairy-tale transformation scene. With his new-found vigour our neighbour started work on a novel and chapter by chapter it was handed to Diana to read. It was a detective story and when it was published the hero, Boysie Oakes, captured the imagination of the public and within no time it was made into a successful film. Our one-time emaciated, introverted, alcoholic neighbour was famous. Several books later, John Gardner was the obvious choice to follow Ian Fleming by writing new stories around the character of James Bond.

How exciting it is to have participated in a true rags-to-riches story.

Back to the theatre. *The Tempest* had opened disastrously. *Julius Caesar* (in which I didn't appear) inauspiciously. *The Comedy of Errors* was a revival from the previous year. So far the season was not exactly brilliant and it was a downcast company that assembled for the first reading of *The Wars of the Roses*.

There have been some excellent productions of Shakespeare's trilogy – *Henry VI Part One*, *Henry VI Part Two* and *Henry VI Part Three* – but they have never been popular at the box office. Although each of the three plays is complete in itself, the public have always been confused; if they can afford the time (and the money) to see all three, they want, quite naturally, to see them in the correct order. Their visit to Stratford may begin mid-week; only to find that on Friday and Saturday Parts Two and Three are being performed: better not see any. If time allows them to see only one part they feel deprived: better see none rather than one. Perhaps if Shakespeare had given the three plays three different titles there would be less opposition.

Another reason for the *Henry VI* plays being so seldom done is that there is no one great leading role to attract a great leading player, but now that Peter Hall had established a splendid ensemble company this was the perfect time to mount these rarely performed plays.

Hall still felt that they were too long and contained too much 'dead-wood' so he asked John Barton, an academic friend from his university days, to edit and adapt the plays into *two* parts, one to be called *Henry VI* and the other *Edward IV*.

The plays concern the wars that took place between the Yorkists and Lancastrians following the death of Henry the Fifth. Henry's father had usurped the crown and many people then felt that Richard Plantagenet, Duke of York, had a far stronger claim to the throne than Henry's heir, his weak, vacillating, introverted son, Henry of Lancaster (Henry VI). As a result of the wars, in which the Yorkists wore a white rose as a symbol and the Lancastrians a red rose, the Duke of York failed in his bid, but two of his sons became kings: Edward IV and Richard III. Shakespeare's play of *Richard III* follows chronologically, so a production of that play would also be mounted and collectively all three plays – *Henry VI, Edward IV, Richard III* – would be known as *The Wars of the Roses*.

Barton did his editing brilliantly. He cut out the 'dead-wood' which included some entire scenes and some repetitious speeches; he cut some characters completely and gave their lines to others. He concertina'ed certain events to clarify the narrative line and when he found that the jagged ends left by his cuts failed to join satisfactorily, the amazing Barton – to whom iambic pentameter is second nature – was not above writing new lines of blank verse: indeed he even wrote two entirely new scenes.

Hall and Barton were to encounter a lot of criticism for tampering with Shakespeare. There are those purists who think it a crime to cut one single line of the Bard's sacrosanct text – however boring and unintelligible. (There would also appear to be five thousand people in Britain who object to losing a single note of Wagner's Ring Cycle even if it would make it more enjoyable to thousands of others.) At the annual conference of Shakespearean scholars one pedant attacked Barton saying, 'I hear that you have had the impertinence to write a complete new scene – what have you done? Admit it.' Barton replied, 'Wait until you have seen the production and then you tell me which scene is mine.'

The pedant failed to pick out either of the offending scenes.

Some sixty actors were required to make up the cast of *The Wars of the Roses* and the group who gathered in the Conference Hall rehearsal room included several faces, new to me, who were members of Hall's team: Brewster Mason, Michael Craig, Jeffrey Dench, John Normington, Charles Kay, Derek Waring, Hugh Sullivan and there – sitting in the front row – Dame Peggy Ashcroft.

I had worked with Peggy in 1949 in *The Heiress* – 'with' is slightly the wrong word: she was playing the lead and I had seven lines – and three times during my years with the Rankery she had suggested me for leading parts opposite her at Stratford, and three times the Rankery as good as refused permission. She signalled to me to join her in the front row. I hate to say this of Peggy, but she and I were possibly the two oldest members of the company. While we waited, one of the youngsters in the team produced a copy of Shakespeare printed in 1910 and illustrated by photographs of (then) contemporary actors and actresses (Tree, Forbes-Robertson, Bourchier, Asche, Ellen Terry, Mrs Patrick Campbell, Mary Anderson, etc).

'What fun,' I said, 'let's see how many I can name.' I was doing rather well until the owner of the book said, 'Good God, Donald – you must be the only member of this company who can remember these people.'

Peter Hall, as director of the production, gave a most informative and enlightening talk on the historical and political background to the power struggles in the play, and we were then shown the model of the set designed by John Bury. The floor of the stage was made of wire mesh – sparks would fly if a sword were dragged across it – and two vast triangular towers, as used in the Ancient Greek theatre and known as periaktoi, on either side of the stage could revolve to present different faces, all covered in steel: the permutations were endless. The whole feel of the set was metallic and brutal – a perfect background for ten and a half hours (for that was the length of the combined plays) of a strident and savage drama.

Then we began the mammoth task of reading through *Henry VI* and *Edward IV*. Was it the presence of Peter Hall and John Barton? Was it a result of Hall's lecture? Was it a dispirited company determined to retrieve the wreckage of the season? Whatever it was, that reading was one of the most exciting things I have experienced.

Peggy Ashcroft as Queen Margaret had already plotted the trajectory of the character which, in the course of the three plays, must age from twenty-seven to eighty. Her French accent was already centred around the pronunciation of the letter 'r'. I wish I could describe it. I have heard Scottish ladies vocalise with a similar sound: it came from the back of the throat as if she were gargling.

The spotty youth, David Warner, whom I had summarily dismissed in *The Tempest* now produced a hauntingly magical performance of Henry: I ate my words – I had been wrong about him.

Brewster Mason is a large man, quite six feet two inches tall, broad-shouldered, with a splendid voice to match. He exudes 'power' – which is exactly the quality required for the character of Warwick, the Kingmaker.

Charles Kay was mysteriously sensitive as George Clarence.

Ian Holm was etching the lines of another of my sons, Richard; one of the best performances I have seen by a young actor.

From previous experience I knew that Roy Dotrice had yet to surprise me. He is a master of make-up and, like Olivier, it doesn't all come together until we see the finished whole.

If I am not careful I will enumerate all the company but I must mention one actress, not (if she will ever forgive me) immediately attractive, but even then in 1963, I thought she had a most original character. She had no part to speak of during the season and was merely walking on in most of the plays – in the production of *Julius Caesar* she was one of the crowd addressed by Mark Antony: 'Friends, Romans, countrymen; lend me your ears . . .' Shakespeare had provided no lines for the crowd but on the first night it was her voice that could clearly be heard answering, 'You can have mine.' I was sure this was an actress to be watched. Her name was Penelope Keith.

If all of the sixty actors who appeared in *The Wars* were to write their versions of that first read-through, every one would be different, so I hope you will forgive me if I tell you only my side of the story. It was a team production, but it will probably seem to be entirely about me. (There is a story of an actor who is playing the very small part of Osric in a production of *Hamlet*: his mother asked him what the play was about. 'Well, it's about a young man who tells someone that someone else wants to challenge him to a duel, and . . .' Sorry, there I go digressing again.)

At Peter Hall's invitation, I had chosen the part of Richard Plantagenet, Duke of York, who was the fifteenth-century equivalent of today's Trotskyite revolutionary – committed to destroying the established status quo and setting himself up in an identical privileged position. In the course of the play he goes off to the war (which he and his followers have instigated) with his three older sons, Edward, Richard and George, leaving his youngest son, seven-year-old Rutland, at home with his mother. First one side is winning, then the other. At a time when the scales have dipped against them and the Yorkists are on the run, York becomes separated from his sons in the heat of battle and is captured by the commander of the Lancastrian forces. The commander is Henry's French wife Margaret. She had been married against her will to the young, possibly impotent, Henry, but she is headstrong and viciously ambitious: if Henry is too weak to command his own forces, she will take charge and she it is who has now captured her arch-enemy, York.

Then follows what must be the most horrific death scene in all Shakespeare: the scene that Peter Hall thought had swayed me into choosing the part, the scene that could make or break my future with the company. I will attempt to give you a précis.

For the Queen merely to kill York would be too simple – he must be tortured and humiliated first. York is tied to a stake – in our production two spears were driven into the ground to form a cross of St Andrew and he was tied to these. Margaret then begins to taunt him: 'Was it you that would be England's King?' York is silent – not a word will he utter to give his enemy satisfaction.

So often in Shakespeare we have to remember that when someone makes a long speech it is only because no one else chooses to interrupt. They could but they don't.

'Where are your sons?' In truth York does not know where they are – but he will not admit it.

'Where is Edward?'

No answer.

'Where is George?'

Still no answer.

'Where is Richard?'

Still York refuses to answer.

'Where is your darling Rutland?'

York is sure that Rutland is safe at home with his mother but Margaret seems to know something that he does not . . . She holds out a bloodstained cloth: 'Look, York – I stained this napkin with the blood that issued from the bosom of the boy – and if thine eyes can water for his death, I give thee this to dry thy cheeks withal . . .' and she slaps the cloth, thick with his beloved son's blood, into his unprotected face, and there it sticks until he can just free a hand enough to pull it away.

His silence makes her more furious and she cries, 'I prithee grieve to make me merry! – stamp, rave and fret, that I may sing and dance!' He wanted to be King, so she places a crown made of paper on his head, and, 'Now off with the crown and with the crown his head!'

York knows he is about to be killed and he can no longer contain himself – before he dies he will tell her exactly what he thinks of her. He launches into a vitriolic attack which leaves her speechless:

> She-Wolf of France, but worse than wolves of France, whose tongue more poisons than the adder's tooth – O tiger's heart wrapped in a woman's hide – See, ruthless Queen, a hapless father's tears: this cloth thou dipped in blood of my sweet boy, and I with tears do wash the blood away. Keep thou the napkin and go boast of this.

York is then ritually stabbed to death and the exultant Lancastrians carry off his body in triumph.

I think you will agree, a very unpleasant but impressive scene. At the first reading in that dismal rehearsal room something happened that I had never known before or since: at the end of that scene the entire company of sixty actors remained in complete silence for quite a minute before continuing with the play – such is the potency of Shakespeare.

So began a period of rehearsal, ten hours a day, seven days a week, for twelve weeks. But just after we had begun, something happened that affected Diana and me, radically changing our private lives. That something was John Barton.

7

CARATACUS OR CARACTACUS

John Barton, born in 1928, was educated at Eton and carries with him that strange mixture of shy diffidence and aloof authority which seems to permeate those boys who do not inherit vast estates or become Cabinet Ministers. He went on to King's College, Cambridge and became an Anglo-Saxon scholar. From 1954, at the age of twenty-six, until 1960 he was a Fellow of King's. Peter Hall had been at the same college and when he took over the administration at Stratford-upon-Avon in 1960 he invited Barton to join him. In photographs taken at the time they both look absurdly young, but this youthful team radically changed the style of Shakespearean production.

In 1963 John was still a bachelor who lived, breathed, thought, ate, slept, drank, dreamed the works of Shakespeare. He and Hall played absurd games – I've seen them do it: 'name the titles of Shakespeare's plays in the order in which they are printed in the First Folio', 'name them in the order in which it is understood they were written', 'give the first line of each play', 'the last line of each play', 'now give the first line spoken by each principal character', and so on. All this left John no time to consider the mundane things of life – like eating and sleeping. As I have mentioned before, accommodation for eleven months is remarkably difficult to find in Stratford – actors have to book months in advance – but John, although he had already spent two years there, arrived for rehearsals in 1963 without accommodation of any kind. For the first three nights he had stayed in three different hotels which had cancellations. The third night he had arrived at the Arden Hotel at midnight: 'Barton?' queried the night-porter as he scanned the list of reservations. 'Ah, room 33, sir.' John stumbled up the stairs clutching his overnight case, opened the door of room 33 and turned on the light. A lady jerked up in the bed and roared, 'Young man! Get out of here!' The horrified John retired immediately and, not wanting to cause more trouble, slept the night on a settee in the lounge. The following morning he discovered that the occupant of room 33 also had the name of Barton. She was his mother and John had quite forgotten about her intended visit.

Unfortunately this situation coincided with Peter Hall collapsing from a mysterious illness. John was co-directing with Peter and now the whole brunt of the massive production fell on his shoulders. If the strain was too much, and if he too collapsed, *The Wars of the Roses* would be lost before they had begun: he must be cosseted. I suggested to Diana that he should come to stay with us, but she was slightly perturbed. Jeremy and Marc were both home from school for the summer holidays so they would have to share a bedroom to allow John to have the single room. She had never met John and had never had the responsibility of having a complete stranger living under our roof – but she realised the importance of the situation and the urgency of a solution, so that very evening John moved into our house in Tiddington.

And there he stayed for three months.

Opinions vary as to whether he was 'no trouble': we saw little of him but what we did see was fairly bizarre. John was now working harder than ever directing the plays as well as continuing to write and rewrite Shakespearean speeches. He usually arrived back at the house around midnight, took two sleeping-tablets and fell into bed, but sometimes he sat up over his papers after taking the tablets and they began to work before he could climb the stairs. On these occasions Diana almost had to carry him to bed. In the morning Diana called him at five-minute intervals from eight thirty on.

I have always hated the mornings and it takes me a long time to surface, so I was delighted to find someone even worse than I. There is little difference between John sound asleep and John arriving downstairs at nine a.m. We had French windows leading out into the garden and the sill of the doors was about two inches high. Every morning John staggered into the room, opened the French windows, tripped over the sill, and went out to take gulps of fresh air. He never looked back to see what had caused him to trip. Once might have been funny or the cause for concern, but he did it every morning for three months, and never knew – or bothered – about the cause.

Returning to the room he took two pills to wake himself up, shook his head violently and, seating himself at the table, spread out a copy of *The Times* on the floor beside him (on the floor, mark you), picked up his knife and fork without seeing them (they had been there yesterday, so they are bound to be there today) and began to eat from a plate which Diana timed to be there just as the fork came down (if she had been late, he would have eaten the table-mat). He had crossed his legs which made it slightly more difficult for him to turn the pages of *The Times*, which he continued to read intently. Then off to rehearsal before anyone had spoken to anyone else.

It was during one of these ritualistic mornings that eight-year-old Marc happened to mention that he was studying Roman History at school.

John's ears pricked up. 'Are you?! What particular period?'

'The Roman occupation of Great Britain from . . .'

Now John's knowledge of the Romans is known internationally: on that subject he is the un-glass-bowled Mastermind of Great Britain; he cannot be faulted. He began, 'When Vespasian defeated Caratacus the actual site of the battle has never been established, but . . .'

'I know,' said Marc, 'but it's not Caratacus – it is Caractacus.'

A sudden silence fell on the room. Knives and forks were slowly lowered. Diana and I secretly looked at each other. Jeremy, who hero-worshipped John, flashed a 'bloody fool' look at Marc. John assumed a schoolmasterly air of 'if you don't let me help you, you will never pass your O-levels' – 'No, Marc – Caratacus.'

'But it isn't,' persisted Marc, 'it is Caractacus.'

This, I felt, was going to ruin an entire day's rehearsals – I had better mediate: although I knew nothing of the subject, I have enormous respect for John's superior knowledge. 'Marc, darling, I'm sure that Mr Barton is right.'

'No, he's not – it is Caractacus.'

This was too much for John who flew upstairs, returned immediately with a book and flicked through the pages as he entered. 'Yes – here we are! As I told you, it is C-A-R-A – oh dear . . . Yes. Well. You are perfectly right, Marc. I must go.' And off he went to rehearsal.

It all seemed as if Diana and I had acquired a third child.

I think I have learned more from John as a director and as a friend than from any other person. I am not academic and I inordinately admire John, who is. I pick his brains unashamedly. I have always had a love for the English language and it thrilled me to find in John someone with a vastly superior knowledge who could guide my inexperienced steps. Just as a small insight into the way his mind works, I am told that in 1961 he was asked, in an emergency, to devise an anthology to be performed at the RSC's new London home, the Aldwych Theatre. Having decided that the theme should be the Kings and Queens of England as seen through their own or contemporary writings, he was able from memory to direct an assistant to the exact works in which all the myriad references were to be found. The result was enormously successful. *The Hollow Crown* is still being performed all over the world.

Of course there are times when I disagree with him or question his theories; for instance, the yardstick that he applies to all actors is Hamlet's advice to the players:

> Speak the speech, I pray you, as I pronounced it to you, trippingly on the tongue; but if you mouth it, as many of your players do, I had as lief the town crier spoke my lines . . .

So far, so good, but John also claims to know how English was spoken at the time of Shakespeare and one of his party pieces is to recite Henry the Fifth's 'Once more unto the breach dear friends, once more . . .' in the way it is believed to have been spoken in Elizabethan England. The sound is like a very strong Somerset accent. The word 'more' is pronounced 'mawerr' and can only be achieved by mouthing it. If Hamlet's advice is spoken in the same Zummerzet burr it makes complete nonsense of 'trippingly on the tongue'.

Again, John can be quite devious. In *Henry VI, Part Two*, Jack Cade interrogates a Clerk from Clapham:

> What is thy name?
> Emmanuel.
> They use to write it on the top of letters . . . away with him
> I say: hang him with his pen and ink-horn about his neck.

I was mystified by this exchange; I failed to understand it and plucked up courage to ask John, 'What does it mean?'
'What?'
'Emmanuel – they use to write it on the top of letters.'
'It is quite clear, isn't it?'
'Not to me.'
'You mean he is not saying it correctly?'
'No – but I don't understand it.'
'What? "Emmanuel – they use to write it on the top of letters"?'
'Yes.'
'Surely it means what it says.'

'Yes, but you know I'm stupid. Why does he say that they used to write Emmanuel on the top of letters?'

Someone less brave than I would have given in at John's expression, but I faced him out. His look softened and he said, 'As a matter of fact, I don't know.'

Rehearsal rooms are minefields to John and where there are no mines there are snares and traps. Everyone else is aware of the hazards but not he. It is customary for a long trestle-table to be set up facing the acting area; behind it, bang in the centre, sits the director, flanked by the various members of the stage-management and technical staff. John is forever jumping up to discuss something with an actor or to rearrange the positions – he seems to have 110 per cent concentration and becomes oblivious to the presence of those on either side with the result that he regularly collides with chairs or people. Some stage-managers have tried to overcome the problem by having two tables – one for John and one for them. This fact seems to have eluded John who then tries to avoid imaginary chairs and has even been known to go over or under the table in his haste.

He always wears a thick chunky cardigan and absent-mindedly produces unlikely things from the pockets. When he was trying to give up smoking he took to chewing gum and on one alarming occasion he produced a wrapped razor-blade from a pocket and proceeded to munch it.

When rehearsals move on to the stage, life becomes even more precarious. A short flight of wooden steps is placed to allow access to the stage from the lower auditorium. It is also a habit of some people to place coffee cups along the edge of the stage so, knowing that John is on the rampage, the stage-manager makes sure that none is in his line of access, but he will choose that time to avoid the steps and jump up on to the stage. The clever stage-manager remembers to have a mopping-up cloth to hand. On leaving the stage John merely hurls himself at the auditorium, sometimes missing the steps entirely. He was once giving notes at the end of a rehearsal and stepping backwards, disappeared down the orchestra pit . . . All the actors rushed forward to render first-aid but John climbed out obliviously, clutching his papers and continued to give his notes. It is the actors who suffer nervous breakdowns.

And this was the man, remember, staying in our house.

One morning he said plaintively, 'Diana, have you seen any of my shirts? I can't find any.'

Diana had expected him to look after his own laundry but that

95

morning, after he had left the house, she went to his room, and, under the bed, behind the chest of drawers, on top of the wardrobe, she found twenty-three dirty shirts. These she took to the fastest laundry in Stratford. Three weeks later John said plaintively, 'Diana, have you seen any of my shirts? I can't find any.' Again, under the bed, behind the chest of drawers, on top of the wardrobe, Diana found twenty-three dirty shirts. But this time she found inside each neck-band a laundry ticket attached with two safety-pins. He had worn the shirts with no sign of discomfort.

A colleague and fellow-director of John's – David Jones – told me that for a time he shared the Barton flat in London. Entering the kitchen he found that a kettle had not only boiled dry on the gas stove but a hole had burned through the bottom of it. A worried David decided he had the answer to John's problem and bought him an electric kettle which turned itself off after boiling. When John came home and saw it, he was despondent: 'Oh dear – I wish you hadn't done that – what am I to do with these?' He opened a cupboard and there were fourteen new, ordinary kettles, all ready for the next burned-out bottom.

I have left the most astonishing Bartonism till last. People don't believe it, but I assure you it is true.

During rehearsals and during performances, John is always giving notes. Of course it is wonderful to have someone who cares as much as he, but no actor can escape – he will hunt you down. He has been known to beard a nervous actor in his dressing-room twenty minutes before the play is due to start – on a first night – and give his notes on a quite different play.

He soon discovered that several of the company popped across to the Dirty Duck during their one-hour-exactly lunch break from rehearsals – what a perfect place to ensnare his prey. He took to wandering around the bar only taking his eyes from his notebook long enough to spy his next victim. Hoping to distract him, actors would invite him to have a drink – but to no avail. He accepted and continued his tracking, glass in hand.

Someone in the management pointed out to him that he had received a number of drinks, but was getting a bad reputation because he never bought any in return. John was horrified and that very lunch-time he raced across to the Duck, flung open the door and announced to a bar full of astonished strangers, 'Drinks are on me.' He made a mental note of each requirement and reeled off the list to the barmaid – 'Three whiskys – two with soda, one with water; four gin and tonics; four vodkas – two with tomato juice, two with bitter lemon; one Guinness; five halves of bitter; two pints; two halves of cider; one brandy and ginger ale; and two bitter lemons.' The order was placed on a circular tray and John was asked for, 'Four pounds, eighteen and ninepence.' He then picked up the tray and turned; forgetting that he had put his foot over the brass rail . . . Twenty-four glasses and their contents crashed to the floor.

John immediately turned back to the barmaid and said, 'Oh dear. Same again, please: three whiskys – two with soda, one with water; four gin and tonics; four vodkas – two with tomato juice, two with bitter lemon; one Guinness; five halves of bitter; two pints; two halves of cider; one brandy and ginger ale; and two bitter lemons.' Meanwhile the assembly had picked up the broken glass. The barmaid started to tot up.

'That will be, er . . .'

'Four pounds, eighteen and ninepence,' interjected John. He picked up the tray and – yes – he had again forgotten his foot in the rail. Down went another twenty-four glasses and their contents.

'Oh dear – I'm so sorry – same again, please: three whiskys – two with soda, one with water . . .'

By now the bar was awash and in a state of turmoil. 'That should be four pounds, eighteen and ninepence,' said John, but before he could lift the tray he was surrounded by a group of helping hands. He was most indignant. 'I can manage perfectly well, thank you.' He extricated his foot and carried the tray in a most dignified manner to a low, round table in the middle of the room and placed it carefully: 'There – you see?!' He sat down on the settle, crossed his legs triumphantly – and kicked over the tray-laden table.

Can you wonder that I treasure John Barton? This is the man who stayed with us, cosseted by Diana, while he bore the full responsibility of rehearsing *The Wars of the Roses* until Peter Hall was well enough to rejoin the production.

8

'TRY IT THE HARD WAY'

Rehearsals were intensified and a complicated schedule was worked out. The two plays (*Henry VI* and *Edward IV*) were each divided into some thirty 'block' numbers. Each 'block' involved a given number of actors and could be rehearsed without keeping other actors hanging about waiting for their entrances. Each 'block' initially was discussed and the basic moves set by Peter Hall. That group would next move on to the rehearsal room where John Barton was waiting and there the same 'block' was repeated, this time with the emphasis on verse-speaking and the understanding of the text. The group then moved on to the dress-circle bar where with the help of Peter Hall's assistant, Frank Evans, they could again go through the same 'block', reminding themselves of ideas and moves. Finally back to the stage for Peter to discuss and set the next 'block'. And so on: seven hours a day, seven days a week, for twelve weeks. And each evening, remember, we were performing other plays.

It took me less than a day to appreciate the genius of Peter Hall. His grasp of the intricacies of the very complicated plays was magisterial. He understood perfectly the politics of the period. This was brought home to me particularly in the many scenes that take place around the Council Table in which the chief protagonists have plenty to say – and sometimes say it at great length – but also present at the table are characters with little or nothing to say. These parts can be quite boring; normally all that an actor who plays one of them can hope to do is to listen intelligently, but with Peter everyone was made to be involved. The actor with a long speech was stopped time and again while Peter asked each person what his attitude was to the last sentence spoken. Was he already in possession of that information? Did he personally approve or disapprove of the sentiments? Everyone present is on the ladder of power, clawing their way up – they could each fall or be pushed off. Who else around the table might agree with him? Flash him a look. If he doesn't agree, why doesn't he? Whose side is he on? Whose side are you on? Can you profit by the information you have just heard? Might you be ruined? In turn, this caused the actors with speeches to play their cards cautiously. Every one of those scenes was electric, sparks flashed around the table and instead of just a lot of talk they became wonderfully dramatic.

It was during one of these rehearsals that Peter made an observation, so brilliant that it should be illuminated in letters of gold above every actor's bed: 'Always remember that when a character speaks he had the alternative of remaining silent.'

Peter made me think. Not that I had never thought before, but he encouraged me to question everything I did; to experiment; never to take the easy way out.

At one point of the play my character, York, returns triumphantly from Ireland ready to seize the crown from the King:

YORK: From Ireland thus comes York to claim his right,
              And pluck the crown from feeble Henry's head:
              Ring, bells, aloud; burn, bonfires, clear and bright,
              To entertain great England's lawful King.
              Ah Sancta Majestas. Who would not buy thee dear?
              Let them obey that know not how to rule;
              This hand was made to handle nought but gold:
              A sceptre shall it have, have I a soul,
              On which I'll toss the flower-de-luce of France.

York's ally, the Earl of Warwick, enters.

WARWICK: Welcome, brave Lord.
YORK: I thank you, Warwick. Is the hour arrived
              When I may openly advance my right?
WARWICK: It is: the realm is now so vilely rent,
              That thou and I with our conjoined powers
              May easily unseat him from the throne.

They then discuss their strategy and finally march off with their combined armies.

With the resources of the Royal Shakespeare Company, I was provided with an 'army' of ten men. Warwick had entered with another 'army' of ten, and at the end of the scene he and I were followed off by the 'conjoined powers' of twenty. Now the RSC is a very democratic company and in the early days of rehearsal, when I discussed this scene with Peter, I was somewhat amazed to find twenty young 'soldiers' telling me how I should play the part. I was still a new boy in the modern school so I remained silent while Peter listened carefully to what they each had to say: 'Yes. Yes. Very good. Very good. Isn't that interesting, Donald? Yes. Thank you. I think in that case, Donald, you should . . .' and he came up with ideas that had nothing to do with anything the twenty 'soldiers' had said. But his diplomacy had paid off. Every one felt he had contributed and not one of them was aware that his ideas were nullified. Clever basket, I thought; but better was to come.

When I first heard that speech of York's I was struck by its similarity to the heroics found in Shakespeare's *Henry V*. I had understudied Henry at Stratford in 1946 and without undue modesty I thought that I could be magnificent in the part – if only someone would ask me to play it. I therefore found no problems in York's speech – I gave it all I had got. I loved doing it and I thought I was rather good.

At the end of one morning's rehearsal Peter enquired, apparently innocently, what I was doing for lunch that day. I had planned nothing. 'Good – then let us have lunch together, quietly. We'll go to the restaurant.'

The following conversation evolved slowly during the hour, interspersed with the usual pleasantries. After ruminating for a moment or two, Peter checked quickly that we could not be overheard, laid down his fork and said, 'Have you ever wanted to play Henry Five?'

My mind raced: I had done one of the speeches for my audition: he must have been impressed: perhaps he is already casting for next season: 'Yes. As a matter of fact, I have.'

'You would be a very good Henry, wouldn't you?'

There was nothing to be gained by hiding my light under a bushel – modesty would get me nowhere. 'Yes, I would!'

Another course was delivered to the table. 'That's where you are so lucky, Donald; unlike so many modern actors, you have no difficulty with the extrovert heroics required – the new generation of actors can't give us the trumpets and the waving banners.'

Better and better, I thought – I'm sure I've got the very part I want next season.

He passed me the salt and pepper: 'Have you noticed that York's speech when he returns from Ireland is very similar to some in Henry Five?'

'Strange you should mention that – yes, I have noticed.'

'– the flag waving, the trumpets, the heroics – you can cope
with it all?'

'Perfectly.'

The waitress cleared away the plates. 'You have no problems
with that scene, have you?'

'None at all.'

'I thought not! – Why not try it the hard way,' and he went on
to outline the alternatives.

Although he momentarily undermined my confidence, from
that moment on I have never taken the obvious, easy way out of
a problem. I try it the hard way.

I have always had a love/hate relationship with directors. Everyone
working in a creative field relies upon the advice of someone whom
he trusts. Is there a writer who doesn't ask a loved one for an
opinion of an early draft? Most painters known to me are quite
prepared to obliterate the morning's work on the advice of their
nearest and dearest. Actors are no exception. With me, Diana,
who knows my work so well and has seen everything I have done
since 1947, will not hesitate to mention that I am reusing some old
trick, pointing out that I first did it in, say, 1957. We all need a
wife/husband/aunt/loved one, but at rehearsals for a play such as
Henry VI we cannot have fifty 'aunties' with fifty different ideas
on how a scene should be played. We must all agree on a common
referee and we call him a director.

I happen to believe in an actors' theatre. The better he is served
by his author, director, designer and lighting, the better will be
the result. The only difference between reading *Hamlet* at home
and seeing it in a theatre should be the actor. When I began my
theatre-going, I was extremely fortunate. Within a few years I was
privileged to see, among others, Gielgud's Hamlet and his Ernest;
Edith Evans' Lady Bracknell; Olivier's Richard the Third and his
Oedipus and Puff; Wolfit's Lear and Volpone; Richardson's Falstaff
and his Peer Gynt; Ashcroft's Hedda and her Duchess of Malfi;
Valk's Othello; Tearle's Othello and his Antony; Redgrave's Macbeth and his Macheath; Portman's Uncle Harry and his Crocker-
Harris. Oh dear me, the theatrical riches of that time, but who
today could put a director's name to many of them? But within
recent years I have seen advertised 'Terry Hand's *Henry IV Parts
One and Two*'; 'Jonathan Miller's *Hamlet*'; 'Peter Brook's *King
Lear*'; even 'Trevor Nunn's *Hedda Gabler*'. Can you name the actors
who played the leading parts in these productions?

Or take the evolution of one play: when *Charley's Aunt* was first seen it was advertised as 'W. S. Penley in *Charley's Aunt*': the next major production was billed as 'Brandon-Thomas' *Charley's Aunt*': more recently we even had 'Cecil Beaton's *Charley's Aunt*'.

My mission in life is to see a return to the actors' theatre or we will all be reduced to Gordon Craig's vision of using puppets. Of course a good director can assist the actors and improve the whole but let us not overlook the fact that the director is a fairly recent phenomenon – he is a product of the twentieth century. Before that the actor was his own director: at the Lyceum all the original ideas were Henry Irving's and his stage-manager merely drilled the 'extras'. Today, sadly, I find actors leaving drama schools and meekly waiting for the god-figure of a director to tell them what to do. Perhaps it is because most of their work is likely to be in television where if they don't do as they are told they will not be seen on the screen.

It is quite impossible to sit in an auditorium and say what ideas have come from an actor or from a director but the myth of the director is perpetrated by many of the critics who happily write about actors being '*under* the direction of . . .' and 'the performances drawn from the actors by . . .'

In the last forty years I have seen more plays spoiled by a director than have been transformed into a success by one.

When Oxford win the boat race due credit is given to the coach, but the public watch the oarsmen, not the man who bicycled along the towpath. How boring it would be if the contest was advertised as being between 'Mr X of Oxford and Mr Y of Cambridge'. Sebastian Coe doubtless relies on the advice of his coach but, when the time comes, Coe is the one who must stamp his authority on the race. In cricket it is the team, led by its captain in much the same way as a leading actor should, who produce the performance. Will we see England playing under the name of its director?

I once asked Lynn Fontanne what her attitude to directors had been.

'Oh my dear – I have always done everything a director asked me to do.'

'Really?'

'Oh yes: unless I disagreed with him.'

Dame Edith Evans in one play had rather taken charge of rehearsals when a plaintive voice came from the director in the stalls, 'Edith, what am I here for?'

'Oh, we'll find something for you to do – don't worry.'

The last word of course must go, as always, to Sir Ralph Richardson who is reputed to have said, 'Directors are like the dog that bit the postman. If he bites him once you forgive him, but if he bites again he has to be put down. Mind you, I always say "Good Morning" and "Did you have a good breakfast?"'

Towards the end of our twelve weeks of rehearsal for *The Wars*, we reached the stage of dress-rehearsals. For much of the time I had to wear full armour which was covered by an enormous cloak for the Coronation scene. I staggered under the weight – surely it must have been the heaviest costume I had ever worn – so one morning I took our bathroom scales into the dressing-room and first weighed myself naked and then picked up everything I had to wear or carry and weighed myself again. Subtracting one from the other I deduced that my costume weighed fifty-six pounds. My belt alone weighed five pounds.

One of John Barton's many excellencies is that he is a superb arranger of stage duels, and for weeks John Corvin, as Clifford, and I, as York, had practised a fight with two-handed swords which had been specially made for the production. They were six feet long, had four-inch-wide blades and each weighed fourteen pounds. What a thrilling sound they made as we scuffed them along on the wire-mesh-covered stage! Corvin and I had reached a perfect understanding and thank goodness we remained on good terms privately because once we had started to swing the lethal weapon at the arm or head of our opponent, there was absolutely no way of stopping it if the other one failed to parry the blow with his own sword. When we had donned our cumbersome armour and begun to wield the weighty swords the fight appeared to be between two lumbering dinosaurs and so gave us a little time to think, but we encountered a new hazard: as we swung the offensive weapon round above our heads, the joints of the armour were in danger of locking.

We came to my death scene. Being tied up in armour was very different from the experience when wearing a shirt and trousers. The soldiers who carried me off noticed the difference too. We got into the wings and, covered in blood and sweat, Peggy Ashcroft and I both collapsed on to a bench from sheer exhaustion. We gulped for air but Peggy managed to say, 'You were best,' to which I replied, 'But you were funniest.' Why did I say that? It was a pure reflex action but Peggy loved it and that silly remark cemented a relationship that has lasted through the years.

The whole company had worked extremely hard for many weeks; too hard actually; we were dropping and we had no reserves of energy, with the result that the final dress-rehearsal was a fiasco and the company was dispirited as we gathered on the stage for notes from Peter and John. The production that we hoped would salvage the reputation of the company seemed a failure to us all and in approximately twenty hours the public and the press would witness another disaster. Some of the company were near to tears. Diana had watched the rehearsal from the dress-circle and had gone round to my dressing-room to wait for me. The next part of the story is really hers.

Over the tannoy she heard Peter's speech to the company. We were too dazed but he complimented us on our work and told us that what we were now doing was absolutely perfect. If we could give that performance tomorrow it would be the realisation of his dreams. If the audience failed to appreciate it the fault was his not ours. As Diana told me later it was like Henry the Fifth rallying his troops – she had never heard a pep talk like it. From our point of view we determined not to let Peter down – and with him, John. The next day we managed to find that little bit extra and luck was on our side – everything went according to plan – *The Wars of the Roses* was a colossal success and I was accepted as a classical actor once again.

Amid all the turmoil, family life had to go on just the same. During their summer holidays from school, the boys were with us in Stratford. They came to see all the plays – several times – and they spent days boating on the river, but they were far removed from their friends in London, amongst whom they were used to spending their holidays. Unexpectedly I had a long weekend free from rehearsal and resolved that we should spend it together – but where?

9

OF PIGS AND TIGERS

We settled on Snowdonia. None of us had been to North Wales before and the boys thought that it would be the next best thing to the Himalayas. I made enquiries and someone suggested that we should stay at a small hotel used by climbers called Pen-y-Gwryd Inn, on the Capel Curig to Beddgelert road.

Off we drove and soon after Oswestry we knew we were in another country: Gobowen, Llangollen (missing out on Rhos-llanerchrugog), Tyn-y-cefn, Cerrigydrudion, Pentrefoelas, Betws-y-Coed and Capel Curig led us straight to our inn at Pen-y-Gwryd. We would not have been surprised had we seen a signpost signalling Reykjavik.

The boys were thrilled – and I have to admit, so was I – to see real climbers returning in the evening light: knitted caps on their heads, coils of rope around their shoulders, anoraks, breeches, stockings and studded boots. At dinner we listened to their conversation and asked them all sorts of naive questions. It was from this inn that great climbers of the not-too-distant past had done their training before scaling Everest. Everest! There was nothing for it: at crack of dawn next morning we must all conquer Snowdon. One of the climbers told us of the various routes to the top: we could climb vertically up the rock faces; we could take a train to within a few feet of the top; we could follow the pig track; or we could take a path with a long slow gradient, used by the tourists. The climber joined his friends in the bar, leaving us to discuss the alternatives.

The boys, including me, would never live it down if we went up Mount Snowdon in a train; we felt that 'Mum' might not manage the rock faces; to be thought of as tourists was too awful: this left the pig track – and if pigs could get to the top, so could we.

After an early breakfast the next morning we set off. Diana, Jeremy and I wore slacks, sweaters, anoraks and sensible shoes.

We never discovered where Marc had acquired his outfit: cord trousers tucked into boots, sweater, anorak, goggles, a haversack and a miniature ice-pick. We all wore identical caps, that I had bought at some time in Ireland, with flaps to come down over the ears. Robbie, the dog, trotted beside us.

After an easy beginning the path began to rise, very gently at first but becoming steeper. Why should pigs of so many generations all choose one route? On and on we trudged. Whenever we reached a vantage point we paused to admire the splendid views. The weather was reasonable and we were surprised that we appeared to be quite alone on the mountain: not another soul did we see. Foolishly we had not enquired how long it might take us. As we sat on a prominence and each ate a bar of chocolate, we heard the sound of feet above us getting closer. Around the bend came a climber in all his trappings: he slithered to a standstill in front of us, looked back up the mountain, thought better of talking to us, and continued downwards. We continued upwards. The track became narrower and the rock/scree slipped beneath our feet. We began to wonder why on earth pigs should choose to go to the top of a mountain: we had seen no vegetation for the past half-hour. Sadly, a mist came down and we were unable to appreciate the views which should have been getting better and better the higher we climbed. We had been in single file for some time, each taking it in turn to be the leader – a position that Marc felt should by rights be his as he was the one with the ice-pick. On and on, up and up. The mist became thicker and we began to have difficulty in seeing the track; now and then we gathered together to discuss which was the actual route. The mist was by now very thick and our voices seemed to be disembodied. Not a sound could we hear but the crackling of the stones that we dislodged, descending into the distance. Individually we all felt rather nervous, but none of us admitted it.

As the father-figure, I was aware of my responsibility but I was certain that we must be near the top so I encouraged my flagging troops. The mist was so thick that we could not see the one in front and the going was so steep that we had to pause every few yards. When our spirits were at their lowest, Marc came into his own: from his haversack he produced four oranges and a bag of sweets (regrettably, no brandy). No travellers ever have been in more need of succour. Off we went again, up and up. Our legs were nearly giving out when we heard voices . . . We called out and heard an answering cry. We renewed our efforts and fought on. To our relief the mist began to clear away in small patches and we saw people – people – about a dozen or so, standing around in groups of twos and threes. We were at the top of Mount Snowdon. How had they got there? We were greeted with amazement – some had come by train, some up the slow gradient but none of them knew of our route. We sat down and looked about us . . . The mist was not a mist: we had come through low clouds!

We were so exhausted that we allowed ourselves the relative comfort of the train to Llanberis for the return journey. That evening we again met our climber friends.

'What have you done today?' we were asked.

'We have been up Mount Snowdon – we went up the pig track.' This was received with some incredulity.

'Dressed like that?'

'Yes.'

'You should only use that route if you are an experienced climber – two-thirds of the way up there is only room for one person at a time – the mountain is on one side and on the other is a sheer drop of hundreds of feet – it is very dangerous and further on you are on a ridge with a drop on both sides.'

'But why should the pigs use a track like that?'

'It is not for pigs! – it is the PYG track – P-Y-G – for Pen-y-Gwryd – it is the track we climbers use to return to the pub.'

If the clouds had not been there, and we could have seen where we were, we would never have dared to go on.

The rest of our weekend we spent safely walking round the battlements of the castles at Conway, Caernarvon and Beaumaris, before the boys returned to school.

We had decided many years previously that, due to the absurd peripatetic nature of my profession, it would give our children more security if they went to boarding prep schools. Jeremy loved it but Marc hated it, so from our own experience we are undetermined whether boarding schools are good or bad for children. Luckily, when they later went on to public schools they both loved them. So what does that indicate? Oh dear, I am about to digress again. I can feel it coming on.

Two of Jeremy's friends at his prep school had gone on to Lancing College in Sussex and he felt that he would like to join them. We applied and their housemaster asked them what young Sinden was like. 'Not very good at games, sir, but he is very witty,' was the immediate answer. As a result two appointments were made, first for us to meet the housemaster at eleven a.m. and then the headmaster at noon. Diana and I drove up the long drive with the magnificent chapel soaring above us and found our way to Fields House. Further enquiries led us along monastic corridors to an iron-studded oak door on which I knocked. Absolute silence. I knocked again, loudly. After a few moments the door was opened a few inches and half a face squeezed into the gap. 'Yes?'

'My name is Sinden . . .'

'Yes?'

'I have an appointment with Mr Halsey . . .'

'Yes?'

'Concerning my son Jeremy . . .'

'Yes?'

'We are hoping that he might come to this house . . .'

'Ah . . . Ah . . . You had better come inside!' The inflection was as if he were saying, 'This is a subject that no decent people discuss in public.'

The room we entered was a perfect example of what we expect a bachelor male academic to have lived in for thirty solitary years: it was surrounded by bookcases, some glass-fronted, but most of the contents seemed to be distributed around the rest of the room. Books were under tables, on tables, beside chairs and piled in corners. The mantelshelf contained the curling detritus of years. Pipe spills stood in two jars. A low armchair with a deep depression in the seat bore the imprint of countless evenings of fireside sitting. A mangy settee held a pile of *Times Literary Supplements*. An octagonal table with a plate, a knife, a cup and saucer, a jar of Oxford marmalade, a half-empty bottle of milk and more than today's crumbs upon it, stood on three legs at the side of the room (the fourth leg rested on a book). A window-seat in the thickness of the wall looked out over the Sussex Downs.

The shy, benign man in front of whom we now stood was about five foot eight inches tall. His face was triangular: a pointed chin widened to a broad forehead roofed by thinning hair. He wore a tweed jacket with sagging pockets, over a cardigan and baggy trousers. He had backed away from us as we entered and we all stood in the centre of the room.

'Yes?'

'My name is Sinden . . .'

'Yes.'

'This is my wife . . .'

'Yes.'

'And we are hoping that our son . . .'

'Yes.'

'. . . will come to the house.'

'. . . aah.'

Diana and I were beginning to wonder if we had made a dire
mistake.

'You've driven from London?'

'Yes – I made an appointment . . . for this morning . . .'

'You should have a cup of coffee.'

'Thank you.'

But we continued to stand uneasily; Diana and I looked at each
other; Mr Halsey – as we presumed him to be – gazed at us
eagerly.

'So you've driven from London?'

'Yes.'

'I think coffee, don't you?'

'Thank you.'

His face suddenly clouded over, he looked suspiciously around
and then began to prowl nervously about the room. Obviously
something serious had happened. He muttered a word that sounded
like 'sauce'. Diana asked if there was anything we could do.
'Saucepan,' he said, and continued his search. From behind a pile
of books he at last produced a pan, filled it with water from a
hidden tap, placed it in the fireplace on a gas ring, lit it after
fumbling in his cardigan for matches, straightened up proudly and
joined us in the middle of the room.

'So you've driven from *London*!'

Over our coffee we talked about Jeremy until I noticed that the
time was five past twelve.

'We really must be going . . .'

'Do you have to get back to London?'

'No. But we have an appointment with the headmaster at
twelve.'

'Oh – I wouldn't bother about that.'

'But I arranged an appointment.'

'Noo – it's not necessary – have another cup of coffee.'

'I think I should at least let him know.'

I picked up the internal telephone that he indicated and waited,
but the line continued to buzz.

'No one answers,' I said.

'No, the porter is not on duty and he operates the switchboard.'

'Could I get the headmaster on an outside line?'

'You could –'

I picked up the receiver of the other telephone.
    '– but I don't know his number.'
    'Have you a directory?'
    'Oh, I've never had one of those.'

Later, over lunch at the local pub, we warmed to this delightful man but not until Jeremy went to Lancing in the following term did we discover that he was known by the affectionate and totally inappropriate name of Tiger and that, due to him, Fields House was the envy of the entire college. Any new boy who stepped out of line was firmly reprimanded by his school-fellows because the unforgivable sin was 'to let Tiger down'. The quiet, inoffensive, charming Tiger instilled self-discipline in all the boys who came in contact with him.

10

'EVENING PADRE'

The Stratford season was drawing to a close. The always successful
Comedy of Errors was recorded for posterity on television. *Richard
III* was added to the repertoire and on several occasions all three
plays that comprised *The Wars of the Roses* were performed on one
day: *Henry VI* began at ten a.m., *Edward IV* followed at two thirty
and *Richard III* at seven thirty. It was an odd experience putting
on theatrical make-up at nine a.m. but it must have been odder
for an audience to be in a theatre by ten in the morning and to
know that, but for short breaks for lunch and dinner, they would
not be released until eleven at night. It became the popular 'in'
thing to do and tickets for the whole day were at a premium.
Peggy Ashcroft as Queen Margaret aged through the thirteen
hours from twenty-seven to seventy-seven: and hers became the
performance of the year.

The company began to worry about future employment. Peter
Hall arranged individual meetings with all the actors. At the
appointed time I made my way to his office: it was as if two great
friends were meeting after a long absence. 'My dear Donald – sit
down – over here – sit down,' and he joined me on the sofa.
'Now, Donald, I want to confide in you – I need your advice – I
would prefer it if our conversation . . . didn't go any further . . .'

'Of course, Peter, of course.'

'Next season . . . Next year – 1964 – as you know, is the
quatercentenary of Shakespeare's birth . . . I've got to do something special at the theatre . . . I have an idea . . . What about
presenting *all* the consecutive histories – *Richard II, Henry IV Part
One, Henry IV Part Two, Henry V*, culminating in *The Wars –
Henry VI, Edward IV* and *Richard III*?'

'It's a wonderful idea.'

'You really think so?'

(I could see the part of Henry Five looming up again.)

'But I have a problem – I cannot do it without you: your great performance as York is the linchpin of *The Wars* . . . if you will come back next season and repeat that performance I can safely go ahead, but if you were to feel that it was not worth your while – I will have to drop the whole idea. I have loved working with you – I hope you have enjoyed working with me . . .'

His eyes were swimming with tears and he gripped my forearm: 'Please, please, say you'll come back. Without you – without your performance of York – I have no season . . .'

Tears sprang to my eyes in appreciation of his confidence but I tried to keep a cool head: 'What about other parts?'

'I couldn't expect you to play another part before York – it would take away the impact of your first entrance, but I have some very interesting ideas for new plays at the Aldwych . . .'

I left his office aware of the enormous trust and responsibility I carried. I could not let Peter down – could I? He had given me my opportunity: after a duff start I was now happy and fulfilled in my work. The thought of being in Stratford for the quatercentenary year was very attractive. But I was broke. I telephoned John Cadell who was dubious: another whole year doing the same thing? The big problem was money: in spite of economising I was finishing the season financially worse off than I had begun – the ends had not met. Peter had asked me to let him know within a couple of days . . . Stratford was professionally where I should be, but try telling that to a bank manager: 'I have twelve months' work – so please may I have an overdraft.' (I wish I understood figures, but some years later an accountant pointed out that to do a season at Stratford actually cost me two hundred pounds.)

Unbeknown to me, a hundred miles away in London, Leslie Phillips had appeared in six episodes of a television series called *Our Man At St Mark's*. The producing ITV company, Associated Rediffusion, wanted to record some more but Leslie was unwilling or unable to do them. John Cadell was asked if I would take over the part: thirteen episodes to be recorded in as many weeks in the spring of 1964. The offer came at a miraculous time; I could afford to return to Stratford and save the season for dear Peter – of course I would do it.

Associated Rediffusion had its offices in St Catherine's House, Kingsway, the building that today houses the Registers of Births, Marriages and Deaths, and its studios were at Wembley. Little did I realise that I was to work there for fourteen weeks a year for the

next three years as the vicar of St Mark's with Joan Hickson as my
housekeeper and Harry Fowler as my verger-cum-sexton. Some
years before, the Sinden family had acquired an Aberdeen Terrier
– a scottie. In effect the dog belonged to Jeremy (Marc was to have
the next one) and he was asked what name it should have. Without
hesitation Jeremy said Robertson. Why? Robertson was his best
friend at school at the time. The name was soon shortened to
Robbie with the result that everyone assumed that he was named
after Robert Burns. I suggested to the TV producer that it might
be a nice idea if the vicar had a dog – a scottie, perhaps – so Jeremy
collected five shillings a week on Robbie's behalf.

Each Tuesday I arrived at the Wembley Studio at nine in the
morning, changed into my vicar's garb of clerical grey suit and
dog-collar, spent the whole day doing rehearsals for the cameras,
recorded the episode between six and six thirty in the evening,
changed out of my vicar's outfit, then drove like hell to the
Aldwych Theatre to be in time for a performance at seven thirty.

I soon realised that if I donned my vicar's clothes when I got up
in the morning and only took them off when I arrived at the
theatre, I could save the time taken by two changes. Thus attired,
I set off one morning in my Morris Mini but was rather annoyed
to find that a short cut I used, between Neasden and Wembley,
was that day barred by a NO ENTRY ROAD WORKS sign. What
nonsense, I thought, I'm sure my little Mini will be able to get
through. A mile up the quiet suburban road I saw the ROAD
WORKS: a large excavator was digging a trench down one side of
the road which left plenty of room for me to get by on the other
side. Very slowly I eased forward, but the driver of the machine
saw what I was about to do, lifted his great trenching implement
with steel teeth out of the hole and placed it firmly on the road in
front of me. I had to stop. He waited for me to reverse back down
the road: I waited for him to remove the implement. I know I was
in the wrong, but he need not have barred my way. I turned off
my engine. He turned off his. We looked at each other coldly. I
was in no particular hurry yet, so ostentatiously I opened my
newspaper. He opened his. It was a battle of wills: both of us were
determined to be bloody-minded. The minutes ticked by until two
bewildered men climbed out of the trench and went over to the
excavator where the driver gesticulated angrily in my direction.
The two men came over to me where one of them, as he bent
down to talk through the Mini window, caught sight of my
dog-collar. He immediately returned and remonstrated with the

driver who apologetically removed his implement and I was allowed to proceed.

On another occasion I was making my way as fast as I could from Wembley to the Aldwych via another short cut at Shepherd's Bush. Where I joined the main road I knew that I had to keep my nerve and edge my way bravely into the rush-hour traffic, but this time I found myself behind a man who, in strict accordance with the Highway Code, was prepared to wait until there was a completely free road to enter. This could take at least half an hour and the play at the Aldwych would have begun. I waited, but he showed no signs of moving, so I selected bottom gear, overtook him and stuck my nose into the traffic. As I did so, I shouted frustratedly, 'You're a stupid bastard.' His riposte, 'And you are a . . .' died on his lips as he saw my collar. I imagined him telling his wife the story. 'You have no idea what I was called today . . . By a vicar!'

I had no idea that a vicar's collar carried so much influence. I was to find it again when Jeremy brought a friend to the studio to see a recording. When it was over, as I was not working that evening at the Aldwych, we went across to the hospitality room where we were joined by two high-up executives of Associated Rediffusion who apologised that they could not stay long as they had to put in an appearance at a particularly starry pop concert at the Wembley Pool next-door (Associated Rediffusion owned the whole of the Wembley Stadium complex). 'Pop concert! – Oh Dad, couldn't we go?' cried Jeremy. The executives explained that unless we already had seats it was quite impossible – most of the famous groups were playing and tickets were like gold dust.

'But wait a minute,' said one executive to the other. 'My ticket admits two and I am going alone – so are you – we could each take one of the boys but "Dad" will have to look after himself.'

I hoped that my face might be well enough known for me to at least get in – even if I had to stand – so off we went.

At the door to the hall we were met by an enormous man – a chucker-out – who scrutinised the tickets proffered by the executives: 'Next! Is this your name? Is this your guest? – right – through that way. Next! Is this your name? Is this your guest? – right – through that way. Next! Oh, evening, padre – straight through, sir.'

Christopher Hodson and Bill Turner were the alternate directors of *St Mark's*; delightful, scatter-brained Joan Hickson and I were in every episode; ebullient Harry Fowler made regular appearances, and each week we had an influx of new characters including attractive girls who in some way or another became embroiled with the young vicar. The casting of every character was splendid – among the girls were the then unknown Ann Bell and Francesca Annis – all of which was a tribute to the impeccable taste of the casting director, Diana Parry.

There was only one problem; and I would like to take this opportunity of apologising to some of my colleagues. For the first few episodes Joan and I did our best to make each week's newcomers feel at home and at ease, but as the strain of rehearsing and recording a new script every six days began to tell on us, we needed to conserve our energy and unhappily found ourselves spending less and less off-stage time with the new arrivals: during the lunch break Joan and I would sit quietly in the canteen reading books or newspapers as we ate, instead of joining the others in jollities.

St Mark's remained in the top ten for every one of its thirty-nine weeks.

We were a close-knit, happy and devoted team. Our executive producer, Eric Maschwitz, in earlier days had written the lyrics for many songs: 'A Nightingale Sang In Berkeley Square' for Judy Campbell to sing in the revue *New Faces*; 'These Foolish Things', and many others, but was perhaps most well known for his pre-war musicals. He told me a story about one of them, *Good Night Vienna*.

Driving down to Kent one Friday evening, Eric saw that the touring version was playing at the Lewisham Hippodrome and he couldn't resist going in and asking the manager, 'And how is *Good Night Vienna* doing in Lewisham?' to which the manager gave the unexpected reply, 'Just about as well as *Good Night Lewisham* would do in Vienna.'

Eric must have told that anecdote to many people, and I must have told it many times myself – certainly it is now known to almost every actor – but before writing about it here I thought I should check the facts. My enquiries eventually spread over two weeks and show just how difficult it is to establish the truth behind a good story.

I first looked up Eric's entry in *Who's Who in the Theatre*, but was surprised to find no reference at all to *Good Night Vienna*. Nor is the name of the musical mentioned in the list of Notable Productions.

I telephoned my friend Richard Bebb. He had a recording

of Jack Buchanan singing – as the label states – '"Good Night Vienna" (Posford) from the film *Good Night Vienna*'. So it was a film – but why Posford and not Maschwitz?

I looked in Halliwell's *Filmgoer's Companion* (6th Edition): *Good Night Vienna* is not mentioned as the title of any film.

I telephoned the Performing Rights Society: the only information they could offer was that the song was composed by George Posford with lyrics by Holt Marvell. Holt Marvell?! – so just where did Maschwitz fit in?

I began to ask everyone to whom I spoke. The impresario John Gale recalled that Eric had also told him the story – but it was Walthamstow and not Lewisham. John, however, was outnumbered – everyone else knew it as Lewisham.

Then at a party given by Martin Tickner I found myself talking to Dame Anna Neagle and I asked if she knew the anecdote about *Good Night Vienna* which ends with, 'Just about as well as *Good Night Lewisham* would do in Vienna'?

She bridled. 'Yes, indeed – but I am sure it is untrue: you see, the film I did with Jack was an enormous success. If you telephone me tomorrow I can give you all the facts.'

I had struck gold: Anna had been Buchanan's leading lady. The next day she told me that in 1931 Eric Maschwitz had taken the words and music to her husband Herbert Wilcox, who immediately snapped them up and made the film which he entitled *Good Night Vienna*.

'But just a minute: what had Maschwitz to do with it?'

'He wrote the lyrics.'

'I'm sorry, Anna, I believe you are wrong: the lyrics were written by Holt Marvell.'

'Oh, didn't you know? Eric was then editor of the *Radio Times* and used to write his lyrics under the name of Holt Marvell.'

So far so good but nothing seemed to be known of the stage version of the musical. Had Eric then asked the question of the manager of a cinema? Unlikely. Since the film was such a success the answer should have implied that *Good Night Lewisham* would have done rather well in Vienna.

Perhaps my friends Ray Mander and Joe Mitchenson would be interested in my enquiries. Ray said that he understood a stage version was indeed made of *Good Night Vienna* but as far as he knew it was only done by amateurs and locally they performed at Lewisham Town Hall.

Did the original story therefore refer to an amateur production?

I telephoned the Lewisham Borough Librarian. She had no records of performances except those that could be found in their old copies of local newspapers – I was welcome to consult these. I might have to spend weeks there to cover a period of thirty years – was it all worth it? A week later I received a telephone call from Ray Mander: he had been researching a totally different subject when out from a file slipped a programme for *Good Night Vienna* starring Bruce Trent, at the Granada, Tooting Bec in 1947. If it played at Tooting Bec the chances were that it also played Lewisham.

Luckily I know Bruce Trent – I had met him in Brighton just after the war and we met regularly at the Green Room Club. I telephoned him: had he played in *Good Night Vienna* at the Lewisham Hippodrome? He remembered that the production had opened in Glasgow but he had no memory of Lewisham. He had never heard Maschwitz's story. Disconsolately I replaced the telephone. A quarter of an hour later it rang: 'Donald – Bruce. You'll never believe this: for years my wife has been trying to get me to throw away a pile of old diaries; I kept meaning to but never got round to it. I've just looked at them and we played the Lewisham Hippodrome for the week beginning the 28th of February, 1948!'

So. Driving down to Kent on Friday evening, the 4th of March, 1948, Eric Maschwitz passed through Lewisham . . .

Good Night Lewisham and back to *Our Man At St Mark's*.

11

'I DON'T REMEMBER THAT BIT'

The four-hundredth anniversary of Shakespeare's birth did not pass unnoticed. Stratford-upon-Avon, of course, surpassed itself. Commemorative medals were struck: Dr Levi Fox and The Shakespeare Birthplace Trust brought out everything from the vaults for a most imaginative display in a building freshly erected next door to the birthplace and opened by Her Majesty the Queen. Richard Buckle mounted an enormous exhibition in a vast temporary tent-like structure in the fields opposite the theatre. It was all quite amazing when you remember that there is no single artefact in the world that was actually owned by Shakespeare. Even the house that he bought and in which he died was pulled down in the eighteenth century.

A Wars of the Roses cricket match was played in which Peggy Ashcroft led the Lancastrians and I the Yorkists. Her team had Cyril Washbrook as honorary captain and mine had Len Hutton. You needed to know your history to appreciate why Brewster Mason as the Earl of Warwick was the umpire. Politically the result of the match had to be a draw.

There was only one sad note to sour the festivities. In Stratford – as in many towns, I understand – it is the time-honoured practice not to oppose the incoming mayor in the local elections. He is usually a man (or woman) who has spent many years of his life in local government and has gradually worked his way up to the crowning achievement of the Mayoralty. In Stratford Sam Tomlinson-Jones was such a man and he was the Mayor-elect for what was to be a most important year – the quatercentenary of the birth of Stratford's most famous citizen.

Suddenly – at the last minute – someone stood against him. Sam had arranged no electioneering campaign; like all his predecessors he imagined that he would be unopposed. The electorate, few of whom had lived in Stratford for as long as Sam, didn't appreciate these niceties and Sam lost his seat – and with it the glory of leading the town in the 1964 festivities.

I had returned briefly for the birthday celebrations on 23rd April. Nothing could be more British and delightful than the annual shindigs on the day of Shakespeare's supposed birth. (We know that he was baptised in the church on 26th April, 1564, and it is to be presumed that he was born two or three days before, but no one knows exactly when. It was a nice eighteenth-century conceit to suggest that our greatest poet was born on St George's Day and that tradition still holds good – except that for convenience the celebrations now take place on the nearest Saturday.) The whole town is en fête; every country in the world sends a representative – usually its ambassador – and they all meet at the theatre before setting off into the centre of the town where hundreds of flagpoles have been erected, one for each nation. On a given signal the flag is unfurled of each representative's country. The procession, now joined by other dignitaries, headed by the Mayor and Corporation and led by a band, sets off to Shakespeare's birthplace, enters through the front door and continues out of the back door (which takes some time), then retracing Henley Street, along the High Street, past the site of the house in which he died, and on to the church where his tomb is soon obliterated by the hundreds of wreaths, sheaves, single flowers and sprigs of rosemary ('for re-membrance') which have been carried by everyone in the pro-cession. Then back to the theatre gardens for lunch in an enormous marquee. Each year someone of eminence is invited to make a speech to propose the toast to The Immortal Memory to which someone else replies for The Theatre.

In 1977 I was asked to make the latter speech and to my everlasting shame I did it disastrously. I love Stratford-upon-Avon. I have spent the happiest years of my life there. I met Diana there. I have been privileged to speak Shakespeare's verse in the very town where he was born, lived, died and was buried. I am for ever in his debt. I could have made the speech of my life, and I mucked it. I tried to be funny and facetious – and it was a hideous mistake.

The business of unfurling the flags sometimes causes problems. One year we had a young American student attached to the company and at the ceremony he proudly joined the United States representatives at the foot of their flagstaff. On cue the cord was pulled and Old Glory fluttered in the breeze – upside down! A contingent of Royal Engineers was to hand and one of them was up the pole like a flash, removed the flag – and dropped it.

The Americans treat their flag with the same reverence that we reserve for the Queen. (Did you know that there is a man permanently employed in Washington DC whose sole job is to run up the Stars and Stripes to the top of the pole on the roof of the Capitol, haul it down, run up another identical flag, then another, then another: all day long? These flags are sent the length and breadth of the United States so that schools, universities, businesses, societies, and the like can boast that their flag actually flew from the top of the Capitol.) Their flag – symbolising so much – must never touch the ground. Our American student did a twelve-foot dive landing flat on his face, but he succeeded in catching the flag just before it landed.

Another year I was asked to unfurl a flag for a country whose representative had not turned up. On my cue I tugged at the cord and nothing happened. I tugged again and again but the bundle at the top of the pole refused to be unwrapped. Again a Royal Engineer came to the rescue. During the official luncheon that followed, I was seated next to the Russian ambassador and I thought that my adventure might be a good conversational gambit so I opened by asking, 'Did you have any problems with your flag this morning?' The ambassador glowered at me and closed the conversation by stating, 'Certainly not! Why should we?'

With all these festivities going on in Stratford, what was London to do? The *Sunday Telegraph* was prepared to underwrite a Festival of Theatre. They approached the impresario Peter Daubeny and as a result the World Theatre Season was mounted in co-operation with the Royal Shakespeare Company. During a period of three months the Aldwych Theatre was visited by companies from seven different countries:

The Comédie-Française presented *Tartuffe* by Molière, and *Un Fil à la Patte* by Feydeau;

The Schiller Theatre from Berlin presented *Andorra* by Max Frisch and *Clavigo* by Goethe;

Peppino de Filippo's Italian Theatre Company in his own play *The Metamorphoses of a Wandering Minstrel*;

The Abbey Theatre Company from Dublin presented *Juno and the Paycock* and *The Plough and the Stars* – both by O'Casey;

The Polish Contemporary Theatre in *What a Lovely Dream* and *Let's Have Fun* by Mrozek, and *The Life Annuity* by Fredro;

The Greek Art Theatre in *The Birds* by Aristophanes;

The Moscow Art Theatre in *Dead Souls* by Gogol, *The Cherry Orchard* by Chekhov and *Kremlin Chimes* by Pogodin.

Fortunately for me this period coincided with my TV work, so being free in the evenings Diana and I were able to see each company and every production. What a feast! I must admit that the prospect was daunting, as I can speak no foreign language, but to have the finest companies that the rest of the world has to offer brought to one's doorstep was an opportunity not to be missed. For those like me, a system of simultaneous translation was provided. For a small fee you could hire a sort of plastic stick which housed a battery at one end and an earpiece at the other. When this was held close to the ear you heard the voices of English actors who had been placed in a soundproof box from which they read a free translation of what was being said by the foreign actors whom they watched through a window. I used one of these things for the first two plays before giving up. Others found them very useful but for me the plastic stick was just the wrong length: it was too short if I placed my elbow on the arm of the seat or too long if I tried to fold my arms. Without it I noticed that those members of the audience who understood the language spoken on the stage would laugh several seconds before those who had to wait for the translation. Lucky actors: two laughs from each joke. I always studied the synopsis of the play and within minutes I was following it quite easily. The good actors stood out a mile from the others and it was simple to follow their thoughts.

And what actors we saw!
Robert Hirsch in the Feydeau farce bowled me over when he executed a stunning piece of 'business'. Shocked when all attention is suddenly focused on him as he stood at the bottom of the staircase, he 'bounced' the whole way up, sideways, without appearing to move his legs or look where he was going;
Peppino de Filippo clowning in the play which he not only wrote, but directed, designed, composed the music and played the lead;
Martin Held in the Schiller Theatre Company;
Actors with almost unpronounceable names in the Polish Company;
Actors with equally difficult names, Hadjimaskos, Kouros and Karakatsanis, in Karolos Koun's stunningly original production of *The Birds*, with Zouzou Nicoloudi's choreography to Hadjidaki's throbbing music;
And then Belokourov, Stanitsin, Kedrov and Boris Livanov, who, before being joined by Stepanova and the great Gribov for *The Cherry Orchard*, performed Gogol's *Dead Souls*.
In one scene of *Dead Souls* Belokourov visited the house of an

aristocratic female dwarf. The curtains opened to reveal her seated on a chair, her feet, just showing beneath a long dress, swung twelve inches or more above the floor. She offered Belokourov tea and her stunted arms worked at the samovar while she continued with the dialogue and had great difficulty reaching her mouth with the cup. Could this be a real dwarf? How would a normal-sized actress cope with the scene? I tried to work it out: the chair would have no seat to it, so that she is actually sitting on the floor with her knees bent up and the costume cleverly made to cover all but her feet. Only her hands would show through her short sleeves. I was still working out the trick when the scene ended and the actress hopped off the chair and waddled out: she *was* a dwarf about forty inches tall! At least so I thought until I met her at the reception after the first night when I discovered that she was five feet four inches tall and had perfected the technique of walking in a crouched position. Alas, I have lost my programme and now I may never again know her name.

At the same reception I made great friends with Boris Livanov, in spite of the fact that he could speak no English and I could speak no Russian: we carried on a conversation in mime and only required an interpreter when we were completely stuck for a word. Boris was (he is now dead) about six feet two inches tall and of massive proportions with a loud basso profondo voice. To my Anglo-Saxon embarrassment he took to picking me up and kissing me on both cheeks each time we met. Halfway down the Strand I heard his bull-like bellow, 'Doonall!' and there he stood like a colossus with his arms spread wide. And in front of the passing office workers I was lifted off my feet and a kiss was implanted on each cheek.

His knowledge of English theatrical history was amazing and his great ambition was to inspect the portraits in the Garrick Club. Unfortunately his visit coincided with the club's annual summer closure. Fortunately I was able to repair the omission when his company made a return visit in 1970.

The London theatre was greatly enriched by these splendid companies and we were overjoyed when Peter Daubeny announced that there would be another season of plays in 1965. Little did we know that they would continue until 1974. For eight months of the year Peter and his wife Molly travelled the world to find the theatrical treasures which they were to display for our delight and then, when the season opened, poor exhausted Peter would sit nervously hoping that his choice would meet with public approval while Molly coped majestically with the inevitable socialising, faultlessly introducing to each other hundreds of people with impossible names and always remembering the protocol involved in the hierarchy.

The British theatre totally lacks a collective co-ordinating body and this was brought home severely to Diana and me during that opening season at the Aldwych. If a head of state visits Britain he is entertained by the Queen as a charge on the nation. A visiting Prime Minister is entertained by our Prime Minister and the government. A trade delegation is entertained by the relevant trade association. In every case a national or collective body can be found to arrange, and pay for, meetings between like-minded people for the purpose of cross-fertilising ideas – except in the arts.

When, for instance, the Royal Shakespeare Company visited the Soviet Union a reception was given by the Ministry of Culture to which Russian actors, writers, designers, directors were invited; each of the main theatres invited our company to meet their resident companies, where endless discussions took place, ideas were exchanged and friendships made. But in 1964 when the various groups arrived to play at the Aldwych, they were accommodated in Bloomsbury hotels and then left to fend for themselves. Of course their own Embassies quite often arranged a first-night party for them but, collectively, the British theatre, on behalf of the British nation, did nothing because, firstly, it lacks a central forum, and secondly, who pays?

Peter and Molly were magnificent and arranged dinner-parties where the leading actors and directors could meet their British equivalents, but they could not possibly have been expected to entertain a company of sixty or more participants – and a different group every two weeks.

It was when we found the Polish Company mooching around Kingsway and doing their shopping in Southampton Row because they 'thought that was London' that Diana and I felt that something – something – should be done. I suggested to Peter Hall that as these foreign groups were using the Royal Shakespeare Company's London home – the Aldwych Theatre – we had a duty: something – something – should be done.

'I quite agree,' he said, 'but the RSC has no money for that sort of thing – but if you feel you can do something I appoint you as our honorary representative.'

So for the 1965 World Theatre Season I had a semi-official

position. I approached the London Tourist Board who gave me piles of maps, guidebooks and leaflets on divers activities which I distributed to each company on arrival and I had beavered away to find individuals or groups who would actually be prepared to cough up the most important commodity – money. Among others the Garrick Club agreed to host a reception for the Greek Art Theatre who had been so successful in 1964 that they were making a return visit.

The Actors Studio Theatre from New York were bringing two separate companies and the ever-generous Lady Barlow (Margaret Rawlings) undertook to host a party at the Mermaid Theatre for one of them while the American Embassy would look after the other.

A friend who was a director of the tobacco firm Peter Stuyvesant consulted his fellow directors who readily agreed to pay for a reception leaving the choice of company and all invitations and arrangements to me, so with that generous offer I apportioned the other companies and then telephoned him with the news, 'The date is the 26th of April and you will be entertaining the Habimah National Theatre of Tel-Aviv.' There was a silence from the other end of the phone.

'An Israeli company? I'm terribly sorry but we will have to withdraw. You see, the Arab countries are among our biggest customers.'

'Ah! Well, just a minute, I will see if I can rearrange things.'

Lady Barlow was most co-operative: she would take on the Israelis and let Stuyvesant have the Americans.

'Hello. New arrangements. The date will be the 3rd of May and you now have the Actors Studio Theatre from New York in a new play by James Baldwin which has an all black cast.'

'But you can't do this to us! Don't you realise that Peter Stuyvesant is a South African firm?'

Some hours later I had persuaded the American Embassy – who had been quite unaware that there were two different companies coming from New York – to entertain the cast of the Baldwin play, leaving Peter Stuyvesant to look after the cast of *The Three Sisters* directed by Lee Strasberg. Although this production included some notable actors such as Kim Stanley, George C. Scott and Sandy Dennis in the cast, it was an unmitigated disaster. All the worst aspects of the Method school of acting were presented – self-indulgence, inaudibility, and every line was prefixed by ums or ers. Half the audience had left before the end of the play and the other half were in no mood to meet the cast at a convivial gathering.

Diana and I decided not to offer our services the following year.

All the other companies were absolutely splendid: the Théâtre de France headed by Jean-Louis Barrault, Madeleine Renaud and Genevieve Page, excelled themselves and London was at their feet. At a special unadvertised matinee, I saw Samuel Beckett's *Happy Days*, in which Madeleine Renaud played Winnie, but it was Barrault's performance in the negligible part of Willie that influenced a decision I was about to make. More of that anon.

For me the most exciting discovery was to see Rosella Falk, Romolo Valli and Elsa Albani in two plays directed by Giorgio de Lullo – *La Bugiarda* and *Six Characters in Search of an Author*. I fell in love with the ladies and was lost in admiration for the men: Diana fell in love with the men and admiringly envied the ladies. Again thanks to Molly and Peter Daubeny they all became our good friends. The following year they returned and this time they presented *The Rules of the Game*, the play around which Pirandello had woven his *Six Characters*. I can still see, in my mind's eye, Valli slicing the top from an egg with a knife, just as his wife's lover is being killed in a duel.

Year after year we saw as many of those World Theatre Season plays as we possibly could: the National Theatre of Greece with Katina Paxinou; the Czech National Theatre – the first time we had seen the innovative designs of Josef Svoboda; the Nō Theatre of Japan and the Bunraku – the puppet theatre, also from Japan; the Schiller Theatre from Berlin; the joyous first encounter with Eduardo de Filippo when he brought his own play and company from Naples. Through him we met Neal Stainton and his Italian-born wife Laura who translates many English plays into Italian and vice versa and at whose houses in London and Rome we regularly met Eduardo and other Italian actors.

Lastly and most exultantly I recall one of the greatest actors I have ever seen: Ferruccio Soleri in *The Servant of Two Masters*. He had made the part completely his own. Whenever the play was revived in Italy he was the only man to play it. If only I could give you a slight taste of his quality . . . The man was not only an actor, he was an acrobat. Serving dinner to his two masters he comes out of the kitchen through a swing-door cut into the wall leaving a shallow 'trip' rail at the bottom: he enters carrying a tray on his upturned hand at shoulder-level; on the tray a china soup-tureen with its lid and a ladle sticking out from it. Failing to see the rail, he trips, performs a complete somersault in the air, and falls flat on his back. Miraculously his hand, extended above his head, still holds the tureen safely on the tray. Superb! Surely it was a trick? But we applaud him while we try to work out how it was done. Obviously the tureen is empty – probably glued to the tray – certainly the lid and ladle must be glued in place. But look! Soleri slowly raises the top half of his body until he is sitting; he swivels the tray round from above his head and rests it on his knees. He then removes the lid, lifts out a ladle full of soup, pours some back and drinks the remainder. Rapturous applause. The man's a genius, his whole performance packed with such expertise. At the end of the meal, both dissatisfied masters throw their plates at him from either side of the stage, a distance of some fifteen feet. These Soleri catches one by one while unconcernedly continuing his speech.

It really was rather bad luck on John Clements who had announced a production of this same play for the forthcoming Chichester Festival with Danny Kaye in the lead. Kaye attended one of Soleri's performances – presumably to pick up a few tips – and promptly cancelled his own engagement. He had found, as indeed we all had, that he was in the presence of the master. Soleri is now dead: we should wait until he is forgotten by audiences before trying to play that part.

But I have digressed again. Where should I be? Oh yes: back I went to Stratford.

Peter Hall had opened the 1964 season triumphantly with *Richard II*, *Henry IV* (Parts One and Two), and *Henry V*, to which *The Wars of the Roses* was now added. Had he not said that his whole season was at risk if I did not repeat my 'great performance' of York? Without my 'linchpin', he would not be able to do the History Cycle?

Several of us were sitting gossiping one evening in the green room when one of the group broke in saying, 'Well, Peter told me last year that without my performance he had no 1964 season – it was the linchpin of *The Wars*.'

'What!' cried another, 'he said that to me. He told me that if I didn't return this year to give my performance, he would have to drop the whole idea!'

He had said the same to every one of us sitting round the table. That is one of the reasons why Peter is such a great administrator.

Once all the plays are on, the daylight hours are likely to lie heavily. All the delightful friends one has made among the residents are only free in the evenings. How is one to fill in the time? I was extremely fortunate that another member of the company, Nicholas Selby, shared my abiding interest in ecclesiology – the study of church architecture. On many mornings he and I set off to explore the churches of Warwickshire, Worcestershire and Gloucestershire. I don't think we left an ecclesiastical stone un-examined. From the parish churches we rose to the cathedrals and I always wrote ahead for permission to visit parts of the building not normally open to the casual visitor. Our first was Worcester, and the Dean, in his reply, suggested that we might like to bring over a whole party. We found several colleagues who were interested, but none of us expected the joys that were to come. As a prelude the Dean had arranged for Bridget Johnson, the honorary librarian, to show us the treasures of the Great Library. Ancient books and manuscripts were taken from shelves and passed around. Bridget bubbled with enthusiasm, '. . . and this is rather fun . . . King John's Will . . .' We could happily have spent a week in her company but the head verger was waiting to take us climbing . . .

As you probably know, the central part of the church is called the nave, and is flanked by two side aisles which, as well as providing extra floor space, serve as supports (buttresses) for the nave walls. The side aisles have slanting roofs and the space inside these roofs is called – for no logical reason – the triforium which extends nearly around the whole building. This was our first stop after mounting a great stone spiral staircase. Thick with dust, the space is enormous and here one finds the most extraordinary things: bits of carved stone, old pews, a broken lectern – all the sort of junk one finds in one's own attic. Here too are the massive pipes of the organ. Taking care we tramped along – an accidental trip over an electric conduit might catapult us through the arches that open on the nave – and then we found a smaller spiral staircase that led us up and up until we arrived at a very narrow passage built into the thickness of the nave walls. This was no place for the faint-hearted. There was only room for one person at a time to edge along. At regular intervals we found windows on our right and corresponding arches on our left, letting the light into the cathedral. Imagine yourself as a very small person walking along your own window-sill; and the window-sill seventy or eighty feet above the floor! This is known as the clerestory (the storey where the windows are), but having invented the word no one is sure how to pronounce it. You might think that *clear story* would be the obvious but many knowledgeable people insist on *cler ess tory*. Perhaps my simplified drawing (opposite) may help.

Once again we could encircle the whole building via this passage but we were considerably relieved when we found another, even smaller, spiral staircase that led us up to the space between the ceiling (vaulting) of the nave and the actual roof where a rickety wooden cat-walk took us through the massive roof trusses until we came to a little door which opened into the belfry, just in time to be deafened by the bell as it struck twelve. Then on up the tower from the top of which the surrounding countryside was spread out like a map. But we were due back on the floor to meet Colin Beswick who was to show us everything on ground-level; the tomb of King John, the chapter house, the two important transitional bays at the west end . . .

And all this while, again at the Dean's instigation, the organist was thundering away, showing us just what that superb organ could do! What a day! We returned to the theatre elated and awed.

Another morning, Nick Selby and I set off for Lincoln. In so many cathedrals the interior view from one end to the other, which could be so impressive, is obscured by the stone choir-screen. Actually it is for this very reason that I prefer the mystery of Gothic buildings to the open-plan design of post-Restoration churches. 'There should always be something "beyond",' as John Betjeman said to me. However Lincoln is one of our largest cathedrals and the view down its length would be quite something – but for the screen.

Dean Peck had arranged for the Clerk of Works, Fred Higgins, to take us climbing, so up we went to the spacious triforium and along to the far west end of the building but even from that height we still could not see over the choir-screen. We continued up the cramped spiral staircase to the clerestory. As at Worcester, it is possible to traverse the entire cathedral along the extremely narrow passage cut through the thickness of the walls and opposite each window an iron bar is all that prevents one from falling seventy or eighty feet to the floor below.

Fred Higgins reached the top first and squeezed to one side to allow Nick to come up. Luckily he and I don't suffer from vertigo and Nick immediately leaned out over the iron bar and exclaimed, 'It is fantastic! From here we can see over the screen – not only to the high altar, but over that to the angel choir beyond. Magnificent!' He then moved aside to allow me to emerge. I must be more cautious than Nick because, before I leaned out, I tested the iron

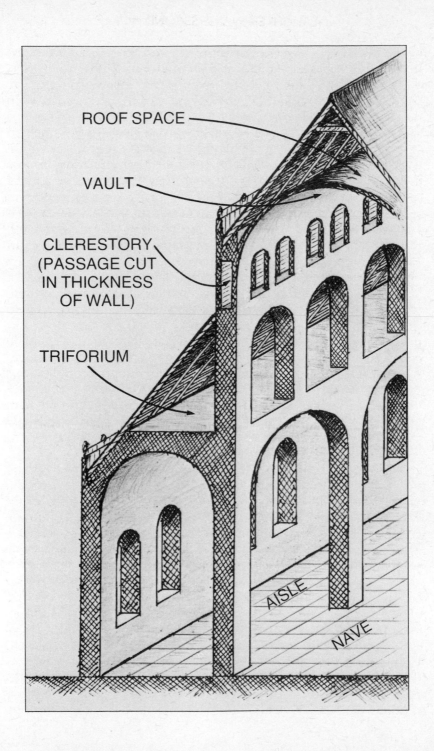

ROOF SPACE

VAULT

CLERESTORY
(PASSAGE CUT
IN THICKNESS
OF WALL)

TRIFORIUM

AISLE

NAVE

bar: it broke away from the stonework and I was left holding it!
Nick nearly had heart failure. It had only been the pressure of his
body that jammed the bar against its mountings.

If you are thrown by a horse the best psychological thing to do
is to remount and keep riding. So Nick and I continued our perilous
way along the narrow passageway. In the belfry we were joined
by the clock winder, George Stowell, and having ascended the
tower we returned to the triforium and began a circuit of the
cathedral at that level, to the north transept where we were faced
with another daunting task.

At some time in the past the immense piers that support the arch
and its vaultings began to bow ominously inwards and to prevent
further damage a great baulk of timber, some eighteen inches
square in section, was fixed between the piers thirty feet above the
floor, and to avoid a long trek around the transept this beam can
be used as a short cut, but it means that one must cross the 'bridge'
relying entirely on one's balance as there is nothing to hold on to.
Thankfully George went first so proving that it could be done and
providing us with a point of focus at which to aim. George made
that trip every day but Nick and I were much relieved when we
reached the other side.

In the cloisters Fred Higgins explained that every member of
the Foundation enjoys the privilege of being buried somewhere
within the precincts: the clergy in the cathedral itself and others
under the paving of the cloisters – but they must first be cremated.
'Do you intend to be interred here?' I asked.

'Oh indeed – that spot is already reserved for me,' and he
showed me a stone set diagonally in the paving.

Some years later, when I was engaged on the third series of *Our
Man From St Mark's*, my character was elevated to the position of
Archdeacon. An Archdeacon is, of course, attached to a cathedral.
To my delight, the television company chose Lincoln and I spent
several happy weeks filming in and around that noble building –
I crossed the hair-raising beam a few times just for fun and with
George's help we even persuaded Diana to cross it. I also attended
Choral Evensong and there discovered the use of the Obit Book.
On the death of any Member of the Foundation, his name is
entered in the book and thereafter, on the anniversary of his death,
the congregation is asked to pray for his soul. The amazing
continuity of an institution such as Lincoln Cathedral is brought
sharply home when you find yourself remembering, for example,
a stonemason who died six hundred years ago!

I was distressed to find the beautiful and impressive Choral Evensong so poorly attended and questioned Dean Peck on the use of such a service when, hypothetically, it might be listened to by no one.

'Over the centuries,' replied the dean, 'there have been many times when men have turned away from the church but they have returned. They will return again, and when they do they will find us ready to receive them. We are the rock and we must provide continuity.'

On my last visit in 1982 I saw the names of *Fred Higgins, Clerk of Works 1953–1978* and *George Stowell, Clock Winder 1960–1980* incised on their stones.

Also in 1964 I indulged in another pastime: I enrolled for an Art class which met every Tuesday afternoon and where most of the other budding Leonardos were past the age of retirement, but we were all enthusiastic and our teacher tactfully refrained from reacting with horror at our abysmal efforts. It was a 'life' class which meant that each week we were faced by a Stratford resident seated demurely and fully dressed on a stool, while twenty of us tried to record her for posterity, in a variety of materials and styles. Some used oil-paint, some water-colour, some acrylic, some pastel, some crayon, some charcoal, some pencil and all the same scale of insignificance. Being colour-blind I used pencil and I spent many happy hours in that quiet room with everyone concentrating like mad and the slosh of paint, the scratching of charcoal and the whispered advice of our teacher as the only sounds. It was meant to be a relaxation but I soon experienced the frustration of seeing, perfectly clearly, that figure sitting before me and yet being quite unable to record it accurately on paper. One day I had thrown away several sheets and was sitting in despair when my attention was caught by one of the younger students: as she hunched over her water-colour I was fascinated by the line of her back: in a flash I understood Botticelli and Modigliani! If I could record that 'line' . . . My pencil flowed down the page and I did it – I did it! It was a line of such perfection! I forced myself not to add to it – I could only spoil it. I still have that sheet of paper with a squiggle running down it which means nothing to anyone who sees it, but I, and only I, know that by rights it should hang in the Tate Gallery.

Immersed in my new-found interest I was able to forget Strat-ford, Shakespeare and the theatre as I laboured to find fulfilment and it was something of a shock to have my concentration broken one day by a voice whispering, 'I hear you're at the theatre.'

Hitherto my fellow students had been too engrossed to notice me. The voice came from a lady on my left whose smock was bespattered with more primary colours than adhered to the large canvas which betrayed her indebtedness to John Bratby. Intent on my own drawing I muttered, 'Yes.'

'Are you in the Histories?'

'Yes.'

The scratching of charcoal and sloshing of paint continued. And so did she.

'*Richard the Second*?'

'No.'

'*Henry the Fourth*?'

'No.'

'*Henry the Fifth*?'

'No,' I hissed – I didn't want to have this conversation but I could think of no way of stopping her.

'*Edward the Fourth*?'

'Yes.'

'What did you play in that?'

'Richard Plantagenet – the Duke of York.'

The occasional head turned toward us and teeth were sucked, but she didn't notice: 'The Duke of York? Now, which one is that?'

There was nothing for it. I laid down my pencil and addressed myself to her ear and away from the others. 'You may remember that he has a singularly unpleasant death scene – one of the most famous and probably the nastiest death scene in the whole of Shakespeare. He is tied to a stake and is taunted by the Queen who has previously murdered his young son and dipped a cloth in the child's blood. She takes this cloth and thrusts it, dripping with his son's blood, into his face before she tortures and kills him.'

This was followed by a deep silence from my tormentor. After inwardly ruminating, she said thoughtfully, 'No . . . No – I don't remember that bit. What else do you play?'

That BIT!!!

Photographed behind the cottage in Kent by my neighbour Edward Mautner.

Henry the Eighth with Peggy
Ashcroft as Queen Katherine, 1969.

Malvolio with the infamous sundial
(page 215).

'That is the fan I used' (Chapter 18).

A theatrical forerunner. Gaiety girl, Topsy Sinden.

John Martin Harvey's hat on Baliol
Holloway's wig on Fred Terry's wig block
(Chapter 18).

I 'stole' Danny La Rue's make-up for Lord Foppington, Henry the Eighth's appearance from Holbein's portrait, and Malvolio's face from Sutherland's Somerset Maugham.

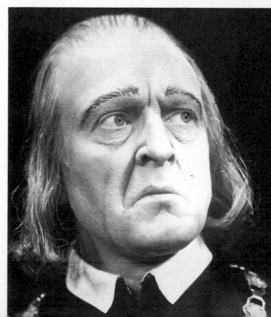

Lindsay Hassett, Ernie McCormick and me at the Melbourne Cricket Club, 1970.

With
Donald Bradman
Adelaide, 1970

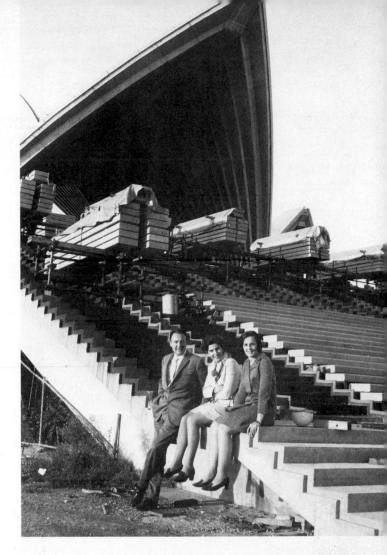

With Diana and Jenny,
the wife of my
Australian cousin
Gordon Fuller at the
uncompleted Sydney
Opera House, 1970
(Chapter 1).

The perspex model of the Opera House (Chapter 21).

Diana drawn by Stanley Parker

12

'EH!'

As the season drew to a close, arrangements were made for the BBC to televise *The Wars* from the theatre at Stratford. The production had been mounted for a proscenium stage and the audience viewed it as if looking at a picture in 3-D, but for the television the audience, through the camera's eye, could actually enter into the action. To this end the semicircle of scenery could be assumed to continue round forming a complete circle. In fact it did not, so each scene needed to be shot twice: for instance, in the many council-table scenes the actors, in the theatre, could only sit on one side of the table to enable them to be seen by the audience; for the television they could sit all round. The scenes were shot in one direction and then the table turned around and the scenes shot again using the identical scenery as a backing. Everybody was seen full-face.

The most hair-raising time came in the battle scenes. John Corvin and I had to fight using swords seven feet six inches long. (In 1963 our swords were six feet long but John Barton, who arranged the fights, maintained that we now made them look too lightweight so two new swords were made eighteen inches longer!) The BBC at that time were experimenting with hand-held cameras with zoom lenses and the director had the bright idea of assuming the camera to be one of the actors. Have you ever tried fighting with a camera?! Not eyeball to eyeball but eyeball to lens, I had to swing the great sword round my head and bring it crashing down – apparently – on an unguarded cameraman. I made only one dent in the camera hood.

Although the Stratford company had first played a season in London at His (now Her) Majesty's Theatre in 1947, it was Peter Hall who originally had the idea that the company should have a permanent base in the metropolis, at the Aldwych Theatre, where the company could produce plays – ancient and modern – by authors other than Shakespeare, and one of the carrots with which he enticed me back for the 1964 season was the prospect of doing a new play there. One unsuspecting day he handed me a script by Henry Livings entitled *Eh!*

I read it and was mystified. I quite failed to understand what it was about – but, insecure as we actors are, I dared not admit it. Obviously Peter, whom I so greatly admired, understood it and I must trust in him.

The play was set in the boiler room of some enormous, but unnamed factory producing an unknown product. All the characters had names and appeared to be individuals but they were also symbols. David Warner was to play Val Brose who symbolised Modern Youth. Brenda Bruce was Mrs Murray/Psychiatry. Nicholas Selby, Rev Mort/Religion. I was to play Mr Price/Bureaucracy.

Due to shortage of space at the theatre, rehearsals began in a cold bare room/shed behind the Red Lion pub in Stratford's Bridge Street. We read through the play and no one else admitted that they didn't understand it: obviously there was something lacking in me. Certainly Henry Livings has a most original and quirky sense of humour and there were glorious moments in the play – such as when the apoplectic Price accuses Brose of growing mushrooms in the boiler room:

PRICE: That says MUSHROOMS on those boxes.
BROSE: Yes, doesn't it?
PRICE: So they're mushrooms?
BROSE: Erm. No. That's the maker's name. Capitals. Capital 'M' Capital 'U'. 'SHROOMS': Mervyn Uhlrich Shrooms, seed merchant.

But some of the humour was obscure, as when Mrs Murray accuses Price of being sexually disorientated:

PRICE: Sex eh? Do you think I ought to do something about it? Glass of cold water by the bed?
Mrs M: Try to let me help instead of regarding me as a challenge.
PRICE: I can feel you doing me good.
Mrs M: You have very powerful drives, you must know that yourself; they can be used or they can be abused.
PRICE: Can I do it a little bit and wear glasses?

It is necessary to remember what schoolboys used to be warned about to understand that. Rather more difficult was:

Mrs M: We should change the job.
Price: What? Go over to oil?
Mrs M: No. Oh what insecure animals men are. We can't get
        the job done properly: change the job.
Price: Like the Russians with their sentries?

Luckily the author was present throughout rehearsals and I was able to ask him, tentatively, what that passage meant.

'But surely you know about the Russian sentries?'

'I'm sorry but I don't.'

'Well. At the time of the Revolution the Bolshevik Army was comprised, mainly, of illiterates. If you put a sentry on guard-duty with orders only to admit those with green passes, he could not comprehend a change in those orders. The only thing you could do was to change the sentry and give the new order only to admit those with red passes.'

Ah-ha. So . . . We can't get the job done properly: change the job. Like the Russians and their sentries . . .

But our audience didn't have the advantage of a private chat with Henry Livings.

I was having enormous difficulties with Price/Bureaucracy, however much I understood his lines: his characteristics, his idiosyncrasies, his motivations, what did he look like? How did he dress? I asked our author: 'Do you think Price wears a bowler hat?'

Henry ruminated for some time and was clearly deeply perturbed by the question. At long last he replied, darkly, 'He probably does – but wishes he didn't.'

Peter Hall also appeared to be perplexed by Price's persona; everything I did seemed to be wrong and he seemed incapable of helping me to put it right. He took to goading me and the more he goaded the more inadequate I became. He clutched at straws, 'Could you try him with a Lancashire accent?'

I have never been any good at regional accents but I found someone in the main company who came from Southport and together we worked hard for three days. The result was passable but Peter was dissatisfied. 'No. No. It doesn't work. Try a Northern Irish accent.' For three days I sweated away, again with help from another actor, until Peter cried, 'No. No. It is not right. Try Scots.' I was miserable and felt like resigning from the production, but I beavered away only to be told by a sarcastic Peter, 'That is terrible – can you do Welsh?'

It was all too much and I lost my temper. Except that I don't actually lose my temper: I shut up like a clam. If inside I am boiling with rage, externally I turn to ice. I threw my script at his feet and stalked from the room with fire in my eyes and steam puffing from my nostrils. I walked on; past the church, over the footbridge and along the fields beside the river. How dare he! The bastard. To humiliate me day after day. Who does he think he is? I fulminated against all directors, the theatre in general and the RSC in particular. I'll catch the next train back to London. I don't care if I never work again. Nothing is worth this misery. Damn! Damn!! Damn!!! Damn Peter Hall and damn the Royal Shakespeare Company!

I walked on and on. The few people I passed must have been bemused by the sight of someone striding at full speed muttering abuse. I walked my fury into the soil. Instead of the rainbow-coloured tunnel I had been peering through I began to notice sheep and cows. Slowly I began to reason with myself: I am an adult; I have a wife and children to support; most other people think I am a good actor – why should I concern myself with what this adolescent thinks of me? Grow up, Sinden. You have been an actor for twenty-two years, don't be browbeaten by this – this jumped up pip-squeak. Now. Go back to rehearsal – give him one more chance – but one more word from Hall – just one word – and – and hit him. Yes. Punch him on the nose. Go out in style. Ha!

I retraced my steps to the Red Lion. I had been absent for two hours.

Now remember, Sinden: one word from Hall and . . . wham! I flung open the door. Hall and the cast were sitting around on benches. Hall looked up and said, 'Let's start with act two.'

I bridled – I suppose he thinks that is funny – he had better not push his luck. We started on the scene and as it moved along I was looking for the slightest slight: my jaw was set, I was edgy and my right fist was poised for the wham! At the end of the play the other actors melted away sensing that their presence was not required. Peter came over to me, placed an arm around my shoulders, and quietly said, 'That is exactly what I wanted – well done.'

Such is the dangerous tight-rope that Peter trod. He was prepared to risk our friendship to achieve his ends. Fortunately the friendship survived.

In 1961 John Gielgud was to play Othello at Stratford with Franco

Zeffirelli directing, and the two met Peter Hall in his office to discuss the casting of the other characters. The story is told that John asked Zeffirelli how he envisaged Iago: 'Iago? Eeahgo. Yago,' he said in his strongest Italian accent. 'I see Iyago as very young: very young, with a baby face, a round, smiling, baby's face – always smiling. But behind that young, round, smiling face is a heart of steel – steel. Do you act, Mr Hall?'

I wish I could say that *Eh!* was an unqualified success. It stayed in the 1965 repertoire at the Aldwych Theatre for several months, but something was never quite right. We were only called upon to give one or sometimes two performances a week. This allowed me time to complete another thirteen episodes of *Our Man At St Mark's* and to take part in a most fascinating new venture. John Irving, the son of my old friend Laurence Irving, was a TV producer at Bristol when he conceived the idea of a programme on antiques in which two amateurs would pit their knowledge against two experts. An antique would be shown to the amateurs who were asked to tell the viewers all they could about the object and to speculate on its age, origin, use, and from what materials it was made. The antique was then handed to the experts who were presumed to know far more about it and after discoursing on it they wrote down, secretly, the price they would expect the object to fetch at auction. The amateurs then put their value on it and the one whose bid was nearest to that of the experts' scored points. One of the experts on *Going for a Song* – as the programme was called – was to be resident and each week a different person – an expert in a particular field – filled the other chair. For the resident expert John Irving chose a local Gloucestershire auctioneer, Arthur Negus, who with his quiet voice, white hair, cherubic face and tactile hands, combined with his vast knowledge of his subject, was a natural and soon established himself as a TV personality. Max Robertson was the chairman/quiz master, and knowing of my interest in antiques John invited me to be one of the amateurs in the first programme and, over the years, I returned on several occasions.

There was only one anomaly in *Going for a Song* and that was the way in which the expert valuation was arrived at. Although each expert wrote down the sum he would expect that object to fetch at auction it was the *average of the two* that was deemed to be its value. On one programme a charming little eighteenth-century desk – called in the trade a bonheur-du-jour – was placed before us. I dated it fairly accurately to 1770 and speculated its value at £400. My fellow panellist put its value at £1000. We discovered later that the visiting expert, whose specialised subject was jewellery, had written down £2000 while Arthur Negus, whose own subject was furniture, had exactly agreed with me at £400. However their average was £1200 and my colleague collected points as being the nearest.

But what a fascinating game it was and I looked forward eagerly to my visits to Bristol.

Meanwhile the run of *Eh!* was drawing to a close and one evening, as we waited in the wings between entrances, I asked Brenda Bruce what she was doing next.

'Rather interesting as a matter of fact – I have been asked to do a British Council tour of South America in two two-handed plays: *Happy Days* and *Dear Liar* and Roy [her husband, Roy Rich] is to direct them.'

'South America! How exciting!' I exclaimed. '– who is your leading man?'

'The tour was only dreamed up yesterday – I'm sure they haven't thought of that yet.'

Remembering Jean-Louis Barrault's performance in the same part I unhesitatingly said, 'Tell them that I'll do it. I'll do it for no salary on condition that Diana can accompany us, all expenses paid.'

And so it came about that a few weeks later Brenda and Roy, Diana and I, with Anthony Chardet as our company-cum-stage-manager, flew off to South America carrying all our essential scenery in a cricket bag.

13

'WHY DIDN'T YOU BRING AN AGATHA CHRISTIE?'

The middle-aged Bernard Shaw had fallen in love with the actress Mrs Patrick Campbell and for many years they corresponded in a series of wonderful letters ranging from the years of their early passion through to his disillusionment while she rehearsed Eliza Doolittle – the part he had written especially for her – in *Pygmalion*. The correspondence was published by Gollancz in 1952 and shortly afterwards Jerome Kilty dramatised it, calling his two-handed play *Dear Liar*. For our tour with this play, drapes of any colour or material that could be found in any theatre became our scenery; an elegant desk and chair were borrowed in each city for Brenda who was playing Mrs Pat. All I required as G.B.S. was a lectern. This was made of three pieces of broomstick slotted into a base and a top with a length of velvet thrown over it. This was the only piece of furniture we carried with us – hence, when dismantled, it fitted in the cricket bag.

We had a slightly bigger problem with our second play, Samuel Beckett's *Happy Days*: in the first act the character of Winnie is buried up to her waist in the ground and in the second act she is buried up to her neck!

The top of my 'lectern' had a hole cut in it big enough to encircle Brenda's waist and in our cricket bag we carried a circle of canvas, thirty feet in diameter, painted the colour of soil/earth, with a hole cut in the centre. This was placed over the 'lectern' and the circumference stapled to the stage. We then searched each theatre to find anything – cardboard boxes, curtains, ropes, sacks – that could be stuffed beneath the canvas to produce an undulating, hill-like, surface. Brenda then crawled under, emerged through the 'lectern' and stood apparently 'up to her waist in the ground'. For the second act she sat on a wooden box and she was then 'up to her neck'.

139

Winnie does all the talking in the play – it could almost be called a monologue – while her husband Willie is seated upstage, partially hidden by the mound, reading a newspaper and occasionally coughing, grunting and hoiking. (But I had seen Jean-Louis Barrault playing the part so I realised the potential.) Brenda's part was enormous and, should she ever have difficulties with her lines, she could never be prompted because there is an implication in the play that the two characters are the last people on earth – so who would be the person prompting? I suggested that I should have the script hidden in my newspaper and then, if the need arose – and it never did – I could prompt her. Night after night I sat there following every word of the play and I marvelled at Beckett's genius. What a play! I don't think it could ever be done on film or television – it is purely a work for the stage. It is unbelievably complex and each night I discovered new things in it and night after night as I sat there I thought, 'Thank God I am not in the audience seeing this play for the first time!'

We opened in Lima, Peru, where we fortunately had time to do some sightseeing and explore the Inca ruins before flying off to Santiago in Chile. Here it dawned upon me for the first time that the name of this city, which one just takes for granted, is actually Sant-Iago – the Spanish for Saint James. How stupid I am.

We had one free day and we were driven in a jeep up and up into the Andes Mountains. The road as such ceased to exist and we continued on foot. I was racing on a good two hundred yards ahead of the others when I rounded a bend and came face to face with four men dressed in ponchos and sombreros with guns . . . I had taken them by surprise and the guns appeared to be levelled at me. Ahhh . . . For the want of something better to do I smiled. They looked at each other and lowered their guns.

(Where were the rest of my party, including the interpreter?)

I advanced slowly and held out my hand and after a lot of muttering one of them took it and showed me that they had been shooting birds and rats which they held up for display. He then pointed to a fifth man who was squatting behind a rock and cooking something in a pan over an open fire. He looked extremely sinister as the flames lit up his gnarled face and stubbled chin. He peered at me through half-closed eyes, then took a pointed knife, stabbed at a piece of meat in the pan and held it towards me. I turned with a questioning look to the four men behind me and they looked unsmilingly at me. One of them gestured with his arm that I should go forward. The hand at the end of the arm happened to be carrying a rifle so I went cautiously across to the man at the fire and took the knife with the meat from him. I cannot pretend that I fancied the idea of eating grilled rat. I looked back at the men and the hand with the gun again jerked towards me. Gingerly I popped the meat into my mouth . . . It wasn't at all bad. We were now at last joined by the rest of my party – from a distance Diana had witnessed the preceding scene with some horror – and the interpreter began to converse with the strangers. He told us later that the men were indeed brigands and had I been alone I might well have been in serious trouble; but I had not actually eaten rat meat – it was a piece of steak they had brought with them for a meal.

Our next stop was Buenos Aires. After the first performance a reception was given at the British Embassy where I was approached by an irate British resident in the Argentine who had hated *Happy Days* – why had we not brought a play by Agatha Christie? Our play had so often been received in stony silence that I was beginning to ask myself the same question.

On a free evening Diana and I were able to attend a performance at the Colon Theatre, and saw Regine Crespin and Giuseppe di Stefano in *Tosca* at one of the great opera houses of the world.

Then off to Montevideo, the capital of Uruguay. Here we were to witness the astonishing effects of inflation. At that time the official rate of exchange was 450 pesos to the pound. The hotel offered us 550 to the pound but the cashier advised us to deal directly with the traders when shopping. We found they would give us goods to the value of 650 to the pound. We were about to take advantage of this when a man we met offered us 950 to the pound against an English cheque!

A very splendid meal at a first-class restaurant cost us the equivalent of one pound fifty for two! Now I know how Americans benefit when they visit London, with the rate of exchange so much in their favour.

Before finishing our tour in Rio de Janeiro we played a week in Sao Paulo, the world's fastest-growing city with possibly the finest gallery of twentieth-century painting.

Rio must be one of the most glamorous cities in the world – especially at night. It is built around scores of curiously shaped mountains, each rising suddenly from the flat terrain and looking like rhinoceros horns. There are so many of them that while we were there the Brazilians were in the process of removing one entire mountain from the middle of the city, where the flattened ground would be of maximum value, and depositing the rock along the coastline on which to build a dual-carriage motorway. Waste not, want not.

On returning from South America I knew that I had the next – and final – thirteen episodes of *Our Man At St Mark's*. My character had resigned his living on being elevated to the position of Archdeacon, and as Archdeacons are attached to a diocese centred in a cathedral the new series had to be renamed *Our Man From St Mark's*. No one noticed the difference. Meanwhile I was left with several free weeks . . .

14

'ARE MY THINGS LAID OUT?'

The salary I could expect from *Our Man From St Mark's*, plus the money I had earned in the previous twelve months, meant that we could take our children away for an extravagant summer holiday. But Diana had already arranged with Jill Cadell to take the combined children on an adventurous holiday using as transport the Sindens' quite large Morris Oxford Estate car.

·For the past year an Italian young man named Luigi had been working for the Cadells as a kind of au pair while he learned English, and he had frequently said that his parents, who lived in a palazzo in Naples, would be delighted to welcome the Cadell family and their friends for a holiday. This was the moment for both our families to take advantage of the generous gesture.

John and Jill Cadell have been our dearest friends since Jill and I worked together in *The Heiress* in 1949, and their children, Simon, and twins Selina and Patrick (my godson), are almost exact contemporaries of our own children Jeremy and Marc.

John could not accompany them to Italy as he was working hard, setting up his own agency (as he was also my own agent I was not unrelieved), and Simon was recovering from a throat infection, but I was now free and suggested that I might join them. However, even our large Estate car could not accommodate three adults and five children; we would need a second car, so our Mini was brought in. Plans began to be made. The Cadells' idea of bliss was to be swimming in the Mediterranean near Naples as soon, and as cheaply as possible so would it not be a good idea to acquire a tent and camp en route?

This was something that none of us had ever done before (I lie – I did it when I was fourteen) so off I went to a firm called Pindisports who explained that any tent to house eight people would be almost too cumbersome to put up and take down at speed each day, but they had quite a large one made in France, called a Marechal. This could easily house six and if Diana and I were to sleep in the Estate car all would be well.

That was really the moment to have called the whole thing off. But we didn't. I bought the Marechal, and took it home greatly encouraged and amused by the advertising matter, which I reproduce opposite.

Did you read every word?

For the next three days, Diana, Jeremy and I, following detailed instructions, laboured to put it up in our garden. Tempers were lost and nerves frayed; metal ribs collapsed around us; fingers were trapped in spring-loaded rods; nearly complete, we discovered that we should have done something else first; but eventually we mastered it.

Came the day when we strapped cases and bags to the roof of the Estate; snorkel and flippers, plastic containers, food and bottles and bottles of pop in the boot; the tent and two Lilos in the Mini; and set off, Jill and Diana taking turns driving the Estate, I driving the Mini, as fast as allowable to the palazzo and sun of Naples.

As we neared Dover I feared that all was not well with the Mini. I had no time to check before it was loaded on the ferry, but when I drove off at Calais I went straight to a garage. Disaster. There was oil on the clutch plate: the whole engine would have to be stripped down and it would be a two-day job.

I, of course, got the blame – why had I not checked everything before setting off? Stupidly we had no address or telephone number to inform Luigi of our problems: our arrangement was to meet him under the clock at Naples railway station at five o'clock on Thursday. Can we really have been so stupid? I have to admit that we were. The only alternative to a two-day wait in Calais was to drive as carefully as possible on a slipping clutch – and pray. So the tent and everything expendable was transferred to the Estate and the children were to take it in turns to travel with me: either the two elder, Simon and Jeremy aged fifteen, or the three younger, Selina, Patrick and Marc aged eleven. Here came the second problem. The twins were inseparable: everything had to be divided equally and everyone must have an equal time sitting in the front. Whichever two sat in the back had their eyes glued to a watch and on the dot of each hour, regardless of traffic conditions, I had to stop while they changed over. I began to dislike all three of the younger ones.

When we stopped at our first camping site I felt that I should

CARE and MAINTENANCE of MARECHAL TENTS

INTRODUCTION

Platts Page and Company Limited, the sole importers and main distributors of Marechal tents in Great Britain have carefully selected the stockists of Marechal tents and a full after sales service is available.

You may be sure if buying a Marechal tent, you are investing in the best.

Marechal tents are manufactured from the finest possible materials, and employ the highest quality workmanship.

All materials are carefully selected and tested extensively prior to being put into production.

The Catalogne frames are manufactured by Llama in France, one of the largest steel factories in the country. All joints are precision made and the entire frame is rust resistant, even under salt water conditions.

The construction of the frame is unique, providing a four-sided roof, with six uprights which are linked together for easy erection. All corners are hinged, allowing for easy erection and dismantling.

Undoubtedly this frame, made exclusively for Marechal, is accepted as the finest frame in Europe.

Outer tent cloths used by Marechal are both water-proofed and rot-proofed. The colours selected have not been chosen haphazardly but are the result of optical research, the combination of blue outer tent and yellow inner tent giving the best protection against glare. All Marechal tents are double, i.e., with flysheet and inner tent, which ensures supreme comfort even under adverse or hot conditions.

Not only the high quality of material, but the reinforcing tapes and the tie tapes used throughout, plus precision sewing with the strongest thread, make Marechal tents unequalled for value and quality. All groundsheets are sewn-in the inner tent coming 4″ up the walls. (All joints are stitched and proofed giving complete protection, and when used with zips closed and mosquito ventilation open, ensure a good night's rest free from all insects.)

Marechal Frame tents are essentially family tents, giving complete headroom in both sleeping and living tent area. Cooking, dressing, and undressing, can be done in complete comfort. In the Catalogne range the verandah porch and doorway are separate units; it is therefore possible to leave the verandah porch erected for the night and yet have complete privacy by letting down the outer tent door and secure with zip fasteners provided.

The range in sizes and prices has been developed from experience, and covers the needs of both small and large families.

ERECTION TIME

This will vary according to the individual and the number of times erected, but generally it is considered that the time required for two persons to erect is 15–20 minutes, and it is of interest to know that the design of this tent enables erection to be accomplished single-handed in only a few minutes longer.

The flysheets to the Catalogne tents are reinforced with double material at all points where the flysheet comes into contact with the frame.

CARE AND MAINTENANCE

Even Marechal tents that are the best in the world require maintenance, and the life of your tent depends largely on careful treatment and storage.

take charge and allocate duties, chauvinist as I suppose I am. Jill (who seemed to have caught Simon's throat infection) and Diana, helped by Selina, were detailed to arrange food, drink, clothing and ablutions while the chaps would get the cars emptied and the tent put up. Here I encountered a third problem. Of the five children only two of them were (indeed, are) practically minded; godson Patrick and our Jeremy. Simon stayed in the car sucking his thumb and lost in his own thoughts and Marc cunningly drifted off to examine this and that. Patrick, as part of the younger group, resented that he was given the lighter chores to do and Jeremy resented that Simon was shirking. The tent that we tried to put up appeared to be quite different from the one we had erected in the garden, and to make matters much worse, it was dark and raining. Everyone was bad-tempered and sulked. We found a local restaurant where we struck problem number four: Selina and Marc flatly refused to sample French cooking. It was with questionable relief that, having tucked up Jill and five children in the tent, Diana and I – because of the rain – tried to undress in the back of the Estate. We climbed into sleeping bags and lay down on two inflated Lilos. 'Just think of our lovely comfortable bed at home,' moaned Diana.

In the morning Jill and Diana drove into the local village and bought croissants, butter and marmalade, most of which were devoured by the young before we packed up the tent and set off again.

It took us two full days of driving to reach Italy and this is where I must remind you that it was mid-August, the sun was belting down and the clutch of the Mini was getting worse by the hour. At Milan we joined one of Italy's great motorways, the Autostrada del Sole, on which, at that time, there was no speed limit – unless you happened to be driving a Mini with a slipping clutch. I had the three youngest with me, when Diana, driving the Estate which followed the Mini in case I broke down completely, began to be rather narked by Simon who continually talked of the splendid status-symbol cars, owned by the parents of other friends, which could travel at unheard-of speeds. Somewhere near Piacenza she could stand it no longer and decided to put her foot on the accelerator and really give the engine an airing. She overtook me at great speed, continued for about five miles, and then stopped at a lay-by until I caught up and overtook her. She then repeated the process. For mile after mile, they overtook us: we overtook them: they overtook us: we overtook them. This procedure provided variety, impressed Simon, and the three youngest could scream out 'Here they come!' and wave as they sailed past. But one vital factor was overlooked: Diana and Jill are great gossips. Jeremy had once remarked that nothing gave him greater security than 'to hear Jill and Mum droning on'.

In the middle of some absorbing topic, Jeremy asked, 'Is the Mini in front or behind?' . . . No one could remember.

Jill and Jeremy thought it was behind – Diana and Simon thought it was in front. They pulled into the side of the road and waited . . . but the Mini didn't come. They raced on to the next intersection . . . but still no Mini. All were now convinced that either the Mini had broken down some miles back or – horror – it had been involved in an accident. At the first opportunity they got on to the other carriageway and retraced their route, all eyes searching for some sign of a mangled heap of Mini and occupants.

Meanwhile, in the Mini, we knew perfectly well that the Estate was behind us and had not overtaken us for some time . . . At the beginning I was not unduly worried but as the mileometer ticked slowly round I was able to keep the children entertained until one observed, 'They haven't been past for a long time . . .' I decided against turning round – they might shoot past at the very moment I drew off the motorway. We went grimly onward . . .

'Where are they?'

'I want Mummy.'

'I want to go home.'

I tried hard to divert their minds but all three were kneeling on the rear seat scanning the retreating road through their tears. Secretly I was now convinced that the Estate had been involved in an accident. But what should I do? After an age I drew up at the Bologna tollbooth. I spoke no Italian and the attendant spoke no English so I had to wait until a helpful German arrived who spoke both – indifferently.

Would the attendant please telephone to the various tollbooths back up the Autostrada and ask if an English family in an Estate car had made enquiries about our Mini. Alternatively – and here I had to make sure the children were not listening – had an accident been reported?

After an agonising wait I was told that there was neither an enquiry nor an accident. I expected that Diana too would try to make a similar contact so I decided to stay where I was: luckily there was a stall with drinks and food to refresh us . . . I was suddenly beckoned by the attendant who was at that moment in contact with his colleague in Piacenza, but for some officious reason he flatly refused to allow me to handle the telephone and the German had by then departed, so I had no help from a translator. After a lot of shouting I gathered that the Estate was at the tollbooth in Piacenza and I was instructed to return there. 'Instructed' is not exactly correct: a stabbing finger pointed at me and then gesticulated northwards as the man behind it roared, 'PIACENZA'.

Piacenza was ninety-two miles back!

Worried silly – I had no idea if the others were alive – and with three bawling, brawling brats in the car spilling sticky drinks on the floor and arguing as to who should be sitting in front, and with a slipping clutch, it took me two and a half hours to get to Piacenza. Will I never forget that name?

The occupants of the Estate had had equal problems. Having retraced their steps, as it were, they arrived back at the Piacenza tollbooth, where Diana, likewise speaking no Italian, enquired after a missing Mini: had one been involved in an accident? The helpful attendant there gestured for them to move the car from the roadway and take it round the corner, saying '*Ospitare, ospitare.*' Poor Diana and Co. immediately thought that he had said *ospedale* and that we were all in hospital around the corner! We learned later that *ospitare* means 'to give hospitality'.

Having sorted that one out, they in turn were 'instructed' to stay where they were because the Mini was returning. (We discovered that the confusion lay in the fact that, by the time we both made our enquiries, we were in the northbound lanes and therefore it was presumed that our destination was to the north.) Shortly before we arrived in P......, Diana and Co. were watching the road when a Mini the same colour as ours hit the central reservation, somersaulted, and burst into flames. They were convinced their loved ones were in it . . .

At last we met, threw ourselves into welcoming arms, cursed each other, and then resumed our journey, the poor Mini covering 180 painful miles more than necessary.

We stopped overnight outside my beloved Florence – not, I'll have you know, to revel in the glories of Brunelleschi and Michelangelo, but merely because the brochure announced that the camping site sported a Cadell-sized swimming pool. We found it empty and being repaired. The next morning we had to make up time and drive right through the heat of the day, so all passengers transferred to the Estate leaving me alone in the Mini.

For the car to keep up a steady 40 mph the engine, because of the slipping clutch, needed to rev at the equivalent of 70 mph. This caused the radiator to overheat, so at each garage I had to refill with water. I found that the engine remained cooler if I turned the car interior heating full on. This would have been all very jolly in Scandinavia but in Italy in August, with the outside temperature at 98° fahrenheit and the equator getting nearer every minute, it was not so funny. With all the windows open I wore only a pair of shorts and held a soup thermos flask full of ice between my knees, lumps of which I continually applied to the back of my neck. Each time I stopped to refill the radiator I turned the hose on myself and topped up with ice.

Twenty miles outside Naples the exhaust of the Estate fell off. The occupants were then nearly as hot as I, but miraculously we found Luigi under the clock at five on Thursday evening. We were all ready to drop into our beds but as he had arranged for us to have an evening meal at his married sister's house, it was not until nine p.m. that we were guided, through sinisterly darkened streets, to the palazzo . . .

The street was lined with tall buildings and we drove through a portal that once held huge gates to an interior cobbled courtyard. Hordes of ragged children descended on us and began to climb over the cars. Dim naked bulbs lit balconies above us. The whole scene was quite Dickensian. Perhaps the building had once been a palazzo but at some time in the nineteenth century it had been converted into apartments and now resembled the worst excrescence of the old Glasgow Gorbals. Within seconds 'Mama' and 'Papa' were there to greet us in Italian. Luigi translated: leave nothing, nothing whatever, in the cars. Could we unscrew the wing mirrors and radio aerials? There was quite a chance they would not be there in the morning. So cases, bags, snorkels and flippers, plastic containers, tents, Lilos, were transported up endless flights of dimly lit stone stairs and into our exotic holiday home: a corridor, two rooms, kitchen and bathroom.

'Mama' and 'Papa' were still in residence and had made up a bed for themselves in the kitchen, leaving their double bed for Diana and me and space on the floors of the bedroom and living room for the six others.

As there was no cistern, the only way to flush the lavatory was to fill the wash-basin, remove the plug quickly, and let the contents gush down the pipe which led, not into the drains, but straight into the loo. It was often necessary to repeat this operation three times.

There was no immediate escape: it was late and we were all exhausted, so while sleeping-bags were prepared, 'Papa' took Patrick, Marc and me for a stroll along the street where, at the next corner, lit by a naphtha flare, a man was selling slices of water-melon from a rusty barrow. 'Papa' bought four slices which were cut with a dirty knife and handed to us. Oh God – now we would all get typhoid! Back we went and wearily settled down for the night – having failed to quench the circle of fairy lights that ringed a plaster statuette of the Virgin Mary on the living-room wall.

At about four in the morning Jill, asleep in the corridor, was awakened by Selina who had caught, and developed to an advanced state, the family throat infection and was running a very high temperature. That meant no more sleep for any of us. It was obviously necessary for Selina to be seen by a doctor and this was when Diana really came into her own.

There are times when she will brook no obstacle – as when some years ago on the one fine day of summer, we donned bathing costumes and lay in the garden. At that precise moment a neighbour decided to light a bonfire. 'Oh really! Tell him to put it out,' Diana instructed me. As I rose I tried to formulate in my mind the exact wording I should use: 'I say, old chap, would you please . . .' or, 'Excuse me, but would you . . .' or, 'I'm sorry about this, but would . . .' Before I got to the hedge Diana had beaten me to it: 'Put that out at once!' she ordered and the neighbour dutifully poured a bucket of water over the offence!

As early as possible in the morning Diana was taken to another apartment, the only one in the palazzo with a telephone, where, surrounded by most of the women and children from the whole building, she called the British Consulate. To her immense relief an English girl answered. Trying not to offend those around her, Diana outlined the situation and said cryptically, 'Have you heard of the Black Hole of Calcutta?' The English girl latched on immediately and asked in what part of Naples we were.

'The area is called San Giovanni.'

'Good God! – you must get out as fast as you can – come straight to the Consulate.'

Within an hour we repacked the car and, making elaborate excuses in mime to 'Mama' and 'Papa', blaming it all on Selina's 'imminent demise', we set off. At the Consulate it was explained that San Giovanni was the worst slum quarter of Naples and the crime centre of the town.

Again thanks to Diana's foresight in taking out full insurance to cover all eventualities, we all transferred to the Vesuvio Hotel until Selina recovered and both cars were repaired. For the remainder of our holiday we pitched camp at the Sorrento camping site on the only vacant plot – next to the public lavatories. Starved of cultural pleasure I managed to persuade my team – after swimming – to visit the famous Naples museum. On arrival I saw my old friend John Warner just leaving. 'It's closing in five minutes,' he cried.

John Cadell had agreed to fly out to Nice and join us for the final leg home; and so we began our return journey on the Autostrada del Sole but when I saw a signpost for ROMA I threw a temperament. Of the eight of us only Diana and I had been there before – it would be a scandal to be so near and not even visit the Eternal City. The others agreed to the detour on condition we made Cap Ferrat that night! With that injunction, what could one see given a bare two hours? Rightly or wrongly I chose the Coliseum and St Peter's. All the young were mightily impressed by the former but could not understand why they should be made to visit a church. As we entered, I led them down the aisle on our right. 'Now,' I began my lecture, 'in the future you may be fortunate enough to see other works by this colossus of the Renaissance – one of the greatest artists the world has produced. You will grow to wonder at the Rondanini Pietà, the Captive Slaves struggling to free themselves from the rock and the amazing symmetry of the Laurentian Library, but here we have a sublime work by the young Michelangelo,' and there, as we rounded the corner, sat the beautiful Madonna with the dead Christ lying in her lap. A heart-stopping moment.

Patrick – my godson – took one look and said, 'Oh Don! – we're not going to spend all day looking at old statues, are we?'

I took them all silently back to the car and up the lovely Autostrada as fast as I could.

We next pitched tent in Cap Ferrat where in the evening, direct from civilisation, John was met at Nice airport and brought back for a meal at a local restaurant. Then, a little tipsy, we returned to the campsite and picked our way over guy-ropes to our tent – we would tell him of our adventures the next day. As he drew near his bed for the night John unconcernedly asked, 'Are my things laid out?'

It really is quite astonishing that the Cadells and Sindens are still great friends.

15

MR DANVERS' DOWNFALL

Some people say that there are no such things as imps and goblins:
others say they really do exist. Some people say there is no Father
Christmas: others say they have seen him. Some people will swear
they have seen a Michael Codron: others deny his existence. But
towards the end of 1965 I was sent a play called *Mr Danvers'
Downfall* with a covering letter signed 'Michael Codron'. Since
then I have firmly believed in imps, goblins, Father Christmas and
Michael Codron – and Codron is the most elusive of all.

It was a very funny play. Very funny indeed. A totally contemporary play – a play that could not have been written before the
new wave of drama that began in 1956. It concerned a middle-aged
man who enjoyed much success with the ladies. His elegant apartment was entirely devoted to the art of seduction: the best champagne on ice; the shaded lamps discreetly dimmed; quiet music
insinuated itself from the record-player and the primrose path led
inevitably to the voluptuous bed in the adjacent room where the
final act of the erotic drama was invariably played. The moment
he was bored with his latest plaything she would be dropped
remorselessly and another willing victim ensnared in his web.

At a party he had encountered several young people of the
nineteen-sixties permissive society and brought an eighteen-year-
old mini-skirted girl back to his love-nest. She was unlike any of
his previous conquests and as he prepared for his performance he
noticed that she was timing his every move. How long would he
take to get her to bed? She almost says, 'If you want to lay me –
just say so and let's get on with it.' The generation gap was
showing.

In the plays of the Thirties and Forties, such men usually had
no visible means of support – in Noël Coward's *Private Lives* we
are never told what Elyot does for a living – so our young author
Terence Frisby looked around at contemporary 'in' jobs, antique-
dealing, advertising, etc: and settled on a Sixties phenomenon, a

professional gourmet-cum-TV-personality. As part of his seduction the spider could cook succulent dishes for his flies.

I knew immediately that it would be a marvellous part for me and the author came to the house to discuss the play. In conversation I learned that he was an actor and this was his first play for the stage. He had already written one for television on the subject of pregnancy entitled *And Some Have Greatness Thrust Upon Them* (a connotation that Shakespeare can never have thought of!) in which a character says, 'My friend, Sylve, told me it was safe standing up.' After the play was recorded, the BBC informed Frisby that that line was to be censored. He in turn took out an injunction to prevent the play being shown in 'mutilated form'. He won his court case but the play was never shown on TV. However, it was later a great success in the theatre under a new title, *The Band Wagon*.

During one long period of unemployment Terry (Frisby) had worked as an omelette chef in one of Lyons' all-night restaurants and had learned from the professionals how to take an egg in one hand, crack it on the side of the bowl and, while still holding the shell, allow the contents to flop into the bowl. He suggested that it would be rather impressive if my character could do the same thing, whisk the eggs in a Kenwood mixer and make an omelette for the young girl in his play. (Diana pointed out that the noise of the machine would drown the dialogue so out we went to our kitchen to prove the point.) A dozen eggs were produced and I began to practise breaking them until I had a better idea: if that was how the professional broke eggs, couldn't I go one step further and break the egg, not by tapping it on the basin, but in mid-air?! With my thumbnail I delicately but firmly pierced the shell and eased the two halves apart; half with my thumb, the other half with my first two fingers. Eureka! I needed to keep my thumbnail at an exact length: too long and it bent under the strain, too short and it could not pierce the shell. Put into the play, that piece of 'business' became quite famous and always drew an amazed reaction from the audience. Diana was right as usual – the Kenwood made too much noise so I whisked the eggs by hand.

An enchanting creature named Barbara Ferris was found to play the young girl. Clive Francis, in his first professional appearance, was her hippy boyfriend. Jon Pertwee played my own great friend, Anthony Sagar was the perfect hall porter and Jill Melford the long-legged epitome of all my character's earlier girlfriends.

All through the four weeks of rehearsal and a six-week provincial

Barbara Ferris

D.S.

tour we encountered problems with the script. What we found funny on the page was sometimes received with stony silence by the audience. We rehearsed every day. Pages and pages of script were rewritten, and rewritten again. At the end of a performance we might be handed three new pages of dialogue to be put in the performance the following night. More important, we could never seem to get the final curtain lines right until I had a brainwave: on the young girl's last exit she gave me a present of a tube of hormone cream which never got the laugh we expected. But during the play, every time my character met a pretty girl he used the same phrase, 'My God but you're lovely!' as a running gag, so, at the end of the play when I was left dejectedly alone, I arranged to have a mirror handy. I then picked up the hormone cream, began to apply it to my face, looked at myself in the mirror and said, 'My God but you're lovely!' The result brought the curtain down in a gale of laughter. That ending was also used in the film version of the play. I rather think Terry Frisby owes me a percentage of the royalties.

In the middle of all the rewrites and rehearsals, we played, on Friday, 13th May, in Nottingham – and it was a classic Friday the thirteenth. Everything went wrong . . .

The H. M. Tennent organisation which owned the lease of London's Globe Theatre was unexpectedly looking for a tenant – a play was just about to close, and as its own production of *Lady*

Windermere's Fan was not ready, the theatre would be empty for six weeks. One of the directors, John Perry, came to Nottingham to see if our play would fill the gap and he chose that very Friday the thirteenth to see it! What he saw was, he thought, obviously going to be a failure but would at least pay the rent for those six weeks, so Michael Codron was able to clinch a very advantageous deal (advantageous to Codron) for our production to open at the perfect theatre for the play, the Globe in Shaftesbury Avenue.

You may be wondering why you have never heard of *Mr Danvers' Downfall*. I have quite forgotten to tell you that in the midst of all our troubles we had realised that *Mr Danvers' Downfall* was not exactly the best of selling titles: it would have to be changed. Everyone made suggestions for an alternative until at last someone thought of *There's a Girl in my Soup*. A stroke of genius – even if W. A. Darlington in the *Daily Telegraph* did open his review by saying, 'Don't be put off by what seems to me to be a very unattractive title . . .'

It makes one wonder if *The Importance of Being Earnest* or *The Merry Wives of Windsor* originally laboured under different titles. Our play was a smash-hit from the first night – it eventually ran for six years – and *Lady Windermere's Fan* had to find another theatre.

Soon after we met, Michael Codron told me that as a schoolboy during the last war he had been evacuated to Leicester where he soon ingratiated himself with the front-of-house staff at the local Theatre Royal and more often than not had a free seat to watch the resident repertory company each week in a different play. They made such an impression on him that he resolved that the theatre must be his life, but he failed, I'm sorry to relate, to remember the name of the leading man. It was I. I nearly said 'it was me', but it has to be I. Which, to digress, reminds me of Henry Irving's first entrance in *The Bells*. The printed version states that:

> (Mathias is seen passing the window. The door opens. Lights up. Chord.)
> MATHIAS: It is I.

Of course you needed to be an actor-manager to arrange for all the lights to be turned up and the full orchestra to strike a chord on your entrance. Gordon Craig, in his biography of Irving, remarks upon his idiosyncratic pronunciation and says that his first line sounded like 'Tsi' ('t's I). Years later Baliol Holloway, who had seen the great man in *The Bells*, explained that he only did that out of necessity because, as he had been seen through the window, the entire audience expected the arrival of their hero and were prepared to greet him with a storm of applause. He had no time to say the full 'It is I'. So the opening of the door, the lights up, the chord, 'Tsi' were simultaneous, a fraction of a second before the applause.

But to return to the point – I feel I should take most of the credit for Michael becoming the most highly regarded of impresarios, one who has mounted a string of successes both with the critics and with the public. He is inexplicably retiring but once the barriers are down he is a delightful companion. Coincidentally his first production was Patrick Cargill's play, *Ring for Catty*, the film version of which, *Twice Round the Daffodils*, I had appeared in a few years before.

Shortly before *There's a Girl in my Soup* Michael had presented a play called *The Killing of Sister George*, which was still running at the St Martin's Theatre, and there he had suffered severe aggravation from a certain lady in the box office. She had many times been accused of being rude to patrons; giving the wrong change or tickets for the wrong night. One afternoon Michael entered the box office unannounced and found her busy knitting, while two telephones were off the hook. He went straight to the owners of the theatre and told them that there would be no performance that evening unless the woman was dismissed that instant. She was. Some months later Michael entered our box office at the Globe and came face to face with the same woman . . .

'Oh, Mr Codron – I don't know what to say – that terrible business at the St Martin's – I don't know what came over me – it had never happened before and I can promise it will never happen again – what can I say? – will you ever forgive me?'

What could poor Michael do but grunt. At that moment a telephone rang which she picked up and announced, 'Palladium'!

Backstage we had our own problems. Jon Pertwee had a wonky hip-joint which might at any moment slip out of its socket; it would then require two men to force it back. In case this should happen on stage he showed Clive Francis and me what had to be done, but when the moment came we were not required.

One evening, as Jon turned on the wrong foot just before he was to exit, we heard a strangulated 'Argh' and saw him look at us in desperation as he said, 'It's gone out!' We had quite forgotten about the hip and were wondering what had 'gone out', when we saw all six feet two inches of Jon stand on tiptoe and, taking little rather effeminate steps, make his way to the door. The rest of the scene was accompanied by grunts and groans from off-stage as Anthony Sagar and the fireman helped to straighten Jon out.

Jill Melford is the most fastidious of ladies and always looks immaculate. One evening I was talking in her dressing-room as I watched her struggling with a hairbrush. It was I believe a Kent Cosby brush and the bristles, mounted in rubber, could be removed from the handle to be washed. She was now failing to get the rubber back in the handle. I suggested that a little talcum powder might lubricate the surface. This reminded me to tell her of a time, some years before, when women wore a garment called a roll-on, made of rather stout elastic which fitted snugly round the hips and held suspenders to which stockings could be clipped. I had been vastly amused on one occasion to see Diana come steaming from her bath and try to struggle into one of these things, contorting her body into the most extraordinary shapes. I put my masculine brain to work on finding a solution: 'Why don't you try talcum powder?' I exclaimed.

But I had not foreseen the workings of the female mind: Diana wheeled on me and accused, 'Who do you know who uses talcum powder?!'

Jill was greatly amused; then her smile faded '. . . and who do you know who uses talcum powder on a hairbrush?'

During the run of *There's a Girl in my Soup* the World Cup football series was played and the final took place at Wembley Stadium between England and West Germany during one of our matinees. Backstage everyone was glued to radios and television sets and our play was in danger of taking second place – actors narrowly avoided missing their entrances until, to the nation's euphoria, England won. At our final curtain call I stepped forward and announced the stupendous news, 'England has won the World Cup!' The totally disinterested silence that followed was deafening until three people clapped their hands together twice in a token of nationalistic pride before they all filed out. We can't win 'em all!

Playing a comedy night after night I became aware of a malaise that had grown worse over the years: the effects of television on a theatre audience. A theatrical performance, at its best, should be cathartic – an emotional release – the meeting in one place of two groups (performers and audience) who collectively share in a life-enhancing experience. Everyone must contribute – the audience just as much as the performers. The price of a ticket is merely to cover the costs that are necessary to provide the ambience for the experience – it is not a question of paying for the piper's tune.

As I write, the Olympics are just about to take place. Given the choice no one would actually choose to watch it on television – we would rather be present in the stadium to cheer and encourage our favourite competitors. If we enter the spirit of the occasion and shout and scream loudly enough, our team is more likely to win. It is no accident that in football more matches are won on the home ground in front of the devoted supporters than matches played away. We come away from a stadium with the sure knowledge that we have contributed to the success of our team. In the athletic field it is also a fact that no record has ever been broken in an empty arena.

Actors, like sportsmen, need and feed on vocalised moral support. In the theatre, 'entrance rounds' are now frowned upon by the intelligentsia, but without this affectionate applause for an actor making his first entrance, both sides of the proscenium arch lose out on an initial and vital form of audience participation. The more responsive the audience the greater the height to which the performer will aspire. An unresponsive audience will meet a lack-lustre performance – not that the performers set out to be dull but we all need the spur to go for the bigger jumps.

The world population now spends many hours a week peering at a flickering box in the corner of the room and they are prey to a hundred distractions: a ring on the telephone or the front door; the cat needs to be let out; somebody puts the kettle on; somebody makes the tea; husband or wife arrives home and needs to be asked what sort of day they have had or to relay an important message.

We are in danger of losing our powers of concentration. We rarely laugh aloud at something on TV – laughter is contagious. In the theatre only a section of the audience will laugh at the first amusing thing, another section will laugh at the next. The rest of the audience will wonder what they have missed and begin to listen a little more attentively. It is the actors' job to treat the audience as a sheepdog does a flock of sheep. His ears are finely attuned: he must listen and isolate that portion of the audience that is quick off the mark and then, not as you might expect, play all the laugh lines to that portion – that would antagonise the remainder – but distribute his next laugh lines to the other parts of the house until the whole audience is acting as one.

When recording, with Elaine Stritch, a TV series called *Two's Company* we had an audience with us in the studio. Both Elaine and I wished we could have done it without them because we found that we were torn between playing to a non-representative 250 people in front of us, and the hidden 15 million sitting in their homes. I asked a group of ladies if, when watching a programme, they liked to hear a studio audience. 'Oh yes,' they replied, 'it gives us some idea when to laugh'!!

What a tragic situation when we need others to tell us what is funny.

These same people, conditioned to hours of home viewing, now bring the same attitude to the theatre: they talk, rustle sweets, remove clothes, stand up, sit down, lie back in their seats – I have even seen someone reading a newspaper. And then we have the coughers. Sir Ralph Richardson once defined acting as 'the art of stopping people coughing'. If only some attempt were made to stifle the cough, but it would appear that the sufferer will wait until he is comfortably seated in the theatre before giving vent to a resounding bark. They are unaware that in an audience of, shall we say, a thousand people, the word on which that one person coughs cannot be heard by the other nine hundred and ninety-nine. If that one word is important the entire audience will miss the point of an entire line. To illustrate:

'Who was that lady I saw you with last night?'
'That was no lady that was my (cough).'

Actors develop a technique of coping with this problem by immediately repeating the word on which the cough happened, or by being able to hear the intake of breath that precedes a cough and then pausing for the length of the interruption. An audience never seems to be aware that we do this. Some years ago I gave a lecture at a university in Japan and as usual encountered – and countered – the odd cougher. Unknown to me my lecture was being recorded on tape and some months later I was sent their magazine with my lecture in print. Reading it I was bemused to find several words repeated: the repetitions occurred where I had been forced to repeat myself to cover a cough.

As I have said, we are losing our powers of concentration – we listen without hearing – and the sad thing is that we are all the losers, audience and performers. The theatre, to survive, must offer something very different from television and the main difference is audience participation.

Russell Thorndike in his biography of his sister Sybil* recalls their visit to *Julius Caesar* at Her Majesty's Theatre:

. . . Sybil and I sat side by side, too thrilled for speech. When the overture began we nearly fainted – the trumpets were beyond our wildest dreams . . . I don't think I can describe our feelings. We held hands when we knew the Senators were coming – we didn't think we could bear it alone – we rose in our seats to join the shouting as the purple-robed Caesar entered. We nearly died of it. From that moment we were in heaven . . . Sybil maintains that audiences must take what they are given and be thankful – their money doesn't pay for what we give them. If they gave as much as *we* give – all of ourselves – then they'll get back something worth having . . . You don't get anything by just paying money for it; you've got to do something yourself. Sitting and eating chocolates just to pass the time, isn't the way to be an audience. You've got to spend *yourself* as the actors have to spend themselves – then you'll come out of the theatre feeling grand.

Dame Sybil remained the perfect theatre-goer for the rest of her life. She paid me the great compliment of coming to see most of the plays I was doing and I could see her, from before the play started, sitting on the edge of her seat alert and tingling with apprehension; she was invariably a split second ahead of everyone else in appreciating every nuance. She laughed; she cried; she reacted to every emotion: for her we were prepared to run a four-minute mile at every performance and the faster we ran the more she applauded. It was joyous. The next time you go to a theatre try to emulate her; notice the difference and how much better you feel.

I had signed a year's contract with Michael Codron. A year means roughly 416 performances. I have found that because there is a different audience each night and no two performances are identical (in 416 showings of a film, each is exactly the same) I can retain my enthusiasm easily for that length of time, but have to admit that on the one occasion I exceeded the year – in the 644 performances of *The Heiress* – I did get rather bored. As my contract drew to a close Michael asked me to sign for a further year – he even offered a considerable rise in salary. I was torn: should I stay with success? I consulted Binkie Beaumont who

* Published by Thornton Butterworth, 1929.

advised me to stay for the entire run – it eventually ran for six years! I was at the point of committing myself when Peter Hall telephoned from Stratford:

'Come and play Lord Foppington in *The Relapse* at the Aldwych.'

16

'WHY DIDN'T WE THINK OF IT BEFORE?'

I declined Michael Codron's generous offer to stay in the *Soup* and decided to return to the RSC.

I had seen Vanbrugh's *The Relapse* in 1947 played beautifully by Cyril Richard, but I couldn't remember it in detail except that Lord Foppington was a splendid part and just the thing I felt I should do next. For his production, Peter Hall had found a young director who had been working at the Belgrade Theatre, Coventry, still wet behind the ears from Cambridge University, named Trevor Nunn. He came backstage to meet me after a performance of *There's a Girl in my Soup*. Of slight build, with a pointed chin, a Mexican-style moustache, rather too much hair and wildly bright eyes. He sat eagerly on a chair and gazed at me like a child.

'I'm so glad I've seen you in this play – it's a lovely bravura performance and you're not afraid to go over the top. In *The Relapse* I want you to go three times as far!'

It is difficult to define the meaning of the theatrical expression 'over the top'. Larger than life? extravagant? expansive? extrovert? All these things?

Whatever it is, I would agree that my performance in *Soup* was as far over the top as I could decently go, but here was a director, part of whose job it is to see that actors do not go over the top, and of the generation who wanted everything underplayed, asking me to go three times further!

I had never done a Restoration play before – of course the restoration of Charles II to the throne of England was in 1660 and *The Relapse* was not written until 1696 when Charles had been dead for eleven years, but we are inclined to lump together all plays written between 1660 and 1714 (when the Hanoverians took over from the Stuarts) and label them Restoration. And how wonderfully earthy they are. Dame Edith Evans once said, 'I don't like the eighteenth century – give me the Restoration – I'm always game for a bit of bawdry!' I got hold of a script as soon as I could and started work.

As we know that the expletive *'Slife* is a corruption of God's life and *Zounds* a corruption of God's wounds, so Lord Foppington's famous phrase *Stap me vitals* is derived from *Stop my vitals* (constipate me) but I know of no other instance of the word *stop* being spelt *stap*. The script contained several other o's spelt as a's. I tried to understand the author's intention in spelling it that way and I think I found the answer. The danger is in thinking that *stap* should rhyme with *slap*. Vanbrugh obviously intended his character to use an affected mode of speech – one might almost say, aristocratic; *orf* instead of *off*; *hice* instead of *house* – and to pronounce *stop* as *stahp*. I delighted in this discovery and throughout the play I pronounced every *o* as *ah*. I even carried it a step further by making every *a* into *awe*. Surprisingly it was still intelligible.

Another hurdle was the convention of the 'aside'. The author many times indicates that a line is said 'aside', and intends that that line should be heard by the audience and not by the other characters on the stage. But how do you do it? I have seen actors speak such a line behind their hand or behind a fan but that is stupid: if the other characters don't even know you are saying it, why use a hand or a fan?

I went off to consult my old friend Baliol Holloway, by then aged eighty-four, who had spent the whole of his theatrical career in the classical repertoire. In his minute flat in Thayer Street, 'Ba' gave me a two-hour lesson in the art of the aside:

An aside must be directed to a given seat in the theatre – a different seat for each aside, some in the stalls, some in the circle. Never to the same seat twice – the rest of the audience will think you have a friend sitting there. If you are facing to the right immediately before the aside, then direct it to the left of the theatre, and vice versa. Your head must crack round in one clean movement, look straight at the occupant of the seat, deliver the line and crack your head back to exactly where it was before. The voice you use must be different from the one you are using in the play. If loud, then soft; if soft, then loud; if high, then low; if low, then high; if fast, then slow; if slow, then fast. During an aside, no other characters must move at all – the time you take does not exist for them.

'Ba' and I practised what he preached, using a scene from – I think – *Still Waters Run Deep* in which two characters speak in asides for twenty or more lines, until he was satisfied that I could do it. It worked and it was a proud moment when 'Ba' later saw a performance and congratulated me.

Foppington's servant is named La Verole. The meaning of that word in modern French is smallpox which is rather a strange name to give a character, unless it is to intimate to the actor that his face should be pockmarked. Luckily I looked it up in my complete, twelve-volume edition of the *Oxford English Dictionary* . . .

Oh dear, I can feel a digression coming on.

A few years before, I had gone out to Majorca to visit my old friend and mentor Charles F. Smith★ who was then in his seventies and had retired to a flat in Palma. I didn't warn him I was coming, but I knew that he could always be found in a certain bar at midday, and indeed sitting there was the man who had given me my first job; who had subsidised me through drama school; at whose flat in Brighton I had met the stellar names of the British theatre; who had such faith in me; who had backed my first overdraft; whose approval of my performances meant so much to me; whom we made godfather to our first-born. I had not seen him for ten years. A more demonstrative man would have burst into tears and embraced me but Charles merely looked up as I called his name and said, 'Hello, what are you drinking?'

After lunch, he suggested we meet next day at the English Club. Only the English in exile huddle together and erect club-like barricades around themselves. Next morning I mounted the stairs at eleven o'clock to find Charles in a deserted room busy at a pink gin as he looked up.

'Hello, what day is it today?'

'Wednesday, Charles . . .'

'Are you sure?'

'Perfectly sure – I arrived yesterday. Tuesday.'

At that moment, a second elderly member arrived.

'Morning, Charles.'

I was introduced to him and after a few pleasantries he turned to Charles.

'What day is it today?'

'Wednesday,' said Charles.

★ See *A Touch of the Memoirs* (1982).

'Are you sure?'

'Well, Donald says it is.'

The newcomer went across to the bar and a third elderly member entered.

'Morning, morning, morning,' and picked up a copy of *The Times* in which he became engrossed before closing it and peering at the top of the front page.

'What day is it today?'

'Wednesday,' said the second member.

'Are you sure?'

'Well, Charles says it is.'

'No I didn't – Donald did.'

And for the next week I became the final arbiter on what was almost the sole topic of conversation – I began to wonder who made the decisions when I was not there. Needing a break from this taxing responsibility, and knowing that Robert Graves also lived in Majorca, I telephoned him. Immediately he invited me to spend a few days with him at his home in Daya on the north side of the island.

'With him' is not really a true description of the few days. I was always two or three steps behind him when either walking or talking. We strode along narrow cliff paths with sheer drops to the wave-lashed rocks. He with his great leonine head thrown back holding forth magnificently on some erudite subject, unaware that because of the pounding sea, I could only hear one word in ten. He had trodden those same paths many times before and knew exactly where we were going, but I had to stumble and slip behind him.

Words, words, words. He realised that as an actor I was involved with the use and colour of words, but was surprised, until I told him of my lamentable lack of formal education, that I had no knowledge of etymology – the root and source of every word I used. Without warning, he would suddenly stop in his tracks.

'What do you call a man who suffers from melancholia?'

Breathless, I tried, 'A melancholic?'

'No, no! A melancholiac. Now you say it – "melancholiac" – how much more beautiful!' Back went the head and off he strode roaring 'melancholiac' to the winds.

I was beginning to regret I didn't have a tape-recorder with me, when I heard his tune change. 'Asphodel – asphodel – I have always thought that such a beautiful word; Swinburne told me it was one of his favourite words – asphodel – the wild asphodel – say it – say it! Wild asphodel.'

He didn't really want me to say it – he just went on saying it to himself. Suddenly he let out a cry. 'Look – look – there it is – the wild asphodel! Have you ever eaten it? No? You have never tasted of the wild asphodel?!!'

The horrors of my misspent youth flooded up. I was so ashamed. I felt that I was already quite low in his estimation – now I would reach rock-bottom. 'No,' I stammered.

'Neither have I! We'll dig it up and have it for supper to-night.'

We prised the plant from the cliff and began our return journey to his house where he presented it to his devoted wife with, 'Donald has never tasted of the wild asphodel!' (No mention, you notice, that he hadn't.) We sat round the scrubbed table while the food of the Gods, the wild asphodel, was served up and Graves tackled it as he would asparagus.

His eyes brightened as he savoured the first mouthful . . . then the second . . . He took up his napkin and vigorously wiped his lips. 'Disgusting!' he bellowed.

Hoping to continue our discussion in the quiet of the house, I was disappointed. Obviously his wife had had enough of his pontificating and the evening was spent in telling each other amusing anecdotes and jokes at which he roared as if he had never heard them before. Suddenly he stopped: 'Don't you have the *Oxford English Dictionary*?'

'I have the concise edition,' I apologised.

'Good God! – you should have the complete twelve-volume edition. The moment you get back to England, you are to buy it – promise me – on one condition: that you look up three words a day for the rest of your life.'

That digression helps to explain why I have at home the complete twelve-volume edition of the *Oxford English Dictionary*, although I have to admit that I have not kept to Graves' edict. However, I looked up the name of Foppington's servant, Verole, and although the present-day translation from the French is smallpox, in the seventeenth century it meant specifically the Pox. How lovely to think that in the original production, when Foppington called for Verole, everyone would have known that he was actually shouting 'gonorrhoea'.

A year or so before, the RSC had employed an expert in business efficiency who was horrified to find that designers bought a different length of material for each costume from various places such as Harrods or Liberty's. He maintained that they should buy in bulk direct from a warehouse – indeed at that very moment he knew of somewhere wanting to dispose of 300 bales of pink silk. For many months, 300 bales of pink silk had been stored untouched in a Stratford warehouse for the simple reason that designers go to extraordinary lengths to make sure that no two ladies will appear in the same material. The time had come when the pink silk had to be used, so our designer, Christopher Morley, had all the costumes, ladies' and gentlemen's, made from it and each one dipped in a different dye. The result was staggeringly beautiful. My own costumes were outrageous. If my performance was to be over the top, so were my costumes – all five of them, and each one topped by a series of wigs that grew in outlandishness as the play progressed.

D.S.

Frances de la Tour

What face could possibly match the outrageousness of the costumes and wigs? In the period of the play, 1696, it was perfectly acceptable for men – especially fops – to use cosmetics. Make-up was not then a female prerogative. So what example did we have in 1967 of a man using make-up to appear other than he is? Why, of course – Danny la Rue. I obtained a colour photograph of Danny in one of his female roles, copied his make-up as a basis and then caricatured it. I finished my pink-coloured base at my chin so that it should actually look like a mask. I have seen ladies who have attempted to disguise their own thin lips by painting cupid bows in lipstick over them. Unfortunately, they always exaggerate – no real lips have such curvaceous bows – why do their friends not tell them? I did this to my lips until they looked like a well-fitted bra in silhouette. I also applied two black 'beauty spots' and glued diamanté to them. The space between my eyes and eyebrows I filled with a bright-blue glitter. With all these technical problems out of the way, Trevor (to whom I had now become devoted) and I discussed the character of Foppington.

He must never appear to be effeminate in spite of his love of himself and his clothes. 'I'm sure his bedroom is covered in mirrors and has all the paraphernalia for seduction,' said Trevor one day over lunch. 'Also, he *thinks* quicker than anyone else in the play– for instance, in the tea-party scene, when the ladies question him on how he spends his days, he knows what they are going to ask before they are halfway through the question.'

My eyes brightened. 'Trevor . . . do you think I dare . . .?'

He guessed exactly what I meant and smirked wickedly, 'Try it at rehearsal this afternoon.'

Without warning the other actors, I spoke the operative word just before they did:

AMANDA:
Does not your Lordship love   reading?
FOPPINGTON: reading?   Oh . . .

BERINTHIA:
How do you dispose of yourself on   Sundays?
FOPPINGTON: Sundays?   Why . . .

When my colleagues had become used to it, everyone agreed it was a splendid idea.

Our superb cast included actors then comparatively unknown, such as Susan Fleetwood, Janet Suzman, Frances de la Tour, Alan Howard, John Kane, Patrick Stewart, Donald Burton, Ben Kingsley and Roger Rees. We were a very happy company, the play opened to rave reviews and every performance was packed to the rafters. It became a collectors' item – many people saw it over and over again.

For the first – and only – time in my career, I had flowers thrown at me at the curtain call – something more often seen in the opera houses. For me Foppington was an important step because I became recognised as a classical comedian, and I was thrilled during the run to be appointed an Associate Artist of the Royal Shakespeare Company. I am often asked what this means. It is purely honorary: the RSC is proud to be associated with the artist and the artist proud to be associated with the RSC.

Four long-lasting friendships came from that period: firstly, of course, with Trevor Nunn, then with the novelist Jeffrey Archer, who, when we first met, was able to quote whole speeches of mine from the play. Thirdly, a friendship was cemented with the Bodens, both highly acclaimed portrait-painters. Leonard painted me as Lord Foppington, a portrait worthy to hang beside a Zoffany or a de Wilde, and Margaret painted our two children. Lastly, with . . . well let me tell you about a most strange encounter.

The Relapse was in repertory so I had several nights off and on one of these Diana and I went to Covent Garden to hear the opera *Otello* and we thrilled as never before to the great duet between Otello and Iago – two stout tree-trunks with voices soaring to Verdi's awe-inspiring music.

At the end of the performance we made our way backstage to greet our old friend Tito Gobbi, who had been singing Iago, and while there I felt that I should also congratulate the superb Otello, American James McCracken. I knocked tentatively on his dressing-room door. A muffled tenor bellow instructed, 'Come in!' I opened the door and there directly in my eyeline was the vast bulk of McCracken, stripped to the waist, washing off his make-up. Chest, arms and face were covered with a black lather. What a moment to try to introduce myself!

'I'm so sorry – do excuse me, but my name is Donald Sinden and I just wanted to . . .'

McCracken vehemently threw the soap into the basin, and roared 'Stap me vitals! I saw you in *The Relapse* last night!' He moved swiftly across the room and embraced me – covering my dinner-jacket with black foam.

We played *The Relapse* on Christmas Eve and I racked my brains to think of something special to do during the performance by way of celebration . . .

Some years before, I had been given a Christmas tree festooned with small fairy lights – each bulb was not much bigger than the head of a match, the size used in electric toy train sets – operated by two six-volt batteries. For the last scene of the play I had been provided with an enormous white wig and I arranged for the bulbs

to be secretly threaded through it and also for a small Father
Christmas to be perched on the top. I hid the large batteries in a
black cotton bag strapped round my waist, one of the wires
attached to a terminal and, just before I made my entrance, I
attached the second wire to the other. As the bulbs were above
my eyeline, I had no idea if they were alight until I entered and
the entire audience and cast were convulsed. One thing I had
overlooked: the play ended in a blackout – or should have done
because on this occasion I was left standing in a cloud of twinkling
lights. I returned to my dressing-room somewhat elated at the
success of my joke when suddenly the door opened and there stood
a glowering Trevor Nunn . . . I tried to excuse myself – after all
it was Christmas Eve – everyone was in a celebratory mood – it
was not just an unforgivable private joke – the audience had
enjoyed it too – I had no intention of doing it again . . . I lapsed
into silence. Trevor continued to glower until, breaking the silence,
he wailed:

'Why didn't we think of it before?!!'

I loved him for that. It was round about this time that Peter Hall
called a meeting of the company and announced that he would be
leaving the RSC to take over the National Theatre and his successor
at Stratford would be . . . we held our breath . . . Trevor Nunn.
The perfect choice.

Someone at a party was trying to persuade Noël Coward to see a
certain play. 'Don't bother with that,' I said bravely. 'Come and
see *The Relapse*.'

'Nothing, my dear Donald . . .' He beamed, as only Noël
Coward could beam. Surely, I thought, that beginning must be
followed by '. . . would give me greater pleasure'? Instead he
continued '. . . would persuade me to see *The Relapse*.'

'Why ever not?'

'I saw Cyril Richard.'

Not to be outdone, I replied, 'I am very much better than he.'

'No doubt. He was abysmal.'

Which play could follow *The Relapse*? What should I do next?

17

NOR PLAUTUS TOO LIGHT

Bernard
Cribbins

Jill
Melford

D.S.

Of all theatrical categories – Comedy, Tragedy, History, Melo-
drama, Farce, High Comedy – Farce is by far the most difficult
– for the writer and the performer. Whatever the play the actor
must explore and build his character. In Comedy, actor and author
must make an audience laugh – if they don't laugh the play is a
non-event. Farce takes a comic situation and stretches it until it is
near breaking-point. The player in Farce must perform his act on
a high wire with no safety-net. David Garrick said, 'Any fool can
play Hamlet but Comedy is a very serious business.' The critic,
James Agate, provided what I think is the best definition of Farce:
'Comedy is unreal people in real situations; Farce is real people in
unreal situations.'

There have been very few great writers of Farce: Labiche, Feydeau, Ben Travers, Philip King, and it was King, master of the technique, who had written *Big Bad Mouse* which in 1966 went out on a pre-London tour with Jimmy Edwards and Eric Sykes in the two leading parts. But all was not well – in fact it was disaster time – audiences did not like it and Edwards and Sykes were unhappy. Its impresario, Michael Codron, asked Ray Cooney – vastly experienced himself in both writing and performing Farce – to see the play where it was being performed somewhere in the north of England and to decide if he could salvage the piece by rewriting it. Cooney saw it and telephoned Codron. It was terrible, he said, and he could see absolutely no way of saving it but if Codron could keep it touring for a few more weeks he would write a brand-new play for the same cast. This offer was gratefully received and Cooney immediately contacted his old friend and collaborator John Chapman. The pair got to work and within three weeks the play was ready and accepted by Codron.

But meanwhile, away in the north, Edwards and Sykes had not been idle. Superb professionals that they are, by incorporating their expertise from the world of Variety, they had transformed failure into success and had made *Big Bad Mouse* into a star vehicle for two clowns which, when it reached London, ran for years. Codron now had not only a success, but a splendid new farce written by Cooney and Chapman called *Not Now Darling* as well. This he sent to me.

All great comedy teams and situations involve one character who is extrovert and domineering and another who is introvert and dominated. Laurel and Hardy, Olsen and Johnson, Tom Walls and Robertson Hare, Morecambe and Wise, Edwards and Sykes. Usually the little man wins in the end, but he is the one who gets hit and the other does the hitting. The confident extrovert is the one who slips on a banana skin and blames the other. *Not Now Darling* was no exception to the golden rule – I was to be domineering and Bernard Cribbins was to be dominated. Bernard is one of the world's finest farceurs, but it was my first farce. Cooney and Chapman had, however, constructed such a splendid framework that our work was made considerably easier. It is quite impossible to tell the complete story of a farce, suffice it to know that the scene is a furrier's showroom on the first floor of Bond Street premises, jointly owned by Cribbins and me. My character is married and has a girlfriend who is also married, but they have not yet progressed to the final act of adultery. He is, however, convinced that if he were to give her a five thousand pound fur coat she would succumb. To avoid suspicion her husband must be led to believe that he has himself purchased the coat. I should add that it is necessary for the nervous, introverted partner to be involved in the deception. From that beginning the plot becomes more and more complicated.

Cooney and Chapman had drawn on a device used in eighteenth-century comedies by giving the characters names that were allied to their characteristics – mine was Bodley, my partner's Crouch – and also by using the device of soliloquy, thus enabling a character to impart a wealth of information to the audience in the shortest possible time.

We opened our pre-West End tour in Birmingham and Diana brought Jeremy and Marc to the first night which was followed by a cast and backers' party. The boys were asked by the author what they thought of the play: Marc aged thirteen said that 'it was quite the funniest play my father has done' and Jeremy, with all the temerity of his seventeen years, said, 'I think you have missed an opportunity; in the lines "Where is she?/At the café across the road./What is the name of the café?/The milk bar," I think that the milk bar should have a real name.'

'What do you suggest?' asked the author.

'The Poor Cow,' said Jeremy.

The dialogue was immediately amended to, 'Where is she?/At the milk bar across the road./What is the name of the milk bar?/The Poor Cow.'

Variations on this new dialogue created several new laughs.

Unbeknown to us Jeremy took advantage of his stay in Birmingham to go over to Stratford-upon-Avon and apply for a job – when he left school – on the stage-management staff of the theatre. He was told that they would consider him seriously if he did a year's work elsewhere. As a result he launched his career at Pitlochry and joined Stratford in 1970.

Not Now Darling opened at London's Strand Theatre on 12th June, 1968, ran for over a year, and on one occasion we were able to experience the difference between Farce and reality. 'My' girlfriend was played, once again, by Jill Melford and at a certain point in the play, with the five thousand pound fur coat over her shoulders and intent on blackmailing the partners, she stands on the balcony overlooking Bond Street and slowly removes her clothes until she is only wearing a 'waspie' – a black corset-cum-brassière with stocking suspenders around its lower edge – which she then threatens to remove. (These 'waspies' are usually laced up at the back but for the purpose of our play a special one was made with buttons down the front.) The partners refuse to capitulate. Very well then – she undoes the top button; then the next; then the next . . . The two partners turn away in horror. She turns away from the audience as the 'waspie' falls to the floor and as she turns back she is holding the mink around her. To all intents and purposes she is naked beneath, but in fact Jill, although braless, wore flesh-coloured stockings and pants.

All was well until Jill was suddenly stricken with laryngitis and Ann Sydney, who was already playing a model, had to take over Jill's role at short notice. Ann had been 'Miss World' in 1964 and had/has a magnificent figure, but her bust measurement was several inches more than Jill's – all of which had to be crammed into the one and only 'waspie' which on that particular evening she threatened to remove. She undid the top button; then the next . . . Bernard Cribbins and I were just about to turn away in horror when the rest of the buttons could no longer stand the strain and like machine-gun bullets, ricocheted around the stage exposing to the full view of the audience a beautiful pair of breasts. Bernard and I could not turn away – we were rooted to the spot gaping. So much for naturalism on the stage. For weeks afterwards people came to the play having been told by friends that they might get a full frontal of a Miss World.

Certainly I found playing Farce the most precise and difficult thing I had ever done. 'Of course it is, dear,' Dame Edith Evans answered when I told her. 'You have no play to help you.' Since then I have played King Lear and Othello and I am still convinced that Farce is more difficult. An actor playing Hamlet has only to come on to the stage and begin, 'To be or not to be . . .' for half the audience to clutch the other half and murmur, 'Isn't it wonderful!'

In athletic terms, King Lear is a marathon and requires much stamina, but you can lag behind for a couple of miles and still win the race. After a performance as Lear I could collapse exhausted into bed and sleep like a baby but *Not Now Darling* was like running and winning a perfect 110-metre hurdle race. Every part of the athlete/actor must be tuned to be ready at the gun – the whole race will only take a fraction of a minute. There is no leeway for the smallest mistake. Every muscle is taut and ready to start on the B of Bang, not even the g. His steps get progressively longer as he nears the first fence. Over goes the left leg with his right trailing – even if he tips a hurdle it will lessen his speed – three more steps to the next hurdle, left leg over – his breathing is totally predetermined, maximum oxygen for maximum effort – nothing has been left to chance, even the hands must present the lowest wind resistance. And then, having cleared the row of hurdles, there is the final dash to the tape – one stumble and the race is lost. Similarly the actor in Farce must crack out every predetermined inflection with split-second timing, surprising his audience with unexpected variations of pace. In Comedy he can give his audience time to savour and respond to a line or situation, but in Farce he must press on at prestidigitatorial speed and only when his highly tuned ears hear the first tinkling of a laugh can he slam on the brakes and give his audience a little release before continuing exactly as if he had not stopped.

Some years ago, when the breathalyser was first introduced, I watched a programme on television in which a random selection of people were put through a test in a simulated car which had only steering-wheel and a brake pedal. When a red light flashed the contestant had to apply the brake and a dial showed how many feet it would have taken the car to stop at 30 mph. The contestants were then each given a large whisky and a short time later undertook the same test. The effect of the alcohol caused each of them to stop (according to the dial) fifteen feet further on. After watching that programme I determined never to drink a drop all day before appearing on stage: if alcohol can impair one's reactions to that extent, just think what it would do to comedy timing.

18

'THAT IS THE FAN I USED'

One of my earliest theatrical experiences was to see Sir John Martin Harvey in *The Only Way* – a dramatisation of Charles Dickens' *A Tale of Two Cities* – at the Theatre Royal, Brighton – and I thought he was awful. He was far too old for the part of Sidney Carton and, if he was too old, what could be said of Nina de Silva, Harvey's wife, who played Lucie? But Charles Smith had previously told me all about the great actor: how he had worked with Irving at the Lyceum and had inherited so many of the chief's leading parts; of his Oedipus at Covent Garden, his Burgomaster of Stilemonde, and so on, so when Charles took me backstage to meet the great man, I was duly impressed. Unbeknown to me Charles acquired the hat that Harvey had worn as Sidney Carton and some time later he gave it to me. This was my first piece of theatricalia.

This hat led me to buy my first book on the theatre, Martin Harvey's autobiography, which cost me sixpence a week, on the never-never, for seven weeks. Then, rapidly, to reading books on Henry Irving (one by Bram Stoker and another by Austen Brereton); Beerbohm Tree; George Alexander; J. L. Toole; Ellen Terry; Charles Hawtrey; and at the same time I was actually meeting actors and actresses who had worked with those legendary figures. Marie Tempest, Irene Vanbrugh, Violet Vanbrugh, Gerald Lawrence and many others. Every actor I met of the older school was amazed to find one so young as I (not yet twenty) who was interested in the theatre of their youth and many gave me things that had belonged to those long dead actors.

My most extensive acquisition came when Julia Neilson, the widow of Fred Terry, died, aged eighty-eight in 1957 and her daughter Phyllis decided to sell the house on Primrose Hill, and its contents that had been the Terry home for many years. Diana and I bought their four-poster bed, a sideboard, several chairs, a clock and, for two pounds ten shillings, a pile of playbills and prints. The following day I arrived to collect the purchases and received my first surprise: the auctioneer's porter found my pile of playbills and prints and checked his list: 'Just a minute – this Lot includes the pictures in the dining room.' These proved to be framed engravings of David Garrick in most of his celebrated parts. All included for two pounds fifty! While they were being taken down I noticed that the door was being held open by an interestingly shaped block of wood. 'Is that part of a Lot?'

'No. No. Rubbish.'

'May I have it?'

'Yes – we've got to empty the house.'

When later I checked with Phyllis she confirmed that I had Fred Terry's wig-block.

Someone else had bought a chest of drawers and had thrown the lining paper into the fireplace leaving a corner of white card protruding. 'Does anyone want this?' I asked as I pulled it out.

'No – all rubbish.'

It was a charming print of Mrs Siddons with 'I bought this at Irving's sale, Fred Terry' written on the back.

At home I rummaged through the pile of playbills and prints and found many exciting things. Who else but her brother would have kept a playbill for the Princess's Theatre on 28th February, 1856, the very night that Ellen Terry made her first appearance on the stage as Mamillius in *The Winter's Tale*? A little print of 'Mr Barrymore' had another inscription by Fred Terry on the back: 'Bought by me at Lewis Waller's sale, F.T.'

When the actress Violet Farebrother, who, I tell you tactlessly, was a girlfriend of Fred's, visited our house for the first time, she stopped in her tracks at the sight of the Terry sideboard. Tears welled in her eyes: 'You've got it – you've got it! I suppose you knew about that sideboard? No? One Sunday evening at Primrose Hill Fred and Julia were having supper alone when Julia said, "Fred – I would like a little more of that ham." Fred went over to that sideboard to carve it for her – and died of a heart attack! – leaning on that sideboard.'

Diana and I were not quite sure how we should react. We took her up to see the bed. A long slow smile of recognition hovered around her lips. 'Ah – I was on tour with Fred when he bought that in Devizes.'

Violet Farebrother put me in touch with Hilda Clarence, the widow of the splendid character-actor O. B. Clarence, who wrote to tell me that she intended to dispose of her husband's library. I raced down to her flat in Hove, but never expected the sight that met my eyes: her dining room was covered in the most fantastic collection of rare seventeenth- and eighteenth-century books and pamphlets on the theatre. I have never been a collector of books purely as books – I am more interested in their contents – but I knew immediately the value of what I saw. I had seen similar books in salerooms and bookshops and I knew the price they fetched. Way beyond my pocket. I felt that I was wasting her time but she allowed me to look through the three or four hundred books that were spread before me and I found about twenty that were surely within my range. I knew of a bookseller by the name of Ifan Kyrle Fletcher who specialised in theatre books of antiquarian interest and I suggested that he would be the man to value them for her: I would pay her whatever price he put on the twenty. Ten days later she wrote to say that Kyrle Fletcher had been down and had suggested I pay her nine pounds for my twenty books – in those days ten shillings (50p) was a fair price for an ordinary second-hand Victorian book. However, shortly after-wards, I received Kyrle Fletcher's latest catalogue and sure enough there were all the other books, 'from the library of O. B. Clarence' or 'with the signature of O. B. Clarence', and each individual book priced between seventy-five and a hundred pounds. It was some time before I saw Hilda again.

'I gather that Mr Kyrle Fletcher bought the rest of the books.'

'Oh yes – what a dear man – he gave me seventy-five pounds for the lot.'

I have never entirely trusted dealers from that time.

Hilda gave me several fascinating things that had belonged to O.B., including the cane used by Charles Mathews in many of his farces and the boots that Irving wore as Iachimo and given by him to an actor whose own shoes had been stolen from the theatre.

Over the years many things came my way, always 'on loan' as it were. I was to hold them in trust and when the time came I would be expected to pass them on to another devotee actor. The perfect example of this handing on was a set of armlets (bracelets) of gilt metal studded with coloured glass resembling precious stones, that had been worn by Edmund Kean as Sardanapalus in Byron's poetic drama. These were passed to his son Charles and from him to Henry Irving, then to Seymour Hicks and then to Roger Maxwell (who, as a young actor, had impressed Hicks). Roger in turn passed them to me together with all the letters that had accompanied the transfers. Mounted, by one of the former recipients, in a mahogany case they graced our dining-room wall,

179

together with J. L. Toole's pocket-book and snuffbox and the mahogany and brass stage-door notice-board which I appropriated when the St James's Theatre was being demolished.

Laurence Irving, the grandson of Henry, gave me the engraved silver shaving mug that H.I. had given to Squire Bancroft who in turn bequeathed it to H.I.'s son (Laurence's father). Laurence also gave me Irving's silver inkstand and the cocked hat he had worn when he was knighted by Queen Victoria at Windsor Castle.

I bought in a sale the silver 'loving' cup presented to J. L. Toole by the Prince of Wales (later Edward VII).

Baliol Holloway gave me his own eighteenth-century wig (which I mounted on the Terry wig-block and topped with the Martin Harvey hat), his Henry the Fifth shield, his Bassanio cap and Irving's Hamlet dagger.

Donald Wolfit bequeathed me his ivory pill-box and his walking-stick – which joined the sticks of James Agate, Lord Alfred Douglas, Sir Noël Coward, Dame Ellen Terry, Johnstone-Douglas, Leslie Faber, J. L. Toole, and more recently, Sir Ralph Richardson.

Athene Seyler gave a bracelet which had belonged to Mrs Kendal and John Gielgud gave me her fan.

None of these things was of great intrinsic value but of enormous sentimental interest to me. I firmly believe that I feel a strong 'contact' with each of their previous owners.

In 1959 I attended a screening at the Institute of Recorded Sound of the film made in 1911 of Forbes-Robertson's Hamlet – incidentally, what a performance he gave and what a tragedy it was that the film was made before the days of sound! I had the temerity to suggest that the greatest Hamlet of our era, John Gielgud, should dub his voice to the film. This was howled down by F.R.'s daughters as a blasphemy; they maintained that Gielgud could never hope to match their father's infinitely superior voice. Only sections of the film had been seen before the complete version was discovered in a loft at the house of Lady Miles, one of Forbes-Robertson's daughters. The screening had been arranged by a group of which I had not previously heard, the British Theatre Museum Association. I was told of its origins.

Laurence Irving had written the definitive biography of his grandfather Sir Henry for which he was able to draw on a massive hoard of archive material still in the possession of his family. After publication in 1951 he received many requests that the archive should be deposited in one of several American universities –

some offering considerable sums of money. In 1955 Irving wrote a letter to *The Times* bewailing the fact that while so much interest was generated in the USA, no British institution was prepared to purchase or house the collection relating to the greatest actor of the nineteenth century and Britain's first actor Knight who alone had raised the status of his profession. His letter triggered off a host of others all in favour of the material remaining in this country and a meeting of all interested bodies was called by the Society for Theatre Research at the Arts Council offices in St James's Square which resulted in the formation of the British Theatre Museum Association, a pressure group committed to the ideal of establishing a museum devoted to the Theatre.

Hitherto I had imagined myself to be the only idiot who collected theatricalia but here were others, many of whom also belonged to the Society for Theatre Research, a learned society which met regularly and published pamphlets on erudite and esoteric matters concerning the Drama. At the reception that followed the *Hamlet* film I talked with a whole roomful of collectors. Some collected theatrical porcelain, some letters, some playbills, some programmes, some prints, some books, some paintings, some designs. Suddenly I was among friends and I was invited to join the committee of the British Theatre Museum Association (or BTMA as it became known), which met once a month in the boardroom of Coutts Bank in the Strand – thanks to its chairman and keen supporter of the Association, Sir Seymour Egerton. Here I met for the first time the chairman of the BTMA, Laurence Irving himself. I immediately fell under his spell. The son of H. B. Irving and Dorothea Baird, the grandson of Sir Henry Irving, Laurence is steeped in theatrical tradition.

During his varied career he had been responsible for the production in 1928 of Masefield's *The Coming of Christ* at Canterbury Cathedral. The enormous success of this verse-play was such that the Dean and Chapter were able to commission a series of poetic dramas including Eliot's *Murder in the Cathedral*. In that same year he went to Hollywood as Artistic Director to Douglas Fairbanks Snr. where he designed the classic film versions of *The Man in the Iron Mask* and *The Taming of the Shrew*. Returning to England he designed many famous stage productions.

He and I met regularly at the Garrick Club and as a family we frequently visited him at his house in Kent where, one year, he designed an entire model theatre production of *Treasure Island* which was performed by the children. His studio is glorious: his own paintings, mounted playbills, portraits, the framed spectacles and the death-mask of his illustrious grandfather, crowd the walls. Glorious too is the book-lined alcove where the privileged join Laurence in two deep armchairs for tea beside the fire. No one else that I know sits in an armchair as Laurence does: his legs stretch out in front from a deep indentation on the very edge of the chair which supports the lower half of his body while the upper half lies back almost horizontal to the floor and his shoulders and head sink into the deep cushions which should be supporting the small of his back. His penetrating mind, wise counsel and aura of infinite calm make any encounter with him a most rewarding experience. I cannot remember what provoked the question but I once asked Jeremy and Marc how they imagined a 'wise' man; they both said Laurence Irving.

Over the years members of the BTMA committee came and went but, among others, Sybil Rosenfeld, Arthur Franks, Jack Reading, Ivor Guest, Barnabas Brunner, G. B. L. Wilson, Antony Hippisley Coxe, Bamber Gascoigne, Alistair Davidson, Kenneth Garside, Ian Keith, Annette Prevost, George Speaight, Duncan Guthrie, Alan Jefferson and Jack Deslandes continued to beaver away year in and year out to achieve our objective.

There are many specialist museums. Every newspaper has its library. There is a Museum of Childhood. The art of war is celebrated at the Imperial War Museum and at numerous Regimental Museums throughout the country. Britain's involvement with the sea is recorded at the Greenwich Maritime Museum. Scientists and inventors are applauded at the Science Museum: airmen and aircraft at the RAF Museums: Natural History at South Kensington and what is the National Gallery but a Museum of painting?

Other nations have produced comparable soldiers, scientists, airmen, painters, sailors and inventors but the one art in which Britain has excelled the world – and excelled it for four hundred years – is the art of Theatre and it is quite astonishing that as a nation we have not built a temple, a central place of reference, a museum (however dusty the word), to glorify the fact. France has three, Germany has several, in Russia each major theatre has one, Denmark has one, Sweden has one, many American universities have one, even Holland, which has practically no theatrical tradition, has one – but Britain had lagged behind.

Our biggest problem was to publicise and lobby an *idea* and to encourage a government to undertake the necessary funding for such a venture. Suddenly our Association needed a new honorary secretary and I proposed that Diana should undertake the job. From that moment all the paperwork was dealt with from our house: subscriptions collected, agendas and minutes circulated and Annual General Meetings arranged.

The BTMA already had a considerable collection of theatricalia centred on the extensive Irving material which Laurence donated 'to the British nation' so our next move was to show to the public and the powers that be what we possessed, and what we still needed to collect. A shop window in fact.

Kensington Borough Council had just opened a new public library in Phillimore Gardens and had vacated the cavernous gallery built some years before in the grounds of Leighton House. With the generous help of Mr Neville Blond, the Coulthurst Trust and later from Lord Delfont, the BTMA were able to lease the gallery, at a nominal rent, from the Council. With colossal cheek we persuaded Sir Hugh Casson – for no fee – to design the interior, which he based on traditional theatre colours; deep plum red, white, gold and the showcases in black. Diana spent many days fast-talking firms like Sandersons (wallpaper) and Strand Electric (lighting) into giving their materials for the good of the cause. We had a band of willing voluntary helpers but it was obvious that we needed a full-time 'curator' and Freda Gaye (then editor of *Who's Who in the Theatre*) was appointed at a derisory salary – but it was all we could afford. On a great day in 1963 Britain's first Theatre Museum was opened to the public on three days a week and was an immediate success. As soon as people saw that we were collecting, material flooded in and we had to rent storerooms in which to keep it. A certain number of things slipped through our net. The actual lighting plots for many of Irving's plays at the Lyceum Theatre were offered for sale. For the whole period before 1900 no others are known to exist and with them it would be possible to reproduce the illumination of an entire production of the nineteenth century and to understand the conditions and the advantages or disadvantages of Victorian lighting. But we had no funds for purchases and they were sold to America.

In the past so much of our theatrical heritage has gone to the United States. I suppose we should be grateful that the material is being preserved but when we think, for instance, of the first edition of Shakespeare's plays where every single copy is different, we are hard pushed to find ten copies remaining in this country while in just one American library – the Folger in Washington – there are seventy-two.

However, exciting things came our way: we received a letter from a gentleman in Kent who, in his retirement, used to accompany his great friend – a surveyor – on his various professional trips. A large detached house had been demolished and, while his friend measured up the two-acre site, he was wandering around the one-time beautiful, now derelict, garden when something caught his eye beneath a large overgrown shrub . . . He pulled out a plaster bust of a lady, covered in grime, took it home and, putting it in his kitchen sink, began to scrub it. Turning it over he discovered that a large hole at the base led up into the hollow head . . . Having removed the caked mud, his hand clutched some papers, in amazingly good condition: one stated that the bust was a self-portrait of Mrs Siddons (who was known to be a good modeller), another accompanied the bust as a gift to her niece and the others followed its chequered history – but none connected it with the last owner of the house. The Kentish man had read of the BTMA and kindly gave us the bust – and the letters. But for him, that unique head of one of our greatest actresses would have been bulldozed into the ground.

The public and scholars flocked to our embryonic museum. Jennifer Aylmer as curator, and Jean Scott-Rogers as administrator, joined our staff, but we became the victims of our own success: as we continued to lobby government for a state-run Theatre Museum we met with the riposte, 'Why do you want us to provide a museum? You have a successful one already!'

The whole saga would fill volumes but I will be as brief as I can. Laurence Irving was succeeded as chairman by Lord Norwich and later I took over and it was during this period that, wearing another of my hats, I attended as president the Annual Conference of the Federation of Playgoers Societies, held that year in Lincoln. Our guest of honour was the Minister for the Arts, Lord Eccles, who was there with his wife Sybil: Diana and I got on rather well with them and a week later received an invitation to dinner. Unashamedly I cornered him on the subject of the Theatre Museum and found him unexpectedly enthusiastic, a firm advocate of 'specialist' museums, and he arranged for me to meet Lord Goodman, then chairman of the Arts Council, to work out the possibilities.

It might confuse the narrative to tell you that other, much newer, groups were seeking government money for vaguely similar undertakings. One group of wealthy businessmen had purchased at auction some items, not strictly of British interest, connected with the Diaghilev Ballet for which they sought an official depository.

I was briefed by my committee and set off to meet Goodman at the Arts Council offices in Piccadilly at four fifteen. Our entire future rested on this meeting. While I waited, four fifteen came and went. At four thirty-five I was met by a secretary and escorted up the stairs to the panelled sanctum. Several people were coming out, some of whom I knew; we exchanged pleasantries and then I saw the massive bulk of Goodman rising behind his desk. He motioned me to sit facing him and subsided into his chair, shoulders hunched, and said, 'Yes – now tell me . . .'

I suddenly felt fourteen and facing my headmaster: I knew all the facts but I had not thought of an opening sentence. However, I launched into my brief but I had not really got under way before the telephone rang – he picked it up. 'Goodman. Yes. Yes. Oh. Yes.'

Politely, I stopped speaking but he put a hand over the mouth-piece and said, 'No – no – carry on . . .' I changed into first gear and continued as best I could. He put down the receiver and pressed a button on the desk while peering intently at my face. A secretary entered and was told, 'Call So and So and tell them that the meeting for next Thursday etc, etc,' and turning to me, 'Continue.' I gathered speed: he was obviously not remotely interested so I might just as well get it over and get out. Again the telephone rang, again he answered it, again he gestured for me to continue and again he pressed the button for the secretary.

While I recounted the past activities of the BTMA, what our hopes were, stressed the need for a museum and outlined how and where government help was required, Goodman answered four telephone calls and three times the secretary was sent for. I was dejected. Fifteen years of dedication were left in tatters on the floor of that panelled room. I was drained, and dripped to a close. He had been studying a paper on the desk and as I finished he looked up. '. . . and that is your case?'

'Yes.'

He pressed the button and in came the secretary. 'Take this letter to Mr Sinden – Chairman, British Theatre Museum Association . . .' He dictated two whole pages in detailed reply to every point I had outlined! And he was on our side!

Others have told me subsequently that Goodman is quite capable of coping with not only two but three or more things at the same time. What a man! I realised how small my own life was.

Lord Eccles then made a brilliant move.

The Victoria and Albert Museum already housed a famous collection of theatrical ephemera – letters, programme designs, playbills, bequeathed to them by Mrs Gabrielle Enthoven – but it was tucked away in an attic, and although consulted by scholars, only a fraction was ever seen by the public. The V & A already had several outlying collections under their 'umbrella' at sub-stations such as the Wellington Museum at Apsley House, the Museum of Childhood at Bethnal Green, Ham House at Richmond, and Osterley Park at Brentford.

Only a minister of the government could bring together our two great theatre collections and house them under one roof.

I was next sent by Lord Eccles to meet the director of the V & A, Sir John Pope-Hennessy. Apparently austere, severe, ascetic, and very shy, this great scholar later revealed a charm and idiosyncratic wit for which I was completely unprepared. I discovered him strongly in favour of the amalgamation – although I was never quite sure if it was only because he badly needed the space in the attics of the museum.

A new committee would need to be formed to be called – in accordance with long-established V & A usage – an Advisory Council, with me as chairman, and we discussed the names of various possible Council members. He warned me that as other groups were in danger of rocking the boat – indeed it could even now founder – it would be far better to incorporate them at this early stage by giving them representation on the Council. Thus all the major collections – bar one – were brought together and we were lumbered with a lot of Russian Ballet material.

Coincidentally the Registers of Births, Marriages and Deaths were then in the process of being moved to new premises at St Catherine's House and leaving the fine rooms at the state-owned Somerset House in the Strand empty. The beautiful panelled rooms with their painted ceilings and carved chimney-pieces had been designed in the eighteenth century by Sir William Chambers specifically as a home for the Royal Academy who remained there until moving to Piccadilly and we – the new Theatre Museum – were now offered them. We accepted with alacrity although they were by no means ideal: the terms of our proposed lease with the Department of the Environment forbade us to obstruct the view of the ceilings or fireplaces, no showcases were to be fixed to the walls and, worst of all, no daylight must be obscured from the windows. Theatrical items are transformed by the magic of artificial light but look quite awful by daylight. But 'a bird in the hand . . .'

We appointed a full-time curator – Alexander Schouvaloff –
for the museum and then sat back and waited for the necessary
money for the move while battle raged between other groups who
had hoped to move into Somerset House.

At about this time Brian Batsford, who was then the Member
of Parliament for Ealing South, gave a dinner party for several
influential people who we hoped would promote the idea of the
museum using the rooms at Somerset House. Everyone was most
enthusiastic, including John Betjeman, who appeared delighted by
the prospect. We were therefore somewhat surprised and hurt a
week or so later when a letter appeared in *The Times*, signed by,
among others, Betjeman, suggesting that the rooms should be
used for the paintings of Turner. I wrote him the following
doggerel – poetic licence applied for – entitled 'The Renegade'.

To dine one night at Norfolk Road
(The House adorned with Early Coade)
On bread and cheese, with mead and bloater
He comes complete in Smithfield boater.

On Architecture we converse;
Cyma Recta: Cyma Reverse.
The London Phil and André Previn:
The Garrick too and Bernard Levin.

The theatre then is to the fore
All gossip, glamour; Folk and Lore
And Brian Batsford then proposes
With Betjeman 'Yeas' and nodding noses –

'Museum of the British Theatre
To celebrate Dramatic Arts' –
Designers, Writers and the Mimes
Preserved for Nation and all times

The Government it seems agreed
To open for the Public's need
The House of Somerset in Strand –
What better use than motley band!'

Ere yet the guilt – self-righteous years
Had left the flushing in 's galled 'Ayes',
He tarried: And then penned to *Times*
'Let Paintings in but not the Mimes'!

Sometime later we were offered alternative premises – the recently vacated Flower Market in the Covent Garden piazza – much larger and much better suited to our needs: 42,000 square feet and most of it without daylight. Lord Goodman telephoned me excitedly. 'Good news, yes, good news; but don't give up Somerset House until you have a signed lease for Covent Garden!' We should have taken his advice. By not doing so we were set back five years because the recession caused the government to delay the granting of money for a new project while they had already committed themselves to Somerset House.

There were bureaucratic delays – the Theatre Museum, through the V & A funded by the Department of Education and Science, would be allocated occupancy of a building on the basis of a lease negotiated by the Department of the Environment from the freeholders, the Greater London Council and countersigned by the Minister for the Arts. How's that for bureaucracy! During these delays the ground floor of the building was designated a Transport Museum in which it was intended to install trains and buses. But would the floor be strong enough to take the weight? By measuring they deduced the floor was twelve inches thick but what was it made of? With a special drill they bored through the floor at several selected points and from the 'filling' of the drill they found which materials had been used. They decided that it could never take the proposed weight. Steel supports, agreed to by the GLC, would be required and erected in *our* basement area!

The Transport Museum premises had an iron and glass roof and brick walls much in need of cleaning. The method used for this was to blast sand and water at it (I'm sure you've seen it done on the exteriors of buildings) but the water found its lowest level – straight through the holes in the floor and into our basement! The Department of the Environment understandably refused to sign a lease for premises filled with water seven feet deep. Even when it was drained the brick walls remained damp for many months and by the time it was completely dry the nation was suffering another recession.

Meanwhile my own collection was growing. It is important to be sure of the provenance of particular pieces. Sometimes they come with an impeccable pedigree: when that splendid actress, beautiful lady and Grande Dame of the British theatre, Marie Löhr, came to our house for the first time she presented me with a long narrow box . . .

'I thought you should have that – it is the fan I used when I played Lady Teazle opposite Beerbohm Tree in 1909.'

Indeed it was beautiful; of painted silk and pierced ivory staves. I had it framed and proudly hung it on the wall.

Some ten years later I hosted a dinner-party given at the Garrick Club in honour of Marie Löhr and during her charming speech she pulled from under her chair a long narrow box saying, 'I would like to give this to Donald – it is the fan I used when I played Lady Teazle opposite Beerbohm Tree in 1909.'

It was indeed beautiful; of painted silk and pierced ivory staves. I had it framed and it made a perfect pair with the first one. Of course it is quite possible for a Lady Teazle to use more than one fan during the course of a performance. When she died aged eighty-four in 1975 I joined her many friends at her memorial service at the Actors' Church, St Paul's, Covent Garden. Sir John Clements, who had been a neighbour of Marie's in Brighton, gave a most moving and loving address. He spoke of her outstanding contribution to the theatre and enumerated her notable performances. He finished by saying, '. . . and I shall always cherish a very special present she gave me – the fan she had used when she played Lady Teazle opposite Beerbohm Tree in 1909.'

Over the years Ministers for the Arts came and went, each one loudly in support of a Theatre Museum, but time and again the financial climate prevented the immediate allocation of government funds. At each delay the whole theatrical profession protested and London's newspaper, the *Evening Standard*, led the media in support of the scheme. At long, long, last – twenty-six years after Laurence Irving's opening letter – the lease was signed by Lord Gowrie and, as I write this, clouds of dust are spewing into Covent Garden as the builders begin their pre-building work.

But alas, when it opens, the silver shaving mug that Henry Irving gave to Squire Bancroft, Irving's own silver inkwell, the silver loving cup given to J. L. Toole by the Prince of Wales, Madge Kendal's bracelet, the armlets worn by Edmund Kean and passed on to Charles Kean, Henry Irving, Seymour Hicks, Roger Maxwell, and several other small silver theatrical items that I was holding in trust, will never be seen there. Our house was burgled in 1979.

I doubt if Diana and I will ever recover from the loss and the shock.

19

WHAT YOU WILL

I really shouldn't have bothered you with all that stuff about the Theatre Museum. It has become so much a part of my life that I imagine others will care just as passionately as I. Actually if you are still reading this you probably do care – and if you don't, well you jolly well ought to!

Before I started on the museum I was telling you about *Not Now Darling* for which I had signed a contract with impresario Michael Codron for a year and this was drawing to a close, although the play was still running to packed houses at the Strand Theatre. Michael asked me to stay on for a second year but as with *There's a Girl in my Soup* I was beginning to feel that staleness was taking over and it was time for me to move on – but to what? This time John Barton came to my rescue: he was to direct *Twelfth Night* for the 1969 season at Stratford-upon-Avon and would I like to play Malvolio? I had not seen the play since I played Sebastian in the 1948 Old Vic production. I reread it as fast as I could. Surely this was not the play I thought I knew? Strangely troubled, I telephoned John: 'I think you may have to cast someone else. I have just read the play and I don't find Malvolio a very funny character – in fact at times I find him tragic.'

'Oh, thank God,' said John, 'I was afraid I might have to talk you into that aspect of his character – so when can you start?'

Having completed 416 performances of *Not Now Darling* I left my part in the hands of Derek Farr and prepared to set off for Stratford, but before I had packed a suitcase another call came, this time from Trevor Nunn: would I also play Henry VIII which he was to direct in the same season? I was to have two wonderful leading ladies: Judi Dench as Cesario/Viola in *Twelfth Night* and Peggy Ashcroft as Henry's wife Queen Katharine. What more could I ask?

Before rehearsals began I read the whole of *Twelfth Night* at least ten times, then my own scenes ten times. I do this with all plays.

This is the way I work. Slowly I come to know my adversary, my character. I like at first to behave as devil's advocate and to regard the character objectively. Slowly – and at the RSC we have seven weeks of rehearsals, an advantage over the usual four in the West End – I hammer myself into the character until by the time the play opens I can step in and out of his shoes. He and I both use the same last but the laces always need adjusting. In studying him I look for any indications in the text of what anyone says or thinks about him and I try to analyse and understand his attitudes to given circumstances – especially his attitude to circumstances outside those in the play.

I have read, marked, learned but not necessarily digested most books on the theory of acting but subscribe to no particular method. I try to judge my own performances on a tenet of Ellen Terry's.

'To act you must make the thing written your own: you must steal the words; steal the thoughts; and convey the stolen treasure to others with great art.'

And the last three words are the most difficult!

Bill Fraser

D.S.

Barrie Ingham

So what kind of man was Malvolio? I saw him as a military man. Unpopular at school (a tell-tale?), he joined the Army and gradually rose in rank – he was so efficient, the authorities had no alternative but to advance him although he possessed no qualities of leadership. At the age of forty-five he found himself a Colonel in something like the Pay Corps with no prospect of further promotion: in a word he was embittered. He was unmarried – he bored every woman he met and none of them could have existed as a wife under his rigid discipline: the kitchen would have been inspected each morning at 08.17 hours precisely. Born a Roman Catholic and still secretly practising in a Protestant world, he was looking for a job. The only man who in any way appreciated his qualities was a certain Count with an estate on the island of Illyria who at that moment required a major-domo to manage it for him: who better than this totally efficient, totally honest, teetotaller?

I like to think that the Count had married an Englishwoman who has a brother, Sir Toby Belch. This would explain his very English knighthood. Sir Toby, his friend Sir Andrew Aguecheek, and an aged priest Sir Topas, formed part of a group of layabouts sponging off the Count. The others included his daughter's governess (for so Maria appeared in John Barton's production, aged fifty) and a fool by the name of Feste who in several abortive attempts has failed to raise a laugh from Malvolio. (Who could?)

No sooner had Malvolio taken control, reduced salaries and emoluments, evicted tenants who were in arrears and made himself indispensable, than the Count died leaving everything to his son and daughter and within a very short time the son, too, was dead. The daughter, Olivia, was in complete charge and being wooed by all and sundry – what would she do without Malvolio?

And so the play begins.

As I rehearsed, my muscles began to react to the tensions within Malvolio. The 'military' years had left their mark, an erect stance nearly always 'At Attention' and when 'At Ease' never fully relaxed. Originally I had wanted to carry a short swagger-stick but as this would have evoked quite the wrong period I settled for a long staff-of-office. Malvolio, however, always felt it an encumbrance – if only he had a third hand he could have used it elegantly. My face began to assume the mask of Malvolio whose mouth was small, tight and mean, the corners turning down. The inner ends of his eyebrows were elevated and the outer pulled down in an expression of permanent supercilious scorn for his inferiors – more vertical lines than horizontal.

Even if the audience thinks that I always look the same in every play, I convince myself that I always look different and I spend a great deal of time observing my fellow-men trying to find copy for my characters. I have frequently found my 'face' in an art gallery and on this occasion I recalled a visit to the Tate. Back I went and, sure enough, there was my Malvolio in Graham Sutherland's splendid elongated portrait of Somerset Maugham. There were the vertical lines of eyebrows, mouth and wrinkles; the knees frozen together; the hair very thin on top but grown long in a mistaken attempt to cover the pate. (How often have I seen men allow thirty-seven hairs to keep growing on one side of their head and comb them across to the other side, deceiving only themselves. I have even seen one man who, to give himself a quiff, grew them at the back of his head and combed them forward over a wad of brown cotton-wool. I would love to have seen him in a high wind.) But the most important thing about Sutherland's portrait was the colour. Yellow! What a stunning idea! Malvolio would be jaundiced. Armed with a postcard reproduction of the painting I had the model for my make-up.

Now for my costume. I wanted to appear as thin as possible. The designer, who had set this production around the year 1603, agreed that I should be dressed in black. Black high-heeled shoes, black stockings, black breeches, black doublet with tight sleeves and narrow shoulders. We looked at hats of the period and I chose one like a black inverted flowerpot. A black overcoat with a large raised collar continued the line of the silhouette from the hat down to the hips. A chain-of-office was made for me; a thin chain with a large circular disc. This of course could run across the chest from shoulder to shoulder but I chose to wear it just around the neck and down – as nearly vertical as possible.

Somerset Maugham's hairstyle was copied for my wig: the bald dome was padded to give it a high egg-shape with long straight hair, just curled under at the ends, surrounding it and thirty-seven hairs combed across the top.

Next I had to establish my relationship with the audience. I have always been surprised how few actors bother about this. If I am to be Malvolio living and breathing the air of Illyria in 1603 and totally involved in events of that time and place, who to Malvolio are those thousand or so people who happen, because of fractured time, to be sitting in a theatre at Stratford-upon-Avon in 1969? Chekhov, Brecht and others have concerned themselves with audience involvement, but to an actor the question is still relevant, especially in a play in which an actor is supposed to speak directly to an audience in a soliloquy. The audience does not disappear the moment the actor resumes his dialogue with other actors. Nowadays, when a television audience can make the tea, put the child to bed, and let the dog out during a play over which the author and actors have sweated blood, I feel that the theatre must offer a valid alternative where the audience is fully involved. The actor must reach out and make that particular audience know that, but for them, that particular performance could never have taken place. It was different yesterday and will be different tomorrow.

So, back to my question: who are those people sitting in the auditorium? To each individual actor they may be quite different, but they must be people who live in the period in which the play is set and breathe the same air as the characters in that play. Each actor will imagine them differently, but for me as Malvolio they became inhabitants of Illyria and as the aristocracy of the island are all involved in the play they would therefore be shopkeepers, fishermen and farm-workers. All are Malvolio's social inferiors who can be expected to be envious and impressed by his elation and, to his acute embarrassment, glory in his come-uppance. I must let the audience know as soon as possible that they are allowed, even expected, to laugh at his predicament, but there I encountered problems with his first scene.

Referring to Feste, Olivia asks, 'What think you of this fool, Malvolio – doth he not mend?' to which Malvolio answers, 'Yes; and shall do, till the pangs of death shake him: infirmity, that decays the wise, doth ever make the better fool.' Not exactly a funny line. Indeed it is quite scathing. How can the audience be expected to laugh at him? I worked away at it until I perfected a way of pronouncing the 'Yes' nasally and making it sound like 'Nnyess' thus getting a laugh on my very first word.

Which reminds me that when I was writing *A Touch of the Memoirs* I received a telephone call from the late Ralph Richardson: 'Hello cocky – I hear you're writing a book about yourself and the acting. Don't tell them how it's done.' Sorry, Ralph; you were probably right.

At the end of that first scene Olivia orders Malvolio to 'Run after that same peevish messenger.' Malvolio would be shocked by this – he has never run anywhere – so I interjected the word 'Run?' which resulted in a very big laugh, but as that extra word did not appear in the text, John Barton strongly disapproved and asked me to leave it out on first nights or when fellow-scholars were known to be in front. On these occasions John allowed me to mouth the word run. The difference was a titter instead of a belly laugh. We had a similar disagreement in the so-called drinking scene where Sir Toby Belch, Sir Andrew Aguecheek, Feste and

Maria are interrupted in their midnight revelry by Malvolio. On the assumption that Malvolio has been awakened from his sleep by the drunken voices he would leap from his bed wearing his nightgown, put on whatever was to hand and go down to stop the row. So what would he put on? His slippers, a coat, his chain-of-office to prove his authority and something to cover his balding head – but what? Most Malvolios wear a nightcap, but I chose my black inverted flowerpot which again received a huge laugh on my entrance because of its incongruity. Again John disapproved. He argued that it was just an easy laugh and made the same stipulations.

Judi Dench as Cesario/Viola wove her magic spell and each night I listened entranced as she told Olivia that she would 'Make me a willow cabin at your gate, And call upon my soul within the house.' She never needed the advice I heard given to an actress many years before when the director stopped a rehearsal crying, 'No, no, no. The willow cabin is a figment of her imagination – a castle in the air. Yours is being built with tree-trunks and six-inch nails.'

Every time I work on a play by Shakespeare I discover new textual niceties. At the beginning of the 'letter' scene Maria tells Belch, Aguecheek and Fabian: 'Get ye all three into the box-tree . . .' so this would imply that there is either a box-tree or hedge on the stage. At the time the play was written the stage had a central inner stage that could be curtained off and an enclosed balcony above it, so what more likely than that a few leafy branches were hung around the upper part and Maria would get a gratuitous laugh by pointedly saying, 'Get ye all three into the *box* . . . tree.'

This great scene also contains what is probably the earliest example of a strange theatrical phenomenon. As we know a soliloquy is a speech in which the audience alone is privileged to hear a character's innermost thoughts, but in the 'letter' scene Malvolio's soliloquy is also overheard by *other characters on the stage*. Malvolio discovers a sealed letter which he believes is intended for him, and reads aloud the words on the outside: '*To the unknown beloved, this and my good wishes*: her very phrases! By your leave, wax. Soft! . . . 'tis my lady. To whom should this be?' He breaks open the letter and reveals the contents to the audience, with Toby, Andrew and Fabian commenting on all the details.

I decided to have some private fun with this line and at the same time increase my bargaining power with John Barton. (In the days of stiff censorship in the theatre, even fairly innocuous words like 'bloody' or 'damn' might be cut by the Lord Chamberlain's office so playwrights would often insert several much stronger four-letter words into the particular script that was sent to the Lord Chamberlain who, predictably, would be horrified and insist on their removal before the play could be performed. The author could then bargain with him and finally settle for taking out the four-letter words on condition that the odd 'bloody' or 'damn' could remain in.) So, during rehearsal, after saying 'By your leave,' I broke off a small piece of the seal, placed it in my mouth and after chewing it for some seconds, I spat it out and announced disgustedly, 'Wax!' As I expected, John thought this was going too far, so, at the next rehearsal, I wickedly went one step further. During the preceding words I screwed my little finger into my ear, pulled it out, peered at the tip and announced, 'Wax – soft!' It is no credit to me that John really thought I meant to do just that in performance. What I did in the end was to touch the wax and declare it 'soft' – therefore only recently sealed.

This scene, which is almost a soliloquy, lasts about twenty minutes and in performance I was exhausted by the end of it. The euphoria, the ecstasy, the excitement, the ebullition, the exhilaration, the intoxication, the effervescence, had to be carefully modulated; rising, falling, rising again, falling again, up and up until it reaches fever pitch. No play that I have done before or since (including *King Lear*) contained any scene that so drained me. I thanked God and John Barton that the interval followed and I had a short rest before changing costumes for the 'cross-gartered' scene. Our designer had discovered that cross-gartering actually meant having a garter hand-tied round the leg below the knee, crossed behind the knee and round the leg again just above the knee. The first time, I tied them so tightly that they became tourniquets – I could hardly walk. I never did again, but I enlarged on the idea and hobbled in pretended pain throughout the scene.

Shakespeare does not prepare his audience for the hideously cruel scene that follows and we have to remember that, at the time the play was written, bull and bear baiting were common sports; the populace flocked to public executions; for minor offences there was the degradation of the stocks (it was a long time before I realised that the pilloried man had to perform all the normal bodily functions in full view of a jeering mob); and the insane were there to be viewed and laughed at.

On the pretext that he is mad, Sir Toby, Maria and Feste imprison Malvolio in a sort of septic tank under the stage covered by a small trapdoor. When this is lifted an iron grille still covers the eight-foot-deep hole. Only by hanging on the bars and pulling himself up can Malvolio force his head through the grille as they torture him mentally and physically. I am convinced that this scene finally unhinges Malvolio who has never been a very stable character. He is to make one final appearance after being released and, significantly, this very prosaic man speaks in verse for the first time after speaking prose for all the rest of the play. The floodgates are open and in verse he can rise to greater heights of passion. He ends by saying, 'I'll be revenged on the whole pack of you,' but it is an empty phrase – he has no means of being revenged on anyone. There is only one way out. Suicide.

With Judi Dench as Cesario/Viola, Emrys James as Feste, Lisa Harrow as Olivia, Bill Fraser as Sir Toby, Barrie Ingham as Aguecheek and Elizabeth Spriggs as Maria, John Barton's autumnal production was an instant success.

The great joy of Shakespeare is that however well you think you know the play there are always fresh delights to encounter. In this production I heard, as if for the first time, lines spoken by Orsino which I now place high on any list of favourites.

> O, fellow! come, the song we had last night.
> Mark it, Cesario; it is old and plain;
> The spinners and the knitters in the sun,
> And the free maids that weave their thread with bones,
> Do use to chant it: it is silly sooth,
> And dallies with the innocence of love,
> Like the old age.

Please do me the favour of saying aloud those words 'the spinners and the knitters in the sun' and feel those recurring 'ns' resonating in the nose. And then listen to 'Do use to chant it' instead of *used* to chant it. Then think about '. . . dallies with the innocence of love, like the old age.'

It is with familiarity that one learns to love Shakespeare.

With Malvolio under my belt I could now start on Henry the Eighth.

20

ALL IS TRUE

Richard Pasco

Henry the Eighth is a bloody awful part.

'I come no more to make you laugh . . .' That is the rather ominous first line of Shakespeare's *Henry VIII* and it pretty well holds good for the rest of the play. Indeed there is hardly a laugh in it, which distresses me as an actor as I enjoy getting laughs. The scholars, who should know about these things, tell us that *Henry VIII* was not the unaided work of Shakespeare but was written in collaboration with a young playwright named John Fletcher. Sometimes these scholars are right, and, having spent a year of my life playing the part of Henry, I find myself agreeing with them wholeheartedly.

Let me tell you my own theory about the authorship of the play. At some time during the middle of his playwriting years, Shakespeare first conceived the idea of a play about the father of Queen Elizabeth the First. Possibly in 1597, which would have been the fifteenth anniversary of Henry's death. Having mapped out his original plan, he found himself in trouble. In all honesty, and he was a playwright who could never be dishonest, he would have to show Henry the Eighth as the ogre and tyrant that he undoubtedly was. This would not have been exactly wise with his daughter Elizabeth still on the throne and herself noted for wielding a pretty bloody axe. But, having done considerable research on the subject, Shakespeare was loth to waste it. What if he were to concentrate on the early years of Henry's reign when Cardinal Wolsey was his Chancellor? What a splendid, colourful character he would be! Henry could be shown as the David who overthrew this Goliath. He could show Wolsey's rather than Henry's fall from grace. Henry's first wife Katharine could be the villain of the piece as well. The audience would sympathise with Henry over the divorce. The young, beautiful and innocent Anne Boleyn could be Shakespeare's heroine because she finally gave birth to, guess who? – Elizabeth, Our Elizabeth, Good Queen Bess. There was, however, no getting away from the fact that Henry the Eighth was the villain. The audience could not be expected to forget that he had chopped off the head of Elizabeth's mum, and possibly the heads of their own parents as well. He had no alternative but to drop the idea. If he offended the Queen and the Court, he and his colleagues would be out of work or, worse still, in the Tower. So Shakespeare put all the relevant speeches he had drafted into his desk and set about writing something less contentious.

The years rolled by and Shakespeare entered the mature years of his playwriting. *Twelfth Night* and *Hamlet* fell from his pen. Queen Elizabeth died in 1603 and James I became King. Merrie England was a thing of the past and Shakespeare set to work on the great tragedies of *Othello*, *Measure for Measure*, *King Lear*, *Macbeth* and *Antony and Cleopatra*. His last play, his swan-song, *The Tempest*, was produced in 1611 and from then on he could enjoy retirement in Stratford-upon-Avon. His place as resident playwright to the King's Men had been taken by a young fellow called John Fletcher who, while clearing out his predecessor's desk, came across a bundle of notes on the subject of Henry the Eighth. He wrote to the grand old man at Stratford and asked if he could please make use of the notes. 'Of course you can, my boy,' replied

Shakespeare. 'You'll find it a very difficult task. Take my advice and make all the speeches ambiguous and call the play *All Is True*. If you need my help just let me know. I enclose two or three speeches you can use, one for Buckingham, several for Wolsey and Katharine. Good luck, and for heaven's sake don't put my name on the playbills. Yours, W.S.'

Well that, as I said, is my own theory. However, the play, under its title of *Henry VIII* first appeared in print as being the work of William Shakespeare in the collected edition of his works edited by John Heminge and Henry Condell in 1623. Poor Fletcher doesn't get a mention.

The play is rarely produced today because of the enormous cost involved. The cast list is the longest of any play by Shakespeare. There are scenes of magnificent pageantry: a great ball given by Wolsey, an enormous courtroom scene, a splendid coronation procession for Anne Boleyn, the dancers who appear to Katharine in a vision and, finally, the impressive baptism ceremony for the infant Elizabeth. Just think of the costumes! The Court of Henry the Eighth did not stint themselves, so when the play is presented today it must look sumptuous. Wolsey is the only character who can get away with only one costume. It would be a cardinal error to dress him in anything but red.

So why bother to do the play? Well, it contains two rewarding parts, Queen Katharine and Cardinal Wolsey, and over the centuries leading actors and actresses have wanted to play them (in our production they were played by Peggy Ashcroft and Brewster Mason). The part of Buckingham is pretty good too, but the part of Henry is a stinker! He is one of those few historical characters whose appearance is known to every man in the street. More than any other monarch, with the possible exception of Queen Victoria, everybody has a preconceived idea of what Henry looked like because of those endless reproductions of Holbein's portrait. There he stands, this great bulk of a man, his feet astride, hands on hips, with vast, hunched shoulders. All the poor actor can do is try to look like that portrait and therein lies the problem. Whereas he is quite safe with Richard II, Henry IV, Henry V and Henry VI, because nobody knows what they looked like, if you don't look like Holbein's Henry, the public think you have failed. I found this to my cost when I played the part.

By measuring the inside of Henry's armour which stands in the Tower of London, we know that he was six foot three inches tall. Very few actors are that tall. (I am six foot.) Then comes the costume – calamity! If you make a study of the human anatomy, you will discover that the distance between the knee and the ground is one quarter of the overall height of a man. Holbein has cheated! In trying to make Henry's vast bulk look in proportion, he has made the distance a *third* of Henry's height! Now no actor will undergo a bone graft, especially not for a part as poor as Henry, so when he dons the skirt-like lower part of the costume his shin-bone is too short and again it appears to be the fault of the actor. In the portrait, Henry's calves are at least six inches in diameter. Well, that at least is easy enough to overcome, so on go enormous padded calves. To underline Henry's virility, Holbein shows a massive codpiece protruding from a split in the skirt. The wardrobe made me one of equal size but at each move the skirt covered it up. Painter's licence I suppose. Then comes the problem of the hat. The one in the portrait is totally two-dimensional. The moment an attempt is made to reproduce it 'in the round' it looks quite wrong unless the actor faces front the whole time. Then on go great padded shoulders and the cloak with enormous sleeves which covers the dagger on the belt, unless the actor keeps his hand on it all the time.

What can one do about the face? I wore a padded wig glued to my forehead to make my head look larger. My own eyebrows were obliterated and false ones stuck in their place. I had a false nose glued on and a moustache and beard were gummed into position. There was Henry's face but where was mine? There I stood, gummed up, stuck up, glued up, padded up, fed up and encased in a costume weighing a ton. I looked stupid and had no freedom to add much of myself to the character.

The important scenes of the play concern the fall of Buckingham, the greatest man in the kingdom, the meeting between Henry and Anne Boleyn, Henry's divorce from Katharine of Aragon to whom he had been married for twenty years, the fall of Cardinal Wolsey whose ambition has overreached itself, the death of Katharine and, finally, the birth of a daughter, Elizabeth, to Anne. Now remember that *All Is True* is the alternative title of the play. But, if you study history, you will find that practically everything shown or talked about in the play is only a veneer of the truth.

The divorce scene is really the centre-piece, so one needs to understand the historical background. Katharine of Aragon had been married as a child to Henry's elder brother, Arthur, when he was also a child. She had always maintained that the marriage was never consummated and when Arthur died, still a child, she was allowed by the Pope to marry his brother Henry, now heir to the throne. During their twenty years of marriage, Katharine produced many children, all of whom either died at birth, or shortly after, except for one daughter, Mary, who thus became heir to the throne. It grieved Henry that he had no son to carry on his line so, when he fell hat over codpiece for Anne Boleyn, he was determined to get rid of Katharine and marry Anne. But how to do it? The Roman Catholic Church did not countenance divorce. Perhaps an annulment, on the grounds that his entire marriage to Katharine was illegal because he should never have been allowed to marry his brother's wife, would be acceptable? It all hinged on two quotations from the Bible, one from Leviticus and the other from Deuteronomy. One maintains that a marriage is a marriage once you have 'taken a wife' whilst the other maintains that a marriage is only a marriage once it is consummated. Ecclesiastics from all over the world argued about that. Henry of course took the side that would suit him best, but the Pope took the other. It was a very difficult situation for Wolsey. As a Catholic who did not want to act against his King, he was caught between King and Pope. Luckily for Henry, all this occurred at the time when the Reformation was gaining ground in Europe. Henry jumped on the bandwagon, made himself head of the Church in England and granted his own divorce.

In the play the divorce scene takes place in and around a consistory court, staged in a sort of fenced-in area in the centre of a large room. Katharine is ordered several times to 'come into the court'. She refuses to acknowledge the court's authority and will not enter because there she would have been under oath. If Henry were to win, their daughter, Mary, would be branded illegitimate. She kneels before the King and makes a long, magnificent and impassioned plea.

Throughout the scene Shakespeare, brilliant as ever, does not allow Henry to speak one word to her. He has been married to her for twenty years but what could he say? Her argument is unanswerable. If he dared to join in, his cause would be lost, so it is better to keep his mouth shut. If he were even to look at her and see her tears, compassion would get the better of him. It is far safer to turn his head away and try not to look or listen. He remains silent until, when Katharine makes her exit, Henry speaks for the first time and shouts after her: 'Go thy ways, Kate.'

That half-line raises an interesting point of how Shakespearean verse should be spoken. We work on a principle at Stratford-upon-

Avon that one should not pause during, but only at the end of
a line. With the major part of Shakespeare written in iambic
pentameters — a beat of five feet to the line — one should keep that
stress going throughout each line. If a full stop is in the middle of
the line, one can break the line, but not stop. The last words of
Katharine's speech are:

> Upon this business my appearance make
> In any of their courts.

HENRY: Go thy ways, Kate.

There must be no pause between her half-line and Henry's. After
he has said 'Kate' he can pause, for an hour if he likes, but before
that he must keep the rhythm going. He's got to slap in his half-line
immediately after Kate's speech. He then embarks upon a very
long, very dreary speech — obviously pure, unadulterated Fletcher
— in which he tries to excuse himself. He finishes up with the very
clever ruse of saying words to the effect of 'If you can't see my
argument that the marriage was *unlawful*, the onus is on you to
prove that it was *lawful*.'

After that boring speech the play moves on to the glorious scene
of Wolsey's downfall. This man has risen from being the son of
an Ipswich butcher to become the greatest man in the kingdom,
only to be finally disgraced. In magnificent phrases that soar and
swoop like an eagle, Shakespeare brilliantly makes us feel sorry
for the man. It illustrates the very English attitude of not wanting
to kick a man when he is down.

We next see Queen Katharine on her death-bed in a tragic scene
in which she sends her blessing to Henry, who has by now married
Anne Boleyn. After this the play might just as well be over and
everybody might just as well go home. The fireworks have all
fizzled out. In what follows it is up to the actor playing Henry to
try to keep the play alive for the next half-hour. Nothing happens
of any real interest until Cranmer introduces the infant Elizabeth
and prophesies what a wonderful reign she will have. (If you were
in — yes; if you were not — no.) All is true? Again we are left with
the question-mark. The play finishes with an epilogue which
begins, ' 'Tis ten to one this play can never please/All that are here.'
Between them Shakespeare and Fletcher had skated over some
very thin ice.

At the end of the play, in Trevor Nunn's production, the
assembled characters sang a magnificent 'Gloria' beautifully set to
music composed by Guy Woolfenden and then left the stage in a

stately procession. Only Henry remained in a spotlight, holding the infant Elizabeth who has just been christened. Here I tried to do a most difficult thing. The end of the play is a cry for peace in the time of the future Queen Elizabeth (the First) and in a few brief seconds I, as Henry with no lines, looked into the future, saw the horror that was to come, questioned why, realised the failure of the hope, crashed into the twentieth century and pleaded silently that where the sixteenth century had failed those of the future may succeed.

Many people told me that it was a most moving moment.

I can't say I enjoyed the part except for certain scenes – and, of course, rehearsals. It was wonderful to be working with Peggy Ashcroft again. Unfortunately she had injured her knee and to assist her in the great trial scene, when she had to kneel for a long time on the steps of the throne, a section of the step was deceptively replaced with foam rubber. This got over her discomfort but added to mine: when I descended from my throne I was inclined to bounce into the court.

At one rehearsal we had all sweated away at that scene for an entire morning session when Trevor Nunn announced that we could all break for coffee. Twenty young actors of our democratic company who comprised the crowd in the courtroom, made a mad rush for the canteen leaving Queen Katharine, King Henry and Cardinal Wolsey (the three who had been doing all the talking) at the end of the queue. By the time we reached the counter we were called back for the next scene.

As always in the special and exciting way things are done at Stratford, John Barton was helping out on the production. We were working on the scene where Cardinal Wolsey gives a ball in his palace which is interrupted by the arrival of King Henry and his courtiers, in disguise and professing to speak no English.

Wolsey – who of course knows very well that only the King would muck about like that – tells his chamberlain to question them. 'I will, my Lord.' Wolsey in the very next line asks, 'What say they?' Therefore, argued Barton, they must have conversed in a foreign tongue, and he decided to invent a language for them. Our new dialogue went something like this:

CHAMBERLAIN: Dnalgne susrev Ailartsua?
HENRY: Taz Swo! Taz Swo!
CHAMBERLAIN: Ta Lavo?
HENRY: On! Ta Sdrol.

COURTIER:	Taz Swo! Taz Swo!
CHAMBERLAIN:	Tab G'ninepo?
HENRY:	Tuoton. Yrad – Nuob. Rouf Snur.
COURTIERS:	Tuoton! Tuoton!
CHAMBERLAIN:	Revo Fodne?
HENRY:	Sey – Revo Nediam.
COURTIER:	Taz Swo.
CHAMBERLAIN:	Etar Revo?
HENRY:	Neetfif. Ha, Th'guac Dna Delwob!
COURTIER:	Taz Swo! Taz Swo!

and so on. You can see that John is a cricket enthusiast, but you have no idea how difficult it was to learn the terminology in reverse.

After rehearsal one day as Trevor Nunn and I walked through the theatre gardens towards the church I asked, 'How do you think it's coming along?'

'All right – but you are still missing something.'

'I know – but what is it?'

'Well, it's not a very helpful thing to say, but you need more – more – more Henry the Eighthness.'

So for the rest of the rehearsal period I spent my days trying to develop my Henry the Eighthness.

Now, for my breakfast I always have a bowl of muesli – in fact I have nine different mueslis and I enjoy the moment of deciding which one it shall be – on which I pour rather too much cream. One morning I filled my bowl from the packet but to my horror found no cream in the fridge. I called out to Diana and she explained that the roundsman had omitted to leave the required order. I have only Diana's words for what happened next. Apparently I bellowed in stentorian tones, 'Kindly see to it that I am not without cream tomorrow!' and strode off to rehearsal. Diana telephoned the manager of the dairy who explained that the regular roundsman was on holiday, he would do his best to see that we had cream tomorrow but he was having problems with the replacement roundsman. He was somewhat stunned when in desperation Diana cried, 'It's all very well for you, but I'm living with Henry the Eighth.'

On 9th October – my forty-sixth birthday – I walked on to the stage for the morning rehearsal and Guy Woolfenden's band struck up 'Happy Birthday' instead of the expected 'Gloria'. This helped to relax our first-night nerves as the play was due to open that very day. Possibly due to my Eighthness exertions, I had developed during the previous ten days a blockage in my eustachian tubes which considerably impaired my hearing – it was the same feeling and pain that I experience when landing in an unpressurised aeroplane – but as I waited in the wings that evening, gummed up, stuck up, glued and padded up, I felt a big glug in my ears and miraculously they cleared just in time for my first entrance. So far so very good but when we came to the trial scene my luck ran out. Peggy knelt at the foot of the steps to my throne and began Katharine's famous speech. Henry's head was turned away to the right, determined not to look at her as he listened and the actor inside his costume marvelled at Peggy's superb performance. On and on she went for eighty or so lines while I remained fixedly glowering away to my right. At the end of her speech Peggy rose from her padded step and swept from the stage to a tumultuous round of applause. I jerked my head round and, almost unheard by the audience, roared after her departing back, 'Go thy ways, Kate!' ready to begin my very long, very boring speech. But the violent movement was too much for the spirit-gum and, with a twang, half of my beard came unstuck . . . I had rehearsed certain movements and gestures all of which had to be forgotten because I was forced to speak sixty-eight intricate lines, and then make an exit, with my arms folded while one hand held the beard to my cheek.

In the audience Diana was sitting near our wig- and-beard-maker Ken ('See a pin and pick it up and all the day you'll have a pin') Lintott, who at the moment of the unsticking rushed from the theatre and wasn't seen again for twenty-four hours. I wished I could have done the same.

21

'SOME OF YOUR LOT'

The Aldwych Theatre as the London base for the Royal Shake-speare Company was now an accepted part of the theatrical scene but in 1969 the company – not for the first or last time – was in serious financial difficulties and we were informed that the expected move from Stratford to London might not take place unless extra revenue were forthcoming. Indeed, if none materialised, we would have to give up our London home altogether.

The company had been invited to Australia to appear at the Adelaide Festival, but the local impresario, who would take over the management, stipulated that it would only be viable if we made it a twelve-week tour by playing in Melbourne before the Festival and in Sydney afterwards. Better and better: in twelve weeks the RSC could make a profit.

The first plan was to take *Twelfth Night* and *Henry VIII*. Peggy Ashcroft, who had never been to the Antipodes, was very excited by the prospect but unfortunately for her it was decided that *Henry* was too cumbersome a production to tour, so *The Winter's Tale* was chosen instead – which was good for me because I would not therefore be required to work every night and, as Diana was to come with me, we could spend our free time seeing something of the country. We all packed up at Stratford and flew off eagerly but apprehensively: it was imperative that the tour was a success: we might – might – retrieve the Aldwych season.

Diana and I grew to love Australia – the country and its people – but our arrival there could hardly have been more miserable. Aeroplanes were not allowed to land in Melbourne after a certain time at night so we had to land in Sydney and stay there overnight before continuing our journey the next day. At the airport the customs officials took a dim view of our young actors who, in the fashion of the Sixties, had very long hair and were wearing tee-shirts and multi-coloured jeans. Everyone's luggage was ransacked – all to no avail. We were bundled into a bus and whisked off to the city. Even from the outside our hotel was grotty. As we crowded into the foyer and queued at the reception desk – it was not really a desk, merely a hole cut through the wall between two rooms – the manager extricated himself from his stool and led me aside. 'Mr Sinden? – I believe you are here with your wife? – I have given you our best room.'

I wish you could have seen it. The walls of the best room crowded in on the double bed and only left space for an alley twelve inches wide on either side. A cracked and grubby wash-basin had a plug tied with string to a tap. Two nails driven into the back of the door were the wardrobe. The bed itself had no headboard and the wall behind bore the marks of many greasy heads. A pair of frayed single sheets failed to cover the ticking of the double mattress which bore far more dubious stains – if it had been soaked in water, the strained-off liquid could have populated the country – but we didn't discover this until early the next morning when we found ourselves lying on it, the sheet having slipped off.

Some of the young men in the company had been so disgusted by their accommodation that they spent the night lying on the warm sands of nearby Bondi beach. A worse fate lay in store for them: the sun had been up for some time before they awoke and they suffered agonising sunburns.

When we arrived in Melbourne later that morning we were interviewed briefly by the press:

'Why are you coming to Australia, Mr Sinden – are you on the skids?'

'No, of course I'm not – why should you think I am?'

'Nobody comes here unless they are.'

I was then whisked away by the impresario who in grave tones told me that there was a lamentable lack of interest in the arrival of the RSC, and very few seats had been sold in advance. Also that the democratic nature of the company with its alphabetical billing meant that there were no 'star' names for the press to latch on to and produce publicity that could help sell seats. It was all very depressing – so much so that the proposed reception after the first night had already been cancelled.

Crestfallen, we were taken to our hotel which we found in the process of reconstruction, and as builders were still at work on the public rooms, we were confined to our individual bedrooms. Here I think I should try to explain a strange anomaly. Everyone seems to expect a leading actor to stay at the equivalent of the Ritz, to drive a Rolls-Royce and buy his wife diamonds. If that actor is making a film, the producing company will pay for his hotel, but if he is on tour with a play he must pay the bill himself and if that leading actor is working for one of the world's best state-subsidised companies he will only be paid a meagre salary. (As Peter Hall said to me in 1963, 'I can easily find a Hamlet for twenty-five pounds a week – but I can't get a Laertes for fifty pounds.') In Australia I was receiving a hundred pounds a week and like each member of the company I was paid a small daily living allowance, but mine had to pay for Diana as well. At the allotted hotel special rates for the entire company had been negotiated so had I chosen to move to somewhere more comfortable I should have to pay the full and higher rates myself and this I could not afford to do. The Melbourne public equated the quality of our actors with the standard of the hotel.

The Winter's Tale opened the season and Diana and I attended the first night. It was humiliating. The Olympians had descended from Stratford to be greeted by rows of empty seats grinning toothlessly from the stalls. The pride of the British theatre was having its face ground in the Australian dust. In the extended interval the few of us present foregathered in the bar for a post-mortem and we were introduced to Dr Jean Battersby of the Australian Arts Council who was shocked by the situation. She had seen the company in England, knew of our reputation, and stated that something must be done. She in turn introduced us to a charming woman who was already the centre of an admiring circle, 'Diana and Donald Sinden – Patricia, Lady Potter.'

Strangely enough, back in England, I had been given an introduction to her husband Sir Ian Potter, one of Australia's wealthiest men, by my old friend, the publisher Hamish Hamilton. Patricia's open friendly smile reassured us as she said, 'We are going to make this a success – it may take a little time but we will do it.'

We joined her group and were told of the many problems surrounding our visit. The Australians are very suspicious of Shakespeare: when Laurence Olivier had opened his *Richard III* in 1948 the Mayor of one city had said, 'I quite liked it – but why didn't they bring the language up to date?'

Referring to the present tour a woman had been overheard to say, 'Oh, Shakespeare? – I'll send my children.'

The Royal Shakespeare Company may have been famous in England but no one seemed to have heard of it in Australia. One fact emerged which under other circumstances we might have found amusing. It had been announced that Her Majesty Queen Elizabeth was to visit Australia the following month and a considerable portion of the population assumed that we were her private troupe of mummers.

From the moment of our meeting, Patricia Potter, Jean Battersby and her husband Charles, and their influential friends, made our tour a success by the inexplicable process of word-of-mouth. The following day more help arrived in the formidable shape of John MacCallum and his wife Googie Withers and we were invited to stay at their house just outside the city.

But before *Twelfth Night* could open a week later, tragedy struck. One of our best young actors, Charles Thomas, was found dead in his bed. I had first worked with Charlie in *The Wars of the Roses* back in 1963 and admired him enormously. He was a regular member of the RSC and was destined for considerable success. His premature death was a terrible blow to all but, in that ridiculous and much abused phrase, 'The Show Must Go On'. But who was to take over his important part of Orsino? Luckily Richard Pasco, who was already playing Leontes in *The Winter's Tale* with the other half of the company, volunteered to play it, but this meant extra intensive rehearsals and our director, John Barton, was back in England. Fortunately Trevor Nunn arrived (having cleverly avoided an overnight stop in Sydney!) and he it was who took charge. We mounted a full-scale dress-rehearsal for him and at the end we gathered round for notes. When we reached Scene Three he said, 'Donald – at Stratford you used to do a very funny thing. I'm sure that when Olivia says, "Malvolio . . . run after that same peevish messenger," you used to say "Run!?" Why have you cut it?'

Following Barton's instructions I had given a 'first-night' version so I explained that John had asked me not actually to vocalise the word.

'Why not?'

'Because it is not in the text.'

Trevor pondered this for a few moments and then, with all the acumen that makes him such a brilliant head of our great company, said, 'Ah! But it *is* in the subtext.'

The word-of-mouth had not worked by the time we opened, but by the end of our stay in Melbourne it was impossible to get a ticket for either play.

I was beginning to love Australia and the Australians – especially when I discovered that they are just as dotty as we are. I was told that after many years of carefree driving on incredibly wide roads in a country where space was no problem, with practically no restrictions, the cities some years previously had begun to encounter problems with the volume of traffic. The government sent a research team around the world to investigate and report on how other countries dealt with the various problems. On their return they submitted their gleanings and one man said that France had instigated the rule that all traffic should give way to vehicles entering from the right and signs had been erected: *PRIORITÉ À DROITE*. Everyone thought this was brilliant and the idea was immediately incorporated into the Australian code. Unfortunately no one remembered that whereas the French drive on the right, the Australians drive on the left. This meant that, for instance, anyone driving towards you on the other side of the road had a perfect right to cut across your bows.

I have somehow omitted to mention so far that I have a particular fascination with Courts of Law. I prefer the Chancery courts because I can watch the cut and thrust of defence and prosecution without being emotionally involved in the outcome – as I find I am at the Criminal bar – and I spend quite a lot of my free time in London at the courts. Over the years I have met a number of judges and barristers who have been kind enough to give me introductions to their counterparts in other countries. Thus it was that I attended the hearing of an appeal in Melbourne. The case was this. A play called *The Boys in the Band*, in which there were a number of four-letter words, had been presented in America and England but when it appeared in Australia, where the laws are different, the actors in the play had been prosecuted for 'uttering obscenities in a public place' (to wit a theatre). Note that it was the actors and not the playwright, director or management who were prosecuted. They were convicted and a nominal sentence was imposed on them. It was all a great joke until it was realised that those same actors could not, for instance, obtain a visa to work in the United States because they had a 'criminal record'. They therefore appealed against their conviction and it became a test case. I attended several days of the hearing and it was slightly bizarre to hear a barrister cold-bloodedly reading out the offending passages from the play.

'My client,' he continued, 'has been prosecuted for uttering these so-called obscenities yet at this very time there is an actor with the

Royal Shakespeare Company – at Her Majesty's Theatre – here in this city – actually spelling out one of these words every night, but because the play is by Shakespeare it would seem there is no offence.'

My blood ran cold. I was the actor who, as Malvolio, reads from Olivia's letter, '. . . these be her very C's her U's, and her T's; and thus makes she her great P's . . .' It has long been a theatrical custom to make the point quite clear by saying, '. . . these be her very C's her U's 'n T's . . .' I was therefore guilty of paraphrasing Shakespeare. Would I be prosecuted? For the rest of our time in Australia, just in case some busybody was in the audience, I was very careful to be precise in my articulation: '. . . these be her very C's, her U's, *AND* her T's . . .'

The time had come to move on to Adelaide. Named after the consort of King William IV, and still possessing many nineteenth-century buildings, this must be one of the world's most delightfully planned cities. Not much more than a mile square the streets are criss-crossed on the grid system as at Winchelsea in Sussex. The central city is surrounded by a green belt of parkland and the suburbs lie beyond: looking along any of the streets the vista is always terminated by greenery.

The director of the Festival was Sir Robert Helpmann who had flown in just before from New York where he had seen the long-running nude revue *Oh Calcutta!* At the airport someone from the press asked him if this meant that we would soon have nudity in the ballet.

'No,' answered Helpmann. 'There are certain parts of the male and female anatomy which keep on swinging after the music stops.'

My memories of Adelaide are nothing but idyllic: walking through the lovely city or taking a taxi down to the beach at Glenelg (a classic example of a palindrome). It was after a hot and sticky matinee that three of us raced from the theatre down to this deserted beach and on arrival found another taxi already there with the driver sitting on a wall beside it. He recognised us (Adelaide is a very small place) and said, 'I've just brought a couple of Limeys – some of your lot – down here.'

We were mystified – who could have got there before us? We trotted down the beach to be met by two white-skinned obvious Limeys coming out of the sea: Benjamin Britten and Peter Pears who were also appearing in the Festival. Some of your lot! They

enjoyed the joke as much as we did and from then on we spent
several free evenings attending each other's performances and
eating together afterwards.

On another glorious day I was transformed into a worshipping
schoolboy. Back in Melbourne I had been introduced to two
cricketing heroes of my youth, Lindsay Hassett and Ernie McCormick whom I had seen playing in England during the 1938 Test
series, and with them I visited the other MCC – the Melbourne
Cricket Club – where for my sole benefit they relived some of the
famous matches played on that splendid ground. I had continually
to remember that 'we' referred to the Australians and not the
English! When I told them that I was moving on to Adelaide,
Hassett said, 'Gee, Don, you must give Don a call – he lives there
and he'd just love to see you.'

Thus it was that I telephoned the great Sir Donald Bradman and
arranged that Richard Pasco, Emrys James, Nicholas Selby and I
should entertain him to lunch. For three hours we encouraged him
to talk about his cricketing days. With the help of extra salts and
peppers, which at his bidding we borrowed from other tables, he
illustrated his points by setting them out as fielders all over the
table and, although he was wearing a neck-brace, every now and
then he jumped to his feet to demonstrate a stroke, hooking an
imaginary six out through the window. In answer to our carefully
disguised innocent questions he took us through the notorious
'bodyline' series showing what it was like to receive a bombard-
ment of deliveries from Larwood. Again I had to remember that
the vehement 'they' referred to the English. What a privilege to
have met him!

With real sadness we left Adelaide and set off for Sydney where,
thanks to resounding words-of-mouth, all seats had been sold well
in advance.

It may sound akin to perversity on my part but I never seem to
like the cities I am expected to like: New York I found merely
tiresome, San Francisco a Victorian rehash of Bristol, and Sydney
– except for the areas of Paddington and Kensington – very disappointing. The much vaunted harbour can only be seen from the
houses that front it, while the bridge (a copy of the one that spans
the Tyne in Newcastle) and the equally famous Opera House, are
only seen at their best when crossing to or from Manly on the
ferry.

Wearing a tin hat I was thrilled to be taken over the Opera

House complex, which was nearing completion at the time, and told of all the trials and tribulations associated with its construction. I am on slightly dangerous ground here because I cannot remember the actual facts and figures.

When the Danish architect Utzon tendered his superb design of curvaceous roofs rising from the harbour he estimated that the cost of building would be $A8,000,000. Enormous piles were sunk deep into the bed of the harbour and a vast concrete platform floated across the top. The piers were continued up for another ten feet to allow for a spacious car park and then another vast concrete platform formed the base for the Concert Hall, Opera House and Theatre that were to be built above. At about this stage the $A8,000,000 were used up. The government stepped in. Utzon was sacked and a team of architects under the direction of a government minister were appointed to take charge. All the costs and estimates were re-examined. On paper it appeared that the car park was costing $A8,000,000. 'Ludicrous!' said someone. 'Cancel the car park.' This order was passed down the official channels until it got to the site. No car park. So the space allotted between the two concrete platforms was duly filled in with more concrete.

Utzon had designed splendid dressing-rooms for the three auditoria, ten feet high with long narrow windows at seated height with panoramic views of the harbour. These were deemed to be too luxurious. If they were given eight-feet-high ceilings, two more floors of dressing-rooms could be accommodated. This was done but they forgot to alter the position of the windows with the result that now one layer of rooms has windows on the level of the floor and another up at the ceiling.

The sail-like roofs produced a more costly problem. They were to be covered with glazed tiles a metre square but as there is not one straight line on any of the roof surfaces, each tile had to be made individually. And once in position how were they to be cleaned? The tallest skyscraper can have cradles lowered from the top on which cleaners can stand but when the surfaces curve in all directions this is not possible. I don't know how they solved that problem.

The car park fiasco still produces the biggest problem. On a wet night the driver must drop his passengers at the foot of an enormous flight of uncovered steps fifty yards away from the entrance and then drive another three-quarters of a mile before he can find a place to leave his vehicle.

But whatever the difficulties, Utzon's vision of a building that gives the impression of wind-filled sails shining like mother-of-pearl, tethered to a raft floating on glistening blue water is one of the wonders of the modern world and has rightly become a symbol of which Sydney may be proud.

In Sydney one of our actors had to extricate himself from a rather embarrassing situation. He had met a girl the day we landed in Melbourne and had taken her with him to Adelaide where they married. Now, less than a month later, she had left him and he was applying for a divorce.

Personally, I have a good reason for being grateful to Sydney. Several of our company went to a performance given by the local company and in return they came the next day to see a matinee of *Twelfth Night*. I racked my brains to think of something extra to do in my performance: something that might only be interesting or amusing to a fellow-actor – caviare to the general. For a whole season we had been nonplussed by the 'stone' sundial that our designer had placed in the centre of the stage for the garden scenes. It was placed exactly where every actor wanted to stand – bang in the centre. Although decorative it was a useless prop. All you can do with a sundial is to check the time – if required – and that was where I got my idea. Around my Malvolio neck I wore a chain with a circular badge suspended from it . . . now if that could be assumed to be a watch . . .

I knew that I must not run the risk of throwing my colleagues, so at the matinee performance I waited until I was left alone for my soliloquy and as I spoke I glanced at the sundial, checked with my watch and saw that the two showed different times. As I continued my speech I peered at the sun – actually the spotlights situated in the gallery – and checked the sundial and my watch again. Yes indeed they were different. Only Malvolio would assume that, of the two, his own watch could not be wrong, so with considerable effort I turned the whole sundial until it showed the correct Malvolio time. The result was just perfect – not only the few Australian actors in front, but the whole audience laughed uproariously. I kept it in for the rest of the run.

While I was occupied at the theatre Diana found various things to do and encountered a prize example of the difference between two common languages. Our visit to the city coincided with the annual Sydney Show, and as 1969 was also the two hundredth anniversary of Captain Cook's discovery of Australia there were special celebrations all over the place. Diana heard that there was to be a ceremony, similar to the lighting of the Olympic Flame,

215

where relays of runners were to carry a flare from Botany Bay – the actual site of Cook's landing – to the central arena at the Sydney Showground where the flare would be used to ignite a resplendent flame. Well ahead of the appointed time Diana arrived only to find that the show occupied several hundred acres – it was like England's Motor Show, Dairy Show, Agricultural Show, Industry Fair, Livestock Show, Chelsea Flower Show, the Ideal Home Exhibition and the Horse of the Year Show all rolled into one. Worried that she might not get to the ceremony in time, Diana approached a woman wearing all sorts of official badges and asked, 'Can you tell me where they do the flares?'

An Australian accent replied scathingly, 'In the flare show, dear.'

Many decades ago, my mother's cousin Albert Fuller and his wife emigrated to Australia and raised a family. Their two sons Gordon and Brian are roughly my contemporaries and it was a delightful surprise when we received a telephone call from them. We met my second cousins for the first time in Sydney and spent many hours together. They lamented that they lived so many thousands of miles from their roots and felt cut off from the rest of our closely knit family. Their father had never shown an interest in the history of the family – did I know anything? I had to admit that I, too, had never been particularly interested, but when I returned to England I would make some enquiries and let them know my findings . . . Just a minute: haven't I told you this before? . . . Oh yes. In the first chapter of this book. It seems therefore a good moment to close, but before doing so I must fill in a few details.

During his visit Trevor Nunn had given me the script of a play first performed in 1840 that, if – if – there were a London season, he would like me to do. I thought I was fairly knowledgeable about Victorian drama, but here was a play of which I had never heard. It was entitled *London Assurance* and contained, Trevor said, a splendid part for me.

Our tour of Australia had become a triumphant success but there were still clouds on the horizon – was there enough cash in the kitty to ensure the London season? By a stroke of good fortune Lord Goodman, who was then chairman of the Arts Council, happened to be visiting Australia and hearing on all sides of our popularity gave us assurances that enough official money would be forthcoming to keep us going for six weeks. After that we would be on our own.

At London airport we were greeted by the whole of an ecstatic

RSC hierarchy: the Aldwych season was on – but if we were to secure the long term we still had to be an immediate success. Our troops had experienced the smell of battle, thanks to Australia we were a finely tuned unit, we were honed to a sharp edge. We accepted the challenge, stiffened the sinews, summoned up the blood and threw ourselves into the fray. Rehearsals began for *London Assurance*, which opened the new season. We won the day. Victory was ours. But that's another story.

INDEX

INDEX

Eh! (Henry Livings), Donald Sinden as
  Mr Price in, 134–7, 138
Eisenstein, S. M., 67
Eliot, T. S., 181
Elizabeth, HM the Queen, 118, 199, 210
Elizabeth, HM the Queen Mother, 69
Ellen Terry Museum, 53
Engel, Susan, 76
Enthoven, Mrs Gabrielle, 186
Eposito, Phil, 7
Eton College, 91
Evans, Dame Edith, 101, 163
  and directors, 102
  on playing farce, 175
Evening Standard, 34, 189

Faber, Leslie, 180
Fairbanks, Douglas (Snr), 181
Faith, Adam, 70
Falk, Rosella, 125
Farebrother, Violet, 178
Farr, Derek, 190
Farrah, Abd'elkader, 76
Federation of Playgoers Societies, 184
Ferris, Barbara, 154
Feydeau, 120, 173
Fil à la Patte, Un (Feydeau), 120, 121
Filmgoer's Companion (Halliwell), 116
Financial Times, 34
Firbank, Ann, 61
Flare Path (Terence Rattigan), 14
Fleetwood, Susan, 169
Fleming, Ian, 85
Fleming, Tom, 76
Fletcher, Ifan Kyrle, 179
Fletcher, John, 198
  and *Henry VIII*, 199–200, 203
Florence, 148
Folger Library, Washington, 183
Fontanne, Lynn, 102
Forbes-Robertson, Sir Johnston, 87, 180
Fortescue, Countess, 81, 82, 83
Fortescue, Earl of, 82, 83
Fortescue, Sir John, 82
Fowler, Harry, 113, 114
Fox, Dr Levi, 118
Francis, Clive, 154, 157
Francis, Raymond, 21
Franks, Arthur, 182
Fraser, Bill, 197
Fredo (playwright), 120
French Without Tears (Terence Rattigan),
  12, 14, 18–19
Frisby, Terence, and *There's a Girl in my
  Soup*, 153, 154, 155
Frisch, Maz, 120
Fuller, Albert, 216
Fuller, Arthur Leslie, 4
Fuller, Brian, 2, 216

Fuller, Gordon, 2, 216
Fuseli, Henry, 83

Gable, Clark, 67
Gadsden, Lionel, and *Peter Pan*, 25–7, 30
Gale, John, 116
Gallipoli campaign, 29
Gardner, John, 85
Garland, Patrick, 33
Garrick Club, 64, 181, 189
  party for Donald Sinden at, 68
  World Theatre Season and, 123, 124
Garrick, David, 172, 178
Garside, Kenneth, 182
Gascoigne, Bamber, 182
Gaye, Freda, 183
Gielgud, Sir John, 76, 101, 180
  as *Othello*, 136, 137
Gill, Eric, 37
Giselle (ballet), 14
Globe Theatre, London, 155, 156, 157
Glove, The (TV play), 39
Gobbi, Tito, 170
Gobowen, 105
Goethe, J. W. von, 120
Gogol, Nicolai, 120
Going for a Song (TV show), 137–8
Gollancz, Victor, publishers, 139
Goodman, Lord, 216
  and BTMA, 184–5, 188
Good Night Vienna (musical), 115–17
Goolden, Richard, 63–4
Gordon, Bernard, 15
Gowrie, Lord, 189
Graves, Robert, 166–7
Great Expectations (Charles Dickens) (TV
  serial), 21
Greater London Council, 188
Greatest Story Ever Told, The (film), 33
Greek Art Theatre, 120, 124
Greet, Ben, 27, 29n
Guest, Ivor, 182
Guilty Party (Ross/Singer), 35, 39
  Donald Sinden in, 61, 63, 64, 68, 70
Guthrie, Duncan, 182

Habimah National Theatre, Tel Aviv, 124
Hadjidaki (composer), 121
Hall, David, 32
Hall, Sir Peter, 21, 75, 133, 162, 163, 209
  Donald Sinden auditions for, 22–3,
    71–2, 79
  and John Barton, 91, 92
  and *The Wars of the Roses*, 85–6, 87, 88, 89
  rehearsals for, 98–101, 104
  plans 1964 season, 111–12, 126
  and World Theatre Season, 123
  directs *Eh!*, 134, 135, 136
  leaves RSC, 171

INDEX

INDEX